Free Legal Aid – A Comparative Approach

Ius, Lex et Res Publica
Studies in Law, Philosophy and Political Cultures

Edited by Barbara Janusz-Pohl and Anna Jaron

Volume 33

Marian Grzybowski / Bogusław Przywora /
Aleksandra Syryt (eds.)

Free Legal Aid – A Comparative Approach

Volume 2

PETER LANG
Berlin - Bruxelles - Chennai - Lausanne - New York - Oxford

Bibliographic Information published by the Deutsche Nationalbibliothek
The Deutsche Nationalbibliothek lists this publication in the Deutsche Nationalbibliografie; detailed bibliographic data is available in the internet at http://dnb.d-nb.de.

Library of Congress Cataloging-in-Publication Data
A CIP catalog record for this book has been applied for at the Library of Congress.

ISSN 2191-3250
ISBN 978-3-631-90533-3 (Print)
E-ISBN 978-3-631-92016-9 (E-Book)
E-ISBN 978-3-631-92017-6 (E-PUB)
DOI 10.3726/b21962

Published by Peter Lang GmbH, Berlin, Deutschland

info@peterlang.com - www.peterlang.com

This publication has been peer reviewed.
www.peterlang.com

Spis treści

Shortcuts

The Constitution of the Republic of Poland of 2 April 1997 (Journal of Laws No. 78, item 483, as amended) – Constitution RP
The Act of 5 August 2015 on free legal aid, free civic counseling and legal education (Journal of Laws of 2021, item 945) – Free Legal Aid Act
Constitutional Tribunal – CT
The act of 14 June 1960 Code of Administrative Procedure (Journal of Laws of 2023, item 775) – Administrative Procedure Code
European Convention for the Protection of Human Rights and Fundamental Freedoms of 4 November 1950 (Journal of Laws 1993, No. 61, item 284) – ECHR
European Court of Human Rights – ECtHR
European Union – EU
The Treaty on Functioning of the European Union (EU Journal od Laws 2016/C 202/1) – TFEU
The Treaty on the European Union (EU Journal od Laws 2016/C 202/1.) – TEU
The Charter of Fundamental Rights of the European Union (Journal of Laws EU C. 2007 303.1) – CRR

Introduction

In today's complex legal landscape, access to justice is a fundamental right that should be available to all individuals, regardless of their socio-economic status. However, countless people around the world face significant barriers when it comes to navigating the legal system and obtaining adequate legal representation. The provision of free legal aid emerges as a crucial mechanism to bridge this gap, ensuring that justice is not limited to those who can afford it.

This book delves into the realm of free legal aid, examining its significance in promoting equal access to justice and addressing the challenges associated with its implementation. While exploring this subject, we recognize the indispensable role of comparative law research in comprehending the diverse approaches and systems employed globally. By analyzing and contrasting legal frameworks across different jurisdictions, we can gain valuable insights into the best practices, potential improvements, and innovative strategies that can enhance the provision of free legal aid.

Conducting comparative law research is vital in the realm of free legal aid for several compelling reasons. First and foremost, it allows us to broaden our perspective beyond the confines of a single legal system. By examining how different countries address the issue of access to justice, we can identify models and mechanisms that have proven successful in overcoming obstacles and achieving desirable outcomes. This comparative approach fosters a rich understanding of the diverse methods employed to deliver free legal aid and encourages the exchange of ideas, experiences, and lessons learned.

Furthermore, comparative law research enables us to identify gaps and shortcomings in existing legal frameworks and policies. By critically analyzing various jurisdictions, we can pinpoint areas where certain systems excel and others fall short. This knowledge empowers us to develop innovative strategies and reforms that can be applied in our own jurisdictions to enhance the effectiveness and efficiency of free legal aid programs.

Moreover, comparative law research provides an opportunity to study the underlying principles and values that shape the provision of free legal aid. Different legal systems are rooted in unique historical, cultural, and social contexts, and by studying these differences, we can gain a deeper understanding of the underlying philosophies and ideals that drive legal aid initiatives. This knowledge enables us to build a more comprehensive and nuanced framework for delivering free legal aid that reflects the needs and aspirations of the diverse communities we serve.

Ultimately, the goal of this book is to illuminate the crucial role of comparative law research in the realm of free legal aid. By examining various legal systems, we can identify effective strategies, highlight best practices, and propose innovative solutions that have the potential to transform the landscape of access to justice. Through a collaborative and informed approach, we can work towards a future where every individual, regardless of their financial means, can assert their rights, seek redress, and participate fully in the legal process.

This book was prepared in particular as part of the activity at the Interdisciplinary Research Centre for Legal Education and Legal Aid and Mediation Jan Dlugosz University in Czestochowa.

Jerzy Jaskiernia

Free Legal Aid in the Axiological System of the Council of Europe

Abstract: The study aims to show the role of free legal aid in the Council of Europe (CoE) axiological system. This organization specializes in creating standards in the area of democracy, the rule of law and human rights, hence it is important to ask the question, what is the importance of free legal aid for the implementation of standards in this area. The author analyzed both the legally binding standards (derived from art. 6 of the ECHR) and the soft law standards, particularly in the recommendations of the CoE's Committee of Ministers. He showed the evolution of the approach, considering the organisation's reaction to new challenges in this area. He verified the following research hypothesis: the CoE played an important inspirational role in promoting free legal aid, and in subsequent documents, it specified the standards in this area, influencing the practice of the Member States.

Keywords: Free legal aid, Council of Europe, axiological system

1. Introduction

Free legal aid is analyzed in contemporary research. Comparative analysis of different Free Legal Aid (FLA) delivery models is taken. They include a normative model of free pre-trial legal aid[1]. Among the analyzed issues are free legal assistance to victims of crime[2] and natural disaster survivors[3]. The are also analyses of free legal assistance to asylum seekers[4] and procedures in the asylum courts[5]. The problem is analyzed in the context of providing legal aid to people with

1 B. Przywora, *Normatywny model przedsądowej nieodpłatnej pomocy prawnej*, Warszawa 2018, p. 32.

2 U.K. Nordenson, *The proposed Swedish systems of free legal assistance and of compensation to victims of crime*, "Zeitschrift für Rechtsmedizin" 1972, nr 2, p. 103.

3 K. Crebo, *Disaster Legal Services: free legal assistance to natural disaster survivors*, "The Affiliate" 2012, nr 1, p. 5.

4 E. Guild, *The Asylum Seeker's Right to Free Legal Assistance and/or Representation in EU Law*, "Issues in International Migration Law" 2015, p. 264.

5 G. Friedl, *Non-Provision of Free Legal Assistance by a Lawyer in the Procedure before the Asylum Court not Unconstitutional*, "Vienna Online Journal on International Constitutional Law" 2009, nr 4, p. 31

low income[6]. It may appear as legal services for the "public good"[7]. The research includes pro bono services[8] and their limitations[9]. The goal is to achieve legal services for all members of society[10]. It is perceived as an element of the "democratization of legal services" process.

This study aims to show the role of free legal assistance in the Council of Europe (CoE) axiological system. This organization specializes in creating standards in the area of democracy, the rule of law and human rights[11], hence it is important to ask the question, what is the importance of free legal aid for the implementation of standards in this area. It is necessary to analyze the legally binding standards of free legal assistance (derived in particular from art. 6 (3) (c) of the ECHR) and the standards of a soft law nature, including in particular in the recommendations of the CoE's Committee of Ministers. The subject of this study will be the evolution of the approach to this problem, considering the organisation's reaction to new challenges in this area. The following research hypothesis will be verified: the CoE has played an important inspirational role in promoting free legal aid, and in subsequent documents, it specified the standards in this area, influencing the practice of the Member States.

2. General characteristics of free legal assistance

Pro bono legal aid is perceived as an instrument of "reducing the civil justice gap"[12]. It is addressed to the poor people[13]. It plays an important role in achieving

6 H. Herskoff, S. Loffredo, *Getting By: Economic Rights and Legal Protections for People with Low Income*, Oxford 2019, p. 49.

7 G. Renouf, J. Anderson, *Legal services 'for public good'*, "Alternative Law Journal" 2003, nr 1, p. 13.

8 A. Faith-Slaker, *What we know and need to know about pro bono service delivery,* "South Carolina Law Review" 2016, nr 2, p. 267; D. Holness, *Recent developments in the provision of pro bono legal services by attorneys in South Africa*, "Potchefstroom Electronic Law Journal" 2013, nr 1, p. 128.

9 D. Bonilla Maldonado, *The Mandarins of the Law: Pro Bono Legal Work from a Comparative Perspective*, "Indiana Journal of Global Legal Studies" 2020, nr 1, p. 131.

10 R.T.Y. Moon, *Access to civil justice: is there a solution? Pro bono efforts can help ensure access to legal assistance for all members of society*, "Judicature" 2005, nr 4, p. 155.

11 J. Jaskiernia, *Funkcje Konstytucji RP w dobie integracji europejskiej i radykalnych przemian politycznych*, Toruń 2020, p. 232.

12 A. Cohn, *Reducing the civil "justice gap" by enhancing the delivery of pro bono legal assistance to indigent pro se litigation: a "field" assessment and recommendations*, "University of Florida Journal of Law and Public Policy" 2017, nr 1, p. 101.

13 B.J. Cardin, R.J. Rhudy, *Expanding pro bono legal assistance in civil cases to Maryland's poor*, "Maryland Law Review" 1990, vol. 49, p. 1.

goals dealing with non-privileged people[14]. Many legal scholars have noted that the Legal Services Corporation (LSC), created to provide civil legal assistance to people experiencing poverty, has not been able to keep up with demand for various reasons, especially the lack of funding and staff[15].

Crime victims often experience a host of negative consequences. In relation to these consequences, crime victims may also need assistance from the criminal justice system and civil legal service providers. Despite this need, crime victims often lack access to civil legal services. One way to potentially improve the availability and accessibility of civil legal services for crime victims is to increase the provision and availability of pro bono services; however, how attorneys perceive pro bono service for crime victims may impede service provision[16].

There is little evidence on the questions of whether pro bono services are effective, whether lawyer charity is a cheaper way to provide them (because it does cost money to do pro bono), or whether it would be more efficient and effective if firms and attorneys stopped giving their time and instead donated money to the organizations already specializing in these clients and causes. Pro bono may or may not be an efficient way of doing socially important work[17].

Middle- and low-income individuals in many jurisdictions obtain only a relatively modest share of lawyers' services. In a society ruled by law, every person should be able to expect key principles of justice to apply. Among the most important dimensions of a right to a fair trial is the right to equal access to an attorney. After all, the attorney is not merely a commercial actor but also represents the legal system. Access to an attorney is a key step in providing justice in practice. Scientific literature distinguishes various forms and instruments of legal aid: the court appointment of lawyers, free or low-cost legal aid provided by public agencies and charitable and fraternal organizations, sometimes mixed with legal expenses insurance, contingency fee and the free services of lawyers

---

14 T.L. Birdsell, *A few minutes of your time can save your client's dime: obtaining pro bono assistance for legal assistance clients*, "The Army lawyer", 1 June 2015, p. 14.

15 J.A. Emrey, *Lawyers' Pro Bono Service and American-Style Civil Legal Assistance*, "The Justice System Journal" 2008, nr 2, p. 233.

16 L.E. Daigle, M.N. Harris, S.J. Mummert, *Crime Victims and Their Unmet Civil Legal Needs: Pro Bono Service Provision Among Private Attorneys*, "Journal of Victimology and Victim Justice" 2019, nr 1, p. 26.

17 R. Maguire, G. Shearer, R. Field, *Reconsidering pro bono: a comparative analysis of protocols in Australia, the United States, the United Kingdom and Singapore*, "University of New South Wales Law Journal" 2014, nr 3, p. 116.

serving pro bono publico. It may be analyzed on the practice present, e.g., in Lithuania and Germany[18].

In the United Kingdom from the 1890s onwards, social reformers, volunteer lawyers, and politicians increasingly came to see access to affordable or free legal advice as a critical part of helping working-class people uphold their rights with landlords, employers, and retailers – and, from the 1940s, with the welfare state. Whilst a state scheme was launched in 1949, it was never fully implemented, and help from a lawyer remained out of the reach of many people[19].

Individual attorneys must engage in pro bono work as it curbs the gap in providing legal assistance to the indigent. Pro bono work isn't only desperately needed by many people, but pro bono legal services are also ethically required of those in the legal profession. Attorneys have an ethical responsibility to perform pro bono work, and the profession has an ethical responsibility to ensure that attorneys act in accordance with the ethical standards set forth by the profession[20].

Lawyers are often criticized for stinting on their responsibilities for public service. Nevertheless, their uncompensated provision of legal services to poor people, or pro bono work, provides a substantial part of available civil legal assistance in the United States. Cross-sectional analysis of data from the late 1990s revealed that reliance on pro bono may render assistance vulnerable to market pressures in obvious and subtle ways. In states where the legal profession takes in more receipts per lawyer, larger proportions of the profession provide uncompensated service to people experiencing poverty. As federally subsidized legal assistance shrinks in scope and scale, growing reliance on pro bono leaves American-style civil legal assistance increasingly vulnerable to market forces[21].

Despite longstanding concern that the commercialization of legal practice is antithetical to professionalism, corporate law firms have dramatically increased their pro bono participation over the past few decades. Pro bono work is only partly rooted in internal organizational dynamics, and the institutional

---

18 E. Gruodytė, S. Kirchner, *Pro Bono Work vs. Legal Aid: Approaches to Ensuring Access to Justice and the Social Responsibility of the Attorney*, "Baltic Journal of Law & Politics" 2012, nr 2, p. 43.

19 K. Bradley, *Lawyers for the poor: Legal advice, voluntary action and citizenship in England, 1890–1990*, Manchester 2019, p. 34.

20 T. DeFilipps, *Attorneys' ethical responsibility to provide pro bono legal services to those in need*, "Buffalo Public Interest Law Journal: in the Public Interest" 2014, vol. 33, p. 1.

21 R.L. Sandefur, *Lawyers' Pro Bono Service and American-Style Civil Legal Assistance*, "Law & Society Review" 2007, nr 1, p. 79.

environment appears more important for explaining variation in pro bono participation. Large firms may be more drawn to pro bono work as a social process tied to professional status and legitimacy than concrete, rational organizational goals[22].

The research has been done to explain how status shapes intersectoral collaboration between large US corporate law firms and public interest legal organizations (PILOs). High-status law firms tend to collaborate with similarly high-status pro bono organizations. This gives rise to a highly unequal playing field where a handful of PILOs have a wealth of connections to high-status law firms. At the same time, the majority of PILOs only collaborate with a few –relatively under-resourced– non-high-status firms[23].

The studies held in the United States describe the practical goal of unbundled legal services for the pro bono family law sector as it applies to limited legal services programs (also known as brief advice clinics) through the use of a goal spectrum, derived from the theoretical goal of access to justice. The service providers in limited legal services programs should explicitly identify and then perform an essential, discrete service that the client needs to have performed to help the client meet his or her ultimate objectives[24].

Free legal assistance play also an important role in Australia. Interesting research was done on the values and private motivations of legal practitioners who provide legal services *pro bono publico*. It was a 2014 empirical study of lawyers in Queensland, Australia, who regularly undertake pro bono work. The findings suggest strong moral and professional motivations for engaging in pro bono legal practice and a distinct "community of practice" of large law firms in forming and sharing sophisticated structures and approaches to addressing social justice needs. However, the study also revealed a range of potential drawbacks arising from the dominance of the large law firm sector in this field[25]. Given the current operation of the legal system and levels of support for publicly

---

22 S.A. Boutcher, *Private Law Firms in the Public Interest: The Organizational and Institutional Determinants of Pro Bono Participation, 1994–2005*, "Law & Social Inquiry" 2017, nr 2.

23 D.F. Leal, *Status and collaboration: The case of pro bono network inequalities in corporate law*, "Social Science Research" 2019, vol. 84, p. 102325.

24 E.A. Anderson, *Unbundling the ethical issues of pro bono advocacy: articulating the goals of limited-scope pro bono advocacy for limited legal services programs*, "Family Court Review" 2010, nr 4, p. 685.

25 F. Bartlett, M. Taylor, *Pro bono lawyering: personal motives and institutionalised practice*, "Legal Ethics", 2016, nr 2, p. 277.

funded legal services, the problem of how the commitment to providing and improving pro bono legal services can be channelled most effectively. In this context, the role of the National Pro Bono Resource Centre in fostering and supporting access to justice for low-income and disadvantaged people in Australia is exposed[26].

The use of artificial intelligence (AI) in law has again become of great interest to lawyers and government. Legal Information Institutes (LIIs) have played a significant role in providing legal information via the web. The concept of "free access to law" is not static, and the evolution of its principles now requires a response from providers of free access to legal information ("a LII response") to this renewed prominence of AI. This should include improving and expanding free access to legal advice[27].

3. The Council of Europe approach to the free legal aid

We may ask what is the place of free legal aid in the axiological system of the Council of Europe.

Among the legally binding documents dealing with free legal assistance, a crucial role plays the ECHR. The right of access to the law and justice is provided for in art. 6 (3) (c) of the ECHR, the other provisions of the Convention and particularly art. 2,3 and 8 are equally applicable to people experiencing poverty, as are the other legal instruments of the Council of Europe, such as the European Social Charter.

Under CoE law[28], an explicit right to legal aid in criminal proceedings is set out in art. 6 (3) (c) of the ECHR. This provides that everyone charged with a criminal offence has a right to free legal aid if they do not have "sufficient means" to pay for legal assistance (the financial or means test), where the "interests of justice" so require (the interests of justice test). Legal aid applies throughout the proceedings, from police questioning to the appeal[29].

Art. 6 (3) (c) of the ECHR also sets out the right to be defended by a lawyer of one's own choosing, which can be subjected to limitations if the interests of justice so require (see Section 4.2.3 on legal assistance of one's own choosing).

---

26 G. Renouf, J. Anderson, op.cit., p. 13.

27 A. Mowbray, P. Chung, G. Greenleaf, *Building sustainable free legal advisory systems: Experiences from the history of AI & law*, "Computer Law & Security Review" 2018, vol. 34, p. 314.

28 *Handbook pf European law relating to the access to justice*, Luxembourg 2016, p. 66–69.

29 ECtHR, *Salduz v. Turkey [GC]*, No. 36391/02, 27 November 2008.

This means there is no absolute right to choose one's court-appointed legal aid lawyer. An individual who requests a change of legal aid lawyer must present evidence that the lawyer failed to perform satisfactorily[30]. Acceptable limitations on the choice of lawyer include requiring specialists for specialist proceedings[31].

Under CoE law, there is no obligation to provide legal aid for all proceedings involving civil rights and obligations[32]. Failure to provide an applicant with the assistance of a lawyer may breach Art. 6 of the ECHR where such assistance is indispensable for effective access to court, either because legal representation is compulsory (as is the case for various types of litigation), or because a case's applicable procedure is particularly complex[33]. Legal systems may establish selection procedures for determining whether legal aid will be granted in civil cases. Still, these may not function arbitrarily or disproportionately or influence the essence of the right to access the court. For instance, refusing legal aid because an appeal did not appear well-founded at the time of application may, in some circumstances, impair the very essence of an applicant's right to a tribunal[34].

In *Airey v. Ireland*[35], the applicant sought judicial separation from her husband but could not obtain a judicial order because she could not afford to retain a lawyer without legal aid. The ECtHR confirmed that, although art. 6 (1) of the ECHR does not explicitly provide legal aid in civil proceedings, states may be compelled to provide it when legal assistance is indispensable for securing effective access to a court. This does not apply to all cases concerning civil rights and obligations. Much depends on the circumstances of each case. In the present case, the relevant factors in favour of granting legal aid were the complexity of the procedure and the issues of law, the need to establish facts through expert evidence and the examination of witnesses; and that this was a marital dispute entailing emotional involvement. The Court found a violation of art. 6 of the ECHR.

---

30 ECtHR, *Lagerblom v. Sweden*, No. 26891/95, 14 January 2003, para. 60.

31 For example, *ECtHR, Meftah and Others v. France [GC]*, Nos. 32911/96, 35237/97 and 34595/97, 26 July 2002, para. 47.

32 ECtHR, *Del Sol v. France, No. 46800/99*, 26 February 2002, para. 20.

33 ECtHR, *P., C. and S. v. The United Kingdom*, No. 56547/00, 16 October 2002, paras. 88–91.

34 ECtHR, *Aerts v. Belgium*, No. 25357/94, 30 July 1998. Following this decision, Belgium amended the law to restrict refusals to manifestly unfounded applications.

35 ECtHR, *Airey v. Ireland*, No. 6289/73, 9 October 1979, para. 26.

Under CoE law, granting legal aid to legal persons (for example, companies) is not, in principle, impossible but must be assessed in light of the relevant national rules and the situation of the company concerned. The ECtHR has noted a lack of "consensus or even a consolidated tendency" among states[36]. A legal aid scheme available only to non-profit-making legal persons does not violate the right of access to justice if there is an objective and reasonable justification for the restriction (for example, because profit-making companies can deduct the legal costs from their tax obligations)[37].

In the area of free legal assistance, important meaning in the axiological system of the Council of Europe also instruments of soft law character, not legally binding but having important political meaning as an inspiration for legislative solutions and practice of the CoE's member states.

In Resolution (76) 5 on legal aid in civil, commercial and administrative matters[38], the Committee of Ministers, considering that to eliminate economic obstacles to legal proceedings and permit persons in an economically weak position more easily to exercise their rights in member states, it is expedient to ensure equality of treatment in granting legal aid to nationals of member states of the Council of Europe and to those aliens for whom such equality of treatment appears to be most justified, has recommended to governments of member states to accord, under the same conditions as to nationals, legal aid in civil, commercial and administrative matters, irrespective of the nature of the tribunal exercising jurisdiction: a. to natural persons being nationals of any member state; b. to all other natural persons who have their habitual residence in the territory of the state where the proceedings take place[39].

In recommendation No. R (81) 7 of the Committee of Ministers to member states on measures facilitating access to justice[40], the CMCE has recommended that Member states should take all necessary steps to inform the public on the means open to an individual to assert his rights before courts and to make judicial proceedings, relating to civil, commercial, administrative, social or fiscal matters simple, speedy and inexpensive. CMCE has recommended, e.g., "No litigant should be prevented from being assisted by a lawyer. The compulsory

---

36 ECtHR, *Granos Organicos Nacionales S.A. v. Germany*, No. 19508/07, 22 March 2012, para. 47and 53.

37 ECtHR, *VP Diffusion Sarl v. France*, No. 14565/04, 26 August 2008.

38 Adopted by the Committee of Ministers on 18 February 1976 at the 254th meeting of the Ministers' Deputies.

39 CMCE Res. 76 (5).

40 Adopted by the Committee of Ministers on 14 May 1981 at its 68th Session.

recourse of a party to the services of an unnecessary plurality of lawyers for the need of a particular case is to be avoided. Regarding the nature of the matter involved, it would be desirable to facilitate access to justice, for an individual to put his own case before the courts, then representation by a lawyer should not be compulsory"[41].

Special meaning for the understanding position of the Council of Europe in free legal aid is the recommendation No. R (93)1 of the Committee of Ministers to Member States on effective access to the law and justice for people experiencing poverty[42]. CMCE held this recommendation concerned the very poor – understood to mean persons who are deprived, marginalized or excluded from society economically and in social and cultural terms. It is considered that this situation of severe poverty continued to deprive men and women of the effective enjoyment of human rights, which must be secured for all without distinction, by art. 14 of the ECHR. CMCE was convinced that efforts to promote access to the law and justice would only be fully effective as part of a comprehensive, coherent, forward-looking policy to combat severe poverty in cooperation with the population groups concerned. CMCE recalled the principle of the indivisibility of human rights, which implied that the enjoyment of civil and political rights such as those enshrined particularly in art. 6, paragraph 3. c, and 13 of the ECHR was not effective if economic, social and cultural rights are not equally protected. CMCE reaffirmed that attachment to human rights was linked to respect for human dignity, especially regarding access to the law and justice for the very poor.

The Committee of Ministers has recommended in recommendation R (93) 1 that the governments of Member States:

1. Facilitate access to the law for the very poor ("the right to the protection of the law") by: a. promoting, where necessary, action to make the legal profession aware of the problems of the very poor; b. promoting legal advice services for the very poor; c. defraying the cost of legal advice for the very poor through legal aid, without prejudice to the payment of a modest contribution by the persons benefiting from such advice where this is required by domestic law; d. promoting the setting up where the need seems to appear of advice centres in underprivileged areas;

41 CMCE Rec (81) 7, § 4.

42 Adopted by the Committee of Ministers on 8 January 1993 at the 484th meeting of the Ministers' Deputies.

2. Facilitate effective access to quasi-judicial methods of conflict resolution for the very poor by a. increasing the involvement of non-governmental organisations or voluntary organisations providing support to the very poor in quasi-judicial forms of conflict resolution such as mediation and conciliation; b. extending the benefit of legal aid or any other form of assistance to such methods of conflict resolution;
3. Facilitate effective access to the courts for the very poor, especially by the following means: a. extending legal aid or any other form of assistance to all judicial instances (civil, criminal, commercial, administrative, social, etc.) and to all proceedings, contentious or non-contentious, irrespective of the capacity in which the persons concerned act; b. extending legal aid to very poor persons who are stateless or aliens, in any event where they are habitually resident in the territory of the member state in which the proceedings are to be conducted; c. recognising the right to be assisted by an appropriate counsel, as far as possible of one's choice, who will receive adequate remuneration; d. limiting the circumstances in which legal aid may be refused by the competent authorities chiefly to those cases in which the grounds for refusal are inadmissibility, manifestly insufficient prospects of success, or cases in which the granting of legal aid is not necessary in the interests of justice; e. simplifying the procedure for granting legal aid to the very poor, and considering the immediate granting of provisional legal aid wherever possible; f. considering the possibility of enabling non-governmental organisations or voluntary organisations providing support to the very poor, to give assistance, in the context of access to the courts, to persons who are in a position of such dependence and deprivation that they cannot defend themselves; this appraisal should concern both proceedings before national tribunals and proceedings before the European Commission and the ECtHR and other international instances of judicial nature.
4. Consult whenever possible, in the framework of their general policy aimed at combating severe poverty, non-governmental organisations interested by the field covered by the present recommendation and voluntary organisations providing support to the very poor[43].

In the 90th meeting of the European Committee on Legal Co-Operation (CDCJ), reflecting the importance of legal aid as recognized by the Secretary General of the Council of Europe, in his 2nd report on the State of Democracy, Human

---

43 CMCE Recommendation No. R (93) 1.

Rights and the Rule of Law in Europe[44], held a debate on the challenges facing free legal aid schemes in Europe with a focus on Council of Europe standard-setting, monitoring and co-operation activities in this area, and with a view to promoting synergies between them. The debate included presentations on the current challenges to legal aid schemes by Peter van den Biggelaar (Chief Executive Officer of the Legal Aid Board, Netherlands) and by Stéphane Leyenberger (Executive Secretary, CEPEJ); on member state initiatives on the role of NGOs and civil society in Bulgaria and Romania by Maria Marinova-Alkalay (consultant) and on the Federal Law on Free Civil Legal Aid of the Russian Federation by Yury Zudov (Ministry of Justice, Russian Federation); and on Council of Europe co-operation projects in the area of legal aid in Bulgaria, Romania, the Russian Federation and Ukraine, presented by their respective project co-ordinators. The CDCJ welcomed the debate and, in particular, the opportunity to receive information on the practical implementation of legal aid schemes within the context of the co-operation projects, and underlined its importance in deciding upon the direction of the committee's future work[45].

The CDCJ has stressed that access to justice is a vital element in the democratic process and one of the basic principles of the rule of law. It is essential to liberty, fairness and dignity and should be guaranteed to all individuals irrespective of their financial situation. It guarantees an individual's ability to protect her/his rights in conformity with human rights standards. Access to legal aid (the provision of legal advice, assistance and/or representation at either no cost or subject to a financial contribution) is crucial to ensure access to justice. Legal aid schemes should cover costs related to legal advice, assistance and representation. During 2016–2017 biennium the European Committee on Legal Co-operation (CDCJ) decided to examine the situation and challenges concerning free legal aid schemes in the member States. For this purpose, it has commissioned a comparative study, to include analysis of existing data on free civil legal aid schemes, obstacles to their effective work and existing gaps in the member States. On the basis of this analysis and its conclusions, the CDCJ decided to entrust a working group with the task of assessing the feasibility of developing policy guidance based on good practice and aimed at improving the efficiency and effectiveness

44 *State of Democracy, Human Rights and the Rule of Law in Europe. A shared responsibility for democratic security in Europe, Report by the Secretary General of the Council of Europe*, Strasbourg 2015.

45 90th meeting of the European Committee on Legal Co-Operation (CDCJ), Strasbourg, 28–20 October 2015, Meeting Report (Extract), Strasbourg, 10 November 2015, CDCJ(2015)24, p. 2.

of legal aid schemes in the areas of civil and administrative law in the member States. This work was carried out in 2018, and on the basis of its work and the positive assessment of the feasibility of preparing policy guidance on improving the effectiveness and efficiency of legal aid schemes and on the scope of such guidance, the drafting group worked on the preparation of the draft guidelines on efficiency and effectiveness of legal aid schemes in the areas of civil and administrative law in 2019 and 2020. The draft guidelines, approved by CDCJ at the 95th plenary session, aim to provide generic solutions that can make national legal aid schemes in the areas of civil and administrative law more efficient and effective, without changing their overall organizational framework[46]. The guidelines were finally adopted by the Committee of Ministers of the Council of Europe on 31 March 2021[47].

4. Conclusions

In the light of the analysis carried out, there is no doubt that the standards of the Council of Europe regarding free legal aid are important for guiding the practice of the Member States in this respect. The legally binding standards derived from art. 6 (3) (c) of the ECHR are directly applicable to the issue of free legal aid for the poor. But the Council of Europe, by means of resolutions and recommendations of the Committee of Ministers, has formulated a number of detailed standards which – although they are only soft law – play an important role in the activities of the Council of Europe member states when they create both statutory provisions on free legal aid and practice.

The fact that free legal aid was highlighted in the 2nd report of the Secretary General of the Council of Europe on the state of democracy, the rule of law and the rule of law in Europe means that the Council of Europe has recognized the importance of this issue. This formed the basis of a comprehensive study initiated by the European Committee on Legal Cooperation (CDCJ). Adopted by the Committee of Ministers guidelines *The Efficiency and effectiveness of legal aid schemes in the areas of civil and administrative law* not only take into account previous experience of the Members States in this area but also direct national systems in a way that will lead to the optimal arrangement of free legal aid in

46 *Legal aid*, https://www.coe.int/en/web/cdcj/activities/free-legal-aid, (accessed: 10.02.2021).

47 *The Efficiency and effectiveness of legal aid schemes in the areas of civil and administrative law. Guidelines adopted by the Committee o Ministers of the Council of Europe on 31 March 2021 and explanatory memorandum*, Council of Europe, Strasbourg 2021.

national regulations, and thus increase their effectiveness in the system of legal protection.

Literature

Bartlett F., Taylor M., Pro Bono Lawyering: Personal Motives and Institutionalised Practice, *Legal Ethics*, nr 2, 2016.

Birdsell T.L., A Few Minutes of Your Time Can Save Your Client's Dime: Obtaining Pro Bono Assistance for Legal Assistance Clients, *The Army Lawyer*, 1 June 2015.

Boutcher S.A., Private Law Firms in the Public Interest: The Organizational and Institutional Determinants of Pro Bono Participation, 1994–2005, *Law & Social Inquiry*, nr 2, 2017.

Cohn A., Reducing the Civil "justice gap" by Enhancing the Delivery of Pro Bono Legal Assistance to Indigent Pro Se Litigation: A "field" Assessment and Recommendations, *University of Florida Journal of Law and Public Policy*, nr 1, 2017.

Crebo K., Disaster Legal Services: Free Legal Assistance to Natural Disaster Survivors, *The Affiliate*, nr 1, 2012.

Daigle, M.N., Harris, S.J. Mummert, Crime Victims and Their Unmet Civil Legal Needs: Pro Bono Service Provision Among Private Attorneys, *Journal of Victimology and Victim Justice*, nr 1, 2019.

Decker K., Harley G., Svirtzev F., *Cross Country Comparison of Regional Mechanisms for Delivery of Free Legal Assistance*, Washington 2004.

Emrey J.A., Lawyers' Pro Bono Service and American-Style Civil Legal Assistance, *The Justice System Journal*, nr 2, 2008.

Faith-Slaker A., What We Know and Need to Know about Pro Bono Service Delivery, *South Carolina Law Review*, nr 2, 2016.

Friedl G., Non-Provision of Free Legal Assistance by a Lawyer in the Procedure before the Asylum Court not Unconstitutional, *Vienna Online Journal on International Constitutional Law*, nr 4, 2009.

Gruodytė E., Kirchner S., Pro Bono Work vs. Legal Aid: Approaches to Ensuring Access to Justice and the Social Responsibility of the Attorney, *Baltic Journal of Law & Politics*, nr 2, 2012.

Guild E., The Asylum Seeker's Right to Free Legal Assistance and/or Representation in EU Law, *Issues in International Migration Law*, 2015.

Herskoff H., Loffredo S., *Getting By: Economic Rights and Legal Protections for People with Low Income*, Oxford 2019.

Holness D., Recent Developments in the Provision of Pro Bono Legal Services by Attorneys in South Africa, *Potchefstroom Electronic Law Journal*, nr 1, 2013.

Jaskiernia J., *Funkcje Konstytucji RP w dobie integracji europejskiej i radykalnych przemian politycznych*, Toruń 2020.

Leal D.F., Status and Collaboration: The Case of Pro bono Network Inequalities in Corporate Law, *Social Science Research*, vol. 84, 2019.

Maguire R., Shearer G., Field R., Reconsidering Pro bono: A Comparative Analysis of Protocols in Australia, the United States, the United Kingdom and Singapore, *University of New South Wales Law Journal*, nr 3, 2014.

Moon R.T.Y., Access to Civil Justice: Is There a Solution? Pro bono Efforts Can Help Ensure Access to Legal Assistance for All Members of Society, *Judicature*, nr 4, 2005.

Mowbray A., Chung P., Greenleaf G., Building Sustainable Free Legal Advisory Systems: Experiences from the History of AI & Law, *Computer Law & Security Review*, vol. 34, 2018.

Nordenson U.K., The Proposed Swedish Systems of Free Legal Assistance and of Compensation to Victims of Crime, *Zeitschrift für Rechtsmedizin*, nr 2, 1972.

Przywora B., *Normatywny model przedsądowej nieodpłatnej pomocy prawnej*, Warszawa 2018.

Renouf G., Anderson J., Legal Services 'for public good', *Alternative Law Journal*, nr 1, 2003.

Sandefur R.L., Lawyers' Pro Bono Service and American-Style Civil Legal Assistance, *Law & Society Review*, nr 1, 2007.

Snyder L., *Democratizing Legal Services: Obstacles and Opportunities*, Lanham 2016.

Agnieszka Franczak, Bogusław Przywora

International and EU Standards for the Protection of Taxpayers' Rights and the Formalized System of Pre-Trial Free Legal Aid in Poland: An Approach to Analysis

Abstract: The study aims to present international standards for the protection of taxpayers' rights and an attempt to evaluate the Polish formalized system of free prejudicial legal aid in Poland in terms of the protection of these rights. In the paper we used the dogmatic and the comparative method.

Keywords: free legal aid, protection of the taxpayer's rights, European Convention on Human Rights, Charter of Fundamental Rights

1. Introduction

The literature often indicates that one of the key challenges of the modern tax administration is maintaining a balance between the rights and freedoms of the taxpayer and the effectiveness of the tax system[1]. Unfortunately, reformers of the Polish tax system in formulating their ideas even ignore the aspect of protection of taxpayers' rights, placing fiscal benefits (otherwise important) above fundamental rights. The complexity of Polish tax law has become so complex that very few taxpayers can afford the luxury of not using a tax advisor and filling out their own tax returns without professional help. The situation thus prompts us to consider the implementation by international state authorities and the EU standard of providing taxpayers with the right to a fair trial in the scope in which it includes access to free legal aid and the creation of an appropriate legislative framework for its implementation.

In this study, the dogmatic-legal method was used, and to some extent the historical-legal and systemic method. The paper adopts the meaning of "pre-trial

1 D. Bentley, *Taxpayers' Rights. Theory, Origin and Implementation*, Kluwer Law International, Alphen aan den Rijn 2007, p. 56.

free legal aid" consistent with the statutory regulations of 2015–2021. In addition to the analysis of the adopted legislative solutions, critical remarks were also presented regarding the currently applicable legal solutions, which mean that international and EU taxpayer protection standards are not fully implemented.

2. A particular need to protect the taxpayer's rights

By its nature, tax law is characterized by a high level of interference in civil rights and liberties. In addition, the method of self-calculation of the tax, which is dominant in the system of tax law, means that it is the taxpayer's obligation to calculate the tax amount and pay it to the account of the competent tax authority. Incorrect interpretation of tax law provisions by taxpayers, as a rule, gives rise to tax liability due to the emergence of tax arrears, the obligation to pay interest for late payment, often the payment of amounts resulting from administrative sanctions imposed on the taxpayer, or fiscal penal liability[2].

We are currently witnessing a growing imbalance between the obligations and rights of taxpayers. We are seeing an increase in taxpayers' obligations, not accompanied by an increase in their rights[3]. This state of affairs results, on the one hand, from the growing tendency in the volume of legal regulations and their increasing complexity, and on the other hand, from the growing aggressiveness of the tax apparatus in the control and enforcement processes of tax obligations[4]. For some time now, we have been dealing with a characteristic striving of various groups of tax system reformers to achieve mainly the fiscal goal by "sealing" the tax system, with a simultaneous disturbing tendency to reduce the importance of taxpayer's rights protection instruments in the process of applying the law, such as, for example, official interpretations of tax law in Poland[5].

Undoubtedly, along with the increase in the complexity and repressive nature of the tax law, it should be counterbalanced with appropriate mechanisms to protect the taxpayer's rights. The purpose of the taxpayer's rights protection mechanisms is to achieve a specific balance between the needs of the state and the rights of the individual[6]. Given the priority political goal of combating tax

---

2 A. Franczak, *Ochrona praw podatnika. Diagnoza sytuacji*, Warszawa 2021, p. 12.

3 M. Cadesky, I. Hayes, D. Russel, *A Model Taxpayer Charter. Preliminary Report. Towards Greater Fairness in Taxation, AOTCA, CFE, STEP*, London 2013, p. 19.

4 B. Brzeziński, *Prawo podatkowe. Zagadnienia teorii i praktyki*, Toruń 2017, p. 565.

5 A. Franczak, *Ochrona praw…*, p. 12.

6 D. Bentley, *Taxpayers' Rights. Theory, Origin and Implementation*, Kluwer Law International, Alphen aan den Rijn 2007, p. 56.

avoidance or tax evasion, mechanisms to protect taxpayers' rights and ensure tax law certainty remained outside the focus of various groups of tax reformers. In Poland, there are also no solutions such as a taxpayer's rights charter (declaration) or an institution of the Taxpayer's Rights Ombudsman, which would realistically allow taxpayers to protect themselves from over-zealous tax authorities. Hence, the institution of free legal aid is of particular importance[7].

3. The Strasbourg standard of a fair trial in the light of the European Convention on Human Rights

The most effective international instrument for the protection of human rights is the ECHR[8]. The main purpose of the ECHR is to ensure protection for an individual, but also to take up problems of public order in the general interest, raise the standards of human rights protection and transfer jurisprudence in this area to the entire community of Member States[9]. In order to ensure the proper functioning of the right-of-aid mechanisms in a democratic society, it is necessary to guarantee, in accordance with the ECHR, the right of the individual to a fair trial[10]. The right to a fair trial is included in art. 6 (1) of the ECHR, according to which everyone has the right to claim their rights before a court or tribunal. Thus, the regulation of this article implements the principle of the right to a fair trial. ECtHR in Delcourt v. Belgium[11] emphasized the special nature of this right. He pointed out that the right to a fair trial cannot be narrowly interpreted, any interpretation of art. 6 (1) of the ECHR would not correspond to both the purpose and nature of this regulation. The right of access to a court must be practical and effective[12]. Thus, the individual must have a clear and practical possibility to challenge the act constituting an interference with his rights[13]. All procedural

---

7 A.Franczak, *Ochrona praw…*, p. 13.

8 See also: B. Przywora, A. Wróbel, *Formalised Access to Pre-jurisdictional Free Legal Aid. Analysis based on Example of Ukraine, Poland, Great Britain and Sweden*, Berlin 2023, p. 26–28.

9 See ECHR judgment in the case of Karner v. Austria of 26.07.2003, application no. 40016/98.

10 A. Kulikowska, *Prawo do pomocy prawnej w świetle orzecznictwa Europejskiego Trybunału Praw Człowieka,* Studenckie „Zeszyty Naukowe" 2016, Vol. XIX, no. 30, p. 40; ECHR judgment in the case of De Cubber v. Belgium of 26 October 1984, application no. 9186/80.

11 ECHR judgment in the Delcourt v Belgium of 07.23.1968, Application No. 1474/62.

12 ECHR judgment in the Bellet v France of 04.12.1995 Application No. 40886/06.

13 Ibidem.

laws of states are intended to guarantee the proper administration of justice and compliance with the principle of legal certainty, and the parties must be entitled to expect that they will be applied[14].

The position of the ECtHR regarding the application of art. 6 of the ECHR in tax matters is basically negative, which was reflected in the often discussed judgment in the Ferrazini case[15]. However, a different position is presented in the literature, according to which this provision also applies in tax matters[16]. The authors of this publication also support the possibility of applying the protection provided for in art. 6 of the ECHR for tax matters.

The right to defense in the ECHR was formulated in art. 6 sec. 3 of the ECHR. Guarantees resulting from sec. 3 Art. 6 of the ECHR should, in the opinion of the European Court of Human Rights, be guaranteed also in the preparatory proceedings[17]. The Tribunal stated that even if the main objective of art. 6 of the ECHR in relation to criminal proceedings, it is to ensure a fair trial before the court which is competent to decide on a criminal accusation, this does not mean that art. 6 of the ECHR does not apply to pretrial proceedings[18].

The provisions of the ECHR regarding the right to a fair trial will leave states a choice of the means of implementing the right to aid in their internal legal systems, while the task of the ECtHR is to control the compliance of the chosen method with the principles of a fair trial[19]. Any exception to access to legal aid must be clearly specified and strictly limited in time. This is particularly true

---

14 ECHR judgment on the Cañete de Goñi v Spain on 15.10.2002, Application No. 55782/00.

15 ECHR judgment in the *Ferrazzini v Italy* of 12.07.2001, Application No. 44759/98.

16 P. Baker, *Should Article 6 ECHR (Civil) Apply to Tax Proceedings?* Intertax 2001, vol. 29, Issue 6–7, pp. 205–2011; S. Frommel, *The European Court of Human Rights and the right of the accused to remain silent: can it be invoked by taxpayers?* Intertax 1993, No. 11, p. 520; N. Lee, *Time for Ferrazzini to be reviewed?* British Tax Review 2010, No. 6, p. 589; B. Brzeziński, *The Issue of the Application of Article 6 Paragraph 1 of the European Covention on Human Rights to Tax Cases* [in:] *System of Financial Law. System of Tax Law*, (ed. M. Radvan), Acta Universitatis Brunensis, Juridica, Editio Scientia Vol. 515, Brno 2016, p. 273; A. Brzezińska-Rawa, A. Franczak, *Poglądy nauki prawa podatkowego na stosowanie art. 6 ust. 1 EKPC w sprawach podatkowych* [in:] A. Franczak (ed.), *Ochrona praw…*, p. 56.

17 ECHR judgment on Pishchalnikov v. Russia of 24.09. 2009, application no. 7025/04.

18 As cited in: E. Cape, Z. Namoradze, R. Smith, T. Spronken, *Effective Criminal Defence and Fair Trial* [in:] *Effective Criminal Defence in Europe*, E. Cape, Z. Namoradze, R. Smith, T. Spronken (eds.), Antwerpia–Oksford–Portland 2010, p. 5.

19 A. Kulikowska, *Prawo do pomocy…*, p. 45.

when allegations of severely sanctioned crimes are brought, as the right to a fair trial must be respected to the highest possible degree[20].

It should also be emphasized that art. 6 of the ECHR is the minimum standard of protection that must be ensured by the states parties to the Convention. Each of the states-signatories to the Convention may therefore provide a broader scope of protection than that provided for by the aforementioned legal act but may not go below the required minimum. Legal norms expressed in the ECtHR are self-executing, i.e., they grant direct rights to individuals, and can also be directly applied by state authorities[21].

From the point of view of ensuring in practice the right to a fair trial (effective protection of the taxpayer's rights), art. 13 of the ECHR (right to an effective remedy) and in art. 14 of the ECHR (the exercise of the rights and freedoms listed in the Convention should be ensured excluding discrimination on grounds such as: sex, race, color, language, religion, political and other beliefs, national or social origin, membership of a national minority, property, birth or any other cause)[22].

From the above-mentioned regulations of the Convention (art. 6, 13 and 14) one can indirectly infer a positive obligation of the state to construct an effective system of legal aid in order to have an effective right of access to a court. The states have the right to choose the forms of action[23]. One of these solutions may be free pre-trial legal aid (free legal counseling, free civic counseling). This form of aid from the state primarily provides access to information about the citizen's rights and obligations (taxpayers' rights and obligations, and at the same time about the legal possibilities of initiating court proceedings in the effective assertion of rights). In this sense, the formalized system of pre-trial free legal aid is an

---

20 ECHR judgment on Salduz v Turkey on 27.11.2008, The Grand Chamber. Application no. 36391/02.

21 See P. Hofmański, *Europejska Konwencja Praw Człowieka…*, p. 38; J. Braciak, *Prawo do prywatności…*, pp. 304–305; K. Skubiszewski, *Konstytucyjne ujęcie stosunku prawa polskiego do prawa międzynarodowego*, „Państwo i Prawo", 1987, z. 10, pp. 138–140.

22 Cf.: M.A. Nowicki, *Komentarz do art. 14 EKPCz*, [in:] *Wokół Konwencji Europejskiej. Komentarz do Europejskiej Konwencji Praw Człowieka*, M.A. Nowicki (ed.), Warszawa 2017.

23 See B. Przywora, A. Wróbel. *Poradnictwo obywatelskie w świetle badań prawnoporównawczych,* Warszawa 2020, pp. 22–23. Also in: K. Flaga-Gieruszyńska, *Idea pomocy prawnej z urzędu w postępowaniu cywilnym*, [in:] *Aequitas sequitur legem. Księga Jubileuszowa z okazji 75. urodzin Profesora Andrzeja Zielińskiego*, K. Flaga-Gieruszyńska, G. Jędrejek (eds.), Warszawa 2014, p. 55.

instrument (bridge) in the effective exercise of the right to a fair trial. It should be remembered that the Convention was constructed with a high degree of generality, and only the case law of the ECtHR specifies the universal standards of the Convention[24], at the same time, it leaves countries free to use mechanisms to ensure the implementation of the Convention standards.

4. The right to an effective remedy and the right to defense under the Charter of Fundamental Rights

The Charter is a collection of fifty fundamental human rights and civic obligations. The CFR is legally binding by the Treaty of Lisbon[25], which entered into force on 1 December 2009. Thanks to the granting of a legal status equal to the treaties, the CFR gained the rank of primary law. The provisions of the Charter in accordance with art. 51 (1) of the CFR are addressed to the institutions, bodies, offices and agencies of the UE with due regard for the principle of subsidiarity and to the Member States when they are implementing UE law.

The right to an effective remedy and to a fair trial is guaranteed in art. 47 CFR. It should be noted that art. 47 of the CFR refers to art. 6 of the ECHR. Pursuant to the first paragraph of art. 47 of the CFR, everyone whose rights and freedoms guaranteed by the law of the Union are violated has the right to an effective remedy before a tribunal. The literature indicates that art. The 47 CFR has two faces: access to fair trial and quality of the procedure. Right to a fair trial (which includes access to an effective remedy to a court with full jurisdiction, independent and impartiality, including the right to legal aid; the right to enforce a final and binding court decision without delay; the right not to challenge a final court decision). The right to a certain quality of the procedure – fair (the right to defense in the form of the right to participation and the right to: be heard, equality of arms, open proceedings, proceedings within a reasonable time).

In turn, art. 48 of the CFR guarantees two procedural rights: the presumption of innocence (paragraph 1) and respect for the rights of the defense (paragraph 2). The explanations to the Charter indicate that art. 48 of the CFR guarantees the rights reflected in art. 6 of the ECHR, in par. 2 and 3, and

---

24 Cf. M. Florczak-Wątor, *Horyzontalny wymiar praw konstytucyjnych*, Kraków 2014, pp. 33–43; B. Przywora, *Normatywny…*, p. 103.

25 Treaty of Lisbon, amending the Treaty on European Union and the Treaty establishing the European Community, signed in Lisbon on 13 December 2007, Journal U. UE 2007/C 306/01.

consequently – considering art. 52 sec. 3 of the CFR, the rights guaranteed in art. 48 The CFR should be interpreted in the same way as art. 6 sec. 2 and 3 of the ECHR.

In order to ensure the right to an effective remedy and the right to defense (including protection of the taxpayer's rights), art. 21 of the CFR, which provides for the prohibition of discrimination. This article extends the scope of protection against discrimination in the EU legal order to include new criteria such as genetic characteristics, worldview, origin, political beliefs and property status. And it is the property status that cannot discriminate against the taxpayer as regards access to legal aid. These provisions of the CFR should be used to search for sources for creating, in particular, forms of free pre-trial legal aid[26].

5. Formalized system of free pre-trial legal aid in Poland – Selected issues

The issue of legal and civic counseling in Poland has been the subject of extensive research and analyzes conducted in recent years mainly by non-governmental organizations and lawyers and sociologists cooperating with them. The result of these works was the adoption of the provisions of the Free Legal Aid Act. Undoubtedly, it can be concluded that the right to free legal aid is an important structural element of the right to an effective remedy and the right to a defense. It is from this perspective that the public authorities' duty to comprehensively regulate this matter should be perceived.

The provision of free legal aid, free civic counseling and legal education belong to the new public administration tasks category. These are tasks commissioned from the scope of government administration, performed by the poviat in consultation with communes or independently. Apart from this power of the state, there are many forms of free legal counseling[27]. This is primarily about aid provided by attorneys, legal advisers, notaries or additional advisers.

The first to be emphasized is the provisions of the Free Legal Aid Act[28]. As is clear from the government's justification of the project, it aimed to implement "the country's development strategy until 2020, set out in Resolution No.157 of the Council of Ministers of 25 September 2012 on the adoption of the National

26 B. Przywora, A. Wróbel. *Poradnictwo…*, pp. 30–31.

27 B. Paxford, *Komentarz do art. 2*, [in:] *Ustawa o nieodpłatnej pomocy prawnej oraz edukacji prawnej. Komentarz*, B. Paxford, R. Rynkun-Werner, M. Wasylkowska-Michór (eds.), Warszawa 2016, p. 5.

28 Item 1255.

Development Strategy 2020 (Monitor Polski of 2012, item 882), which provides for better access to legal information and legal services, including access to legal aid for people in difficult life situations that they cannot overcome using their own powers, resources and possibilities"[29]. The project was also an important element of the Prime Minister's exposé delivered on 1 October 2014, i.e., it fulfills the assumptions of the strategy of the "Law for everyone" program. This program assumed the cooperation of government administration, local government units, and non-governmental organisations to guarantee free access to the reduction of the financial barrier present in Poland through good legal service[30]. The introduced regulations were to constitute the next stage of "building a coherent system of aid to citizens within the broadly understood administration of justice"[31] based on EU and international documents, e.g., art. 47 of the CFR and Recommendation No. R (93) of the Committee of the Council of Ministers of the Council of Europe to member states on effective access to law and justice for the poorest[32].

As a rule, an attorney or legal advisor provides legal aid in person based on a civil law contract concluded with the poviat. On the other hand, it is envisaged that an advocate or legal adviser may use the aid of, for example, trainees, and in the event that the point of free legal aid is entrusted to run a non-governmental organization conducting public benefit activities, apart from attorneys and legal advisers, legal aid will also be provided by tax advisers[33].

From the point of view of the subject, it is necessary to indicate the amendment of the analyzed act. The designer was the President of the Republic of Poland[34]. The purpose of the amendment was:

(a) extending both the subjective and objective scope of the act,
(b) streamlining the regulation of the Act in the field of selecting non-governmental organizations that provide free legal aid and enabling them to provide free civic counseling under the Act,
(c) limitation of exemptions[35].

---

29 Justification, Sejm Paper/7th term, No. 3338; http://www.sejm.gov.pl/Sejm7.nsf/druk.xsp?nr=3338, p. 1. (accessed: 24.02.2021).
30 Justification, Sejm Paper/term VII, No. 3338, p. 2.
31 Ibidem, p. 2.
32 Ibidem, p. 3.
33 Ibidem, p. 12.
34 Sejm Paper No. 1868; http://www.sejm.gov.pl/sejm8.nsf/druk.xsp?Nr=1868 (accessed: 24.02.2021).
35 Justification, Sejm Paper/VIII term, No. 1868, p. 1.

The low effectiveness of the regulation was also indicated as an argument in favor of the change. In the first year of the Act's implementation, ie in 2016, "377,506 legal advice was provided, including: 237,389 advice at 882 points run by attorneys-at-law or legal advisers and 140,117 advice at 642 points run by non-governmental organizations. Thus, for one point run by advocates or legal advisers there is on average slightly more than 269 advice, and for one point run by non-governmental organizations – slightly more than 218 advice. Moreover, the collected data indicate that in 2016, in 76.68 % of cases, the time needed to provide one advice was 15 to 60 minutes (15–30 minutes accounted for 42 % of consultations, and 30–60 minutes – 34.68 minutes of consultations), while in 14.16 % of cases the time necessary to provide one advice was over 60 minutes, and in 9.41 % of all cases this time did not exceed 15 minutes"[36].

6. Assessment of the Polish system of free legal aid in terms of the implementation of international and EU standards of taxpayers' rights

The scope of pre-trial free legal aid it covers is significant for the protection of the individual (including the taxpayer's rights):

1. informing a natural person about the applicable legal status and his/her rights or obligations, including in connection with pending preparatory, administrative, court or administrative court proceedings, or
2. indicating the authorized person how to solve their legal problem, or
3. preparation of a draft letter, except for pleadings in pending preparatory or court proceedings and letters in pending administrative court proceedings, or
4. free mediation, or
5. drawing up a draft letter for exemption from court costs or appointing an ex officio attorney in court proceedings or appointing an attorney, legal advisor, tax advisor or patent attorney in administrative court proceedings and providing information on the costs of the proceedings and the financial risk related to bringing the case to court (art. 3 of the Act).

The importance of this provision for a person using legal aid should be emphasized. Persons providing legal aid are obliged not only to inform about the applicable regulations, but also about possible costs of conducting court proceedings and the time for their completion in connection with the exercise of procedural

36 Justification, Sejm Paper/VIII term, No. 1868, p. 2.

rights. In addition, a positive assessment should be made of the solution under which an entitled person may benefit from aid in the form of a draft letter (excluding pleadings in pending preparatory or court proceedings and pleadings in pending administrative court proceedings). In practice, such a solution is especially useful for people who are elderly or who are unable to cope with a difficult life situation on their own[37].

Free legal aid and free civic counseling are available to an entitled person who is unable to bear the costs of paid legal aid, including a natural person running a sole proprietorship who does not employ other persons in the last year (art. 4 (1) of the Act). Doubts as to compliance with the standards of taxpayers' rights may also be raised by the method of determining the catalog of persons entitled to such aid, applicable in the act. This catalog was drawn up in a fairly general, unverifiable way (the taxpayer makes a declaration that he is unable to bear the costs of paid legal aid), and on the other hand, it is narrow, without the objective income criterion (taxpayers conducting sole proprietorship employing other persons in during the last year). De lege ferenda, this problem could be solved by changing the subjective scope of persons entitled to help[38]. An example here could be, for example, the regulation of the German Act on Legal Aid and Legal Representation for People with Low Income, analogous to the Polish Act, which stipulates that any person whose economic and personal situation does not allow for the costs of such advice on their own and who has no other means of obtaining such advice (e.g., under insurance from a social organization, trade union or state body)[39].

Free legal aid at points entrusted to run a non-governmental organization may be provided by: (1) a tax advisor – in the field of tax law, excluding tax matters related to running a business; (2) a person who: (a) graduated from legal studies and obtained a master's degree or obtained a foreign law degree recognized in the Republic of Poland, (b) has at least three years of experience in performing activities that require legal knowledge directly related to the provision of legal aid, (c) takes full advantage of public rights and has full legal capacity, (d) has not been punished for an intentional offense prosecuted by public prosecution or a fiscal offense; (3) mediator in the field of free mediation (art. 11 (3) of the Act).

37 B. Przywora, *Normatywny model…*, pp. 395–396.

38 A. Ploszka, *Publicznoprawny status jednostki skrajnie ubogiej*, Warszawa 2019, LEX/el.

39 § 1 Gesetz über Rechtsberatung und Vertretung für Bürger mit geringem Einkommen (Beratungshilfegesetz), https://www.gesetze-im-internet.de/berathig/BJNR006890980.html (accessed: 26.02.2021).

The adopted solutions should be assessed as not fully effective due to the lack of implementation of the basic assumptions, which should support and lead to ensuring proper access to free legal aid in the field of tax law, especially at the pre-trial stage. The adopted solution raises doubts, in particular from the point of view of professionalism in providing legal aid in the field of tax law. Incorrect legal advice may result in far-reaching losses by the taxpayer who asks for the advice, including: the obligation to pay default interest, pay the amounts resulting from administrative sanctions imposed on the taxpayer, or even incur fiscal penal liability. The authors postulate that the catalog of persons providing this aid should be narrowed down to persons having, on the one hand, appropriate powers (e.g., attorneys-at-law, legal advisers, tax advisers), and on the other hand, several years of relevant experience in the area of tax law application.

Further doubts arise from paragraph 11. 3a of the Act, i.e., concerning the institution itself, the so-called free civic counseling in terms of the subject matter with free legal aid. First of all, the problem arises with regard to the persons indicated in this article as authorized to provide this counseling. The Act stipulates that free civic counseling may be provided by a person who:

1. has a university degree,
2. completed with a positive assessment training in the provision of civic counseling, or having experience in providing civic counseling and obtaining a certificate confirming having knowledge and skills in this field issued by an entity authorized to conduct training and an additional training.

Civic counseling aims to raise the legal awareness of a person in terms of their rights or obligations and to support them in solving problems independently. These activities, if necessary, boil down to drawing up, together with the authorized person, an action plan and aid in solving the problem. The scope of free civic counseling includes "in particular advice for indebted persons and advice in the field of housing and social security" (art. 3a (1) of the Act) and free mediation (art. 3a (2) of the Act). In our opinion, this aid should be provided by persons who have qualifications proving professional preparation to provide such aid, e.g., the following qualifications: attorney-at-law, legal advisor, tax advisor, patent attorney. The adopted solution proves the lack of a comprehensive approach to providing the individual (taxpayer) with legal aid at the highest level.

7. Conclusions

The ECHR and the CFR constitute the basis for formulating solutions to protect taxpayers' rights. One of the instruments for the implementation of these standards is the formalized system of free pre-trial legal aid. The introduction of this solution meets social expectations. Thus, Poland joined the group of countries in which the system of free legal aid was introduced in order to implement the right to a fair trial. In this study, we highlighted the basic issues related to the functioning of this aid in the field of tax law. The formulated de lege ferenda conclusions may contribute to more effective protection of the taxpayer's rights. In our opinion, there is no single solution to the problems related to providing taxpayers with effective, free pre-trial legal aid. Nevertheless, examining how the application of the standards for the protection of taxpayer's rights provided for in the Convention and the Charter looks like in the Polish system of formalized free legal aid at the pre-trial stage requires detailed research. These findings constitute a seed of remedial action as well as the adoption of a certain model of conduct. The findings made in the study provoke reflection on the need to improve the system of free legal aid and skilful involvement of various entities/persons in the provision of this aid.

Literature

Araszkiewicz M., *Nieodpłatna pomoc prawna – przegląd badań i materiałów z zakresu ekonomicznej analizy prawa*, Warszawa 2012.

Baker P., Should Article 6 ECHR (Civil) Apply to Tax Proceedings? *Intertax*, Vol. 29, No. 6–7, 2001.

Bandarzewski K., Udzielanie nieodpłatnej pomocy prawnej jako zadanie zlecone powiatowi, [in:] *Charakter i konstrukcja zadań samorządu terytorialnego*, M. Stec, S. Płażek (eds.), Warszawa 2017.

Bentley D., *Taxpayers' Rights. Theory, Origin and Implementation*, Kluwer Law International, Alphen aan den Rijn 2007.

Bentley D., *Taxpayers' Rights. Theory, Origin and Implementation*, Alphen aan den Rijn 2007.

Brzeziński B., The Issue of the Application of Article 6 Paragraph 1 of the European Covention on Human Rights to Tax Cases [in:] *System of Financial Law. System of Tax Law*, M. Radvan (ed.), Acta Universitatis Brunensis, Juridica, Editio Scientia Vol. 515, Brno 2016.

Brzeziński B., *Prawo podatkowe. Zagadnienia teorii i praktyki*, Toruń 2017.

Brzezińska-Rawa A., Franczak A., Poglądy nauki prawa podatkowego na stosowanie art. 6 ust. 1 EKPC w sprawach podatkowych [in:] *Ochrona praw podatnika*, A. Franczak (ed.), Warszawa 2021.

Cadesky M., Hayes I., Russel D., *A Model Taxpayer Charter. Preliminary Report. Towards Greater Fairness in Taxation, AOTCA, CFE,* STEP, London 2013.

Calderón J.M., Taxpayer Protection Within the Exchange of Information. Procedure Between State Tax Administrations, *Intertax*, Vol. 28, No. 12, 2000.

Cape E., Namoradze Z., Smith R., Spronken T., Effective Criminal Defence and Fair Trial [in:] *Effective Criminal Defence in Europe*, E. Cape, Z. Namoradze, R. Smith, T. Spronken (eds.), Antwerpia–Oksford–Portland 2010.

De Flora M.G., Protection of the Taxpayer in the Information Exchange Procedure, *Intertax*, Vol. 45, No. 6–7, 2017.

Debelva F., Mosquera I., Privacy and Confidentiality in Exchange of Information Procedures: Some Uncertainties, Many Issues, but Few Solutions, *Intertax*, Vol. 45, No. 5, 2017.

Diepvens N., Debelva F., The Evolution of the Exchange of Information in Direct Tax Matters: The Taxpayer's Rights under Pressure, *Ec Tax Review*, No. 4, 2015.

Flaga-Gieruszyńska K., Idea pomocy prawnej z urzędu w postępowaniu cywilnym [w:] *Aequitas sequitur legem. Księga Jubileuszowa z okazji 75. urodzin Profesora Andrzeja Zielińskiego*, K. Flaga-Gieruszyńska, G. Jędrejek (eds.), Warszawa 2014.

Florczak-Wątor M., *Horyzontalny wymiar praw konstytucyjnych*, Kraków 2014.

Franczak A., *Ochrona praw podatnika. Diagnoza sytuacji*, Warszawa 2021.

Frommel S., The European Court of Human Rights and the Right of the Accused to Remain Silent: Can It Be Invoked by Taxpayers? *Intertax*, No. 11, 1993.

Huang X., Ensuring Taxpayer Rights in the Era of Automatic Exchange of Information: EU Data Protection Rules and Cases, *Intertax*, Vol. 46, No. 3, 2018.

Jabłoński M., Prawo do nieodpłatnej pomocy prawnej jako „element treści konstytucyjnego prawa do sądu" – uwagi na tle postanowień ustawy z 5.8.2015 r. o nieodpłatnej pomocy prawnej oraz edukacji prawnej, [in:] *Ochrona praw człowieka. Zagadnienia praktyczne*, A. Hauser, M. Urbaniak (eds.), Poznań 2019.

Kulikowska A., Prawo do pomocy prawnej w świetle orzecznictwa Europejskiego Trybunału Praw Człowieka, *Studenckie Zeszyty Naukowe*, Vol. XIX, nr 30, 2016.

Lach D.E., Nieodpłatna pomoc prawna jako instrument zabezpieczenia społecznego, *Ruch Prawniczy Ekonomiczny i Socjologiczny*, Rok LXXVIII, z. 3, 2016.

Lee N., Time for Ferrazzini to Be Reviewed? *British Tax Review*, No. 6, 2010.

Nowicki M.A., Komentarz do art. 14 EKPCz, [in:] *Wokół Konwencji Europejskiej. Komentarz do Europejskiej Konwencji Praw Człowieka*, M.A. Nowicki (ed.), Warszawa 2017.

Paxford B., Komentarz do art. 2, [in:] *Ustawa o nieodpłatnej pomocy prawnej oraz edukacji prawnej. Komentarz*, B. Paxford, R. Rynkun-Werner, M. Wasylkowska-Michór (eds.), Warszawa 2016.

Płażek S., Nowe usługi powiatu w zakresie nieodpłatnej pomocy prawnej, [in:] *Działalność gospodarcza jednostek samorządu terytorialnego – dopuszczalność i granice jej prowadzenia*, M. Mączyński, M. Stec (eds.), Warszawa 2016.

Ploszka A., *Publicznoprawny status jednostki skrajnie ubogiej*, Warszawa 2019.

Przywora B., *Normatywny model przedsądowej nieodpłatnej pomocy prawnej w Polsce*, Warszawa 2019.

Przywora B., *Free Legal Assistance as an Instrument in Protecting the Rights of Foreigners in the Republic of Poland – A Contribution to the Discusion*, Vol. XX, z. 1, 2020.

Przywora B., Wróbel A., *Poradnictwo obywatelskie w świetle badań prawnoporównawczych*, Warszawa 2020.

Przywora B., Wróbel A., Formalised Access to Pre- jurisdictional Free Legal Aid. Analysis based on Example of Ukraine, Poland, Great Britain and Sweden, Berlin 2023.

Skubiszewski K., Konstytucyjne ujęcie stosunku prawa polskiego do prawa międzynarodowego, *Państwo i Prawo*, z. 10, 1987.

Wiliński P., Karlik P., Komentarz do art. 42 Konstytucji RP [in:] *Konstytucja RP, t. 1, Komentarz. Art. 1–86*, M. Safjan, L. Bosek (eds.), Warszawa 2016.

Winczorek J., O potrzebie badań empirycznych nad dostępem do prawa, *Państwo i Prawo*, Nr 12, 2016.

Winczorek J., *Dostęp do prawa. Ujęcie socjologiczne*, Warszawa 2020.

Michał Bożek

Free Legal Aid in the Federal Republic of Germany

Abstract: The study aims to present the legal provisions for free legal aid in the Federal Republic of Germany. The scope of the research will not only cover legal measures, but also the practices of law implementation, including the social and political environment. The core research question posed in the paper is the modeling of German solutions in this regard, as well as the issue of the reception of a possible German model in the legal systems of other European countries.

Keywords: legal aid, Federal Republic of Germany, constitutionalism

1. Introduction

The purpose of the study is to present the issues of free legal aid in the Federal Republic of Germany. The subject of the considerations will be, first of all, an analysis of laws and regulations in this regard. Secondly, an attempt will be made to answer the question about the originality of the German legal solutions concerning the title issue. Then, attention will be focused on assessing the practice of applying the said laws and regulations. As part of the so-outlined research subject, it will also be necessary to sketch the genesis of the applicable legal solutions and determine the impact of German historical experience on their shape. The paper will end with conclusions forming both *de lege lata* and *de lege ferenda* reflections.

The basic research method applied in the study will be a dogmatic method, consisting in an analysis of applicable laws and regulations. Subsidiarily, a historical method will be used, justified by the necessity to show the influence of historical arguments on the shape of the applicable legal solutions. An empirical method, which is necessary to show a practical dimension of the analysed laws and regulations and formulate an assessment of their formal rationality and actual functionality, will be used as the final one.

2. Free legal aid: Legal bases

Free legal aid is governed by the Act on Legal Services (*Rechtsdienstleistungsgesetz*). It forms part of the Act on New Regulations of Legal Cancelling Law (*Gesetz zur Neuregelung des Rechtsberatungsrechts*[1]), which was adopted on 12 December

1 BGBl. I, p. 2840.

2007 and – with some exceptions[2] – entered into force on 1 July 2008. Apart from the Act on Legal Services, this Act also includes an Introductory Act to the Act on Legal Services (*Einführungsgesetz zum Rechtsdienstleistungsgesetz*), as well as a number of provisions introducing numerous amendments to statutes governing court procedures.

Based on the Act on Legal Services, the Federal Ministry of Justice issued an executive regulation to this Act on 25 June 2008 (*Verordnung zum Rechtsdienstleistungsgesetz*)[3], which entered into force on 1 August 2008.

2.1. Genesis

The first attempt to regulate the issue of legal aid in Germany was made at the beginning of the 1920s. However, it was never implemented, despite the fact that both the Reichstag and the Reich Government worked on relevant bills. Ironically, it was materialized in the form of the Act on Protection against Abuses in Legal Counselling (*Gesetz zur Verhütung von Mißbräuchen auf dem Gebiete der Rechtsberatung*)[4] adopted on 13 December 1935 only after the actual liquidation of the democratic systemic order of the Weimar Republic and the seizure of power by the National Socialist camp. An important objective motivating the authors of this Act was the intention to prevent lawyers of Jewish origin, who were deprived of the right to practice in 1933, from engaging in legal counselling services in other forms than by providing attorney's services. Interestingly, despite the clearly anti-Semitic and exclusive nature of part of its provisions, this Act was, in a high degree, a legal instrument free from the influence of the National Socialist ideology, and it regulated the issue of legal aid in a systemic and innovative manner. These words are confirmed by the fact that in the law assessing the Third Reich's legal order, adopted on 20 September 1945 by the Allied Control Council, only those provisions of the Act on Protection against Abuse in Legal Counselling were repealed that were openly of an anti-Semitic nature. However, the Act itself was upheld, becoming the legal basis for legal counselling in the Federal Republic of Germany for many years, first in the West German state and after the reunification throughout Germany. On 1 January 1964, only its title was changed to the Act on Legal Counselling (*Rechtsberatungsgesetz*). It

2 Several provisions of the Act on Legal Services did not enter into force until 18 December 2008. Por. B. Przywora, *Normatywny model przedsądowej nieodpłatnej pomocy prawnej w Polsce*, Warsaw 2019, p. 311.

3 BGBl. I, p. 1069.

4 RGBl. I, p. 1478.

is also worth adding that the provisions of this Act were repeatedly reviewed in terms of their constitutionality by the Federal Constitutional Court, which consistently confirmed the compliance of these provisions with the Basic Law in its judicial decision[5].

Over time, the solutions contained in the Act on Legal Counselling more and more often became the object of criticism. The blade of this criticism was pointed especially at the absence of appropriate regulations on legal aid. This Act lacked a definition of legal aid, which made it practically impossible to draw a line between payable and free legal aid. As a result, a charge was also often laid that the Act on Legal Counselling was, in fact, an instrument to protect the interests of professional attorneys-at-law at the expense of citizens' access to legal aid and their right to choose an appropriate form of such assistance. It was also argued that the German solutions in the field of legal aid were in conflict not only with regulations contained in EU laws but also with the internal orders of the Member States. This criticism was voiced particularly strongly during the 58th Congress of German Lawyers in 1992. One of its participants stated then that in none of the EU Member States he knew, legal counselling was reserved only for attorneys-at-law and such far-reaching legal limitations on access to legal assistance as those in the Federal Republic of Germany were present nowhere else[6].

The criticism of the Act on Legal Counselling became an impulse for the Bundestag and the Federal Government to start working on a comprehensive law on legal counselling, and thus legal aid law, befitting the new era. Finally, at the beginning of 2006, the Bundestag received a bill drafted by the Federal Government, which was passed in 2008 in the form of the said Act on Legal Services as part of the Act on New Regulations of Legal Cancelling Law. As one can read in the explanatory statement of this bill, the initiators' intention was to completely repeal the Act on Legal Counselling of 1935 and replace it with a completely new legal instrument. The purpose of such an instrument was to protect the interests of all people seeking legal aid and to strengthen civic involvement in the legal counselling process. That was why deregulation and de-bureaucratisation of legal aid were to underlie the new statute. Moreover, the Act also had to standardize the existing terminology used in the Act on Legal Counselling. Instead of a few terms known to the Act of 1935 and several other statutes relating to legal advice, the new Act needed to include a collective

5 T. Weber, *Die Ordnung der Rechtsberatung in Deutschland nach 1945*, Tübingen 2010, pp. 77–79.
6 Ibid, p. 81.

definition of various forms of legal counselling. According to the bill originators' design, the best term was the category of "legal services". This category was later included in the title of a separate statute. Considering the fact that only out-of-court services became the subject of the Act on Legal Services, it became necessary to adopt relevant amendments to statutes governing court procedures along with the Act. For that reason, the Act on Legal Services was passed as part of the Act on New Regulations of Legal Cancelling Law[7].

3. Act on Legal Services

The subject matter of the regulation as formulated in the explanatory statement of the bill was clearly confirmed in Section 1 of the Act on Legal Services. This subject matter is the right to provide out-of-court legal services in the Federal Republic of Germany. If such services were to be provided outside the Federal Republic of Germany, the Act might only apply if their subject is German law. This provision also specifies the purpose of the Act, which is to protect people seeking legal aid, legal transactions, and the legal order from unqualified legal services. Simultaneously, this provision declares the integrity of the provisions of other statutes governing the rights to provide legal services.

Section 2 of the Act defines legal services. These are only those activities that are undertaken in someone else's case and that require specific legal knowledge in the form of the ability to make legal assessments (subsumptions). The explanatory statement of the bill, in which the requirement of "special legal knowledge" was defined as the ability to make substantive legal assessments rather than merely the ability to apply the law, serves as a commentary on the so-defined legal service[8]. It involves the ability to make a full and comprehensive legal assessment of a specific situation rather than general knowledge of the provisions applicable in such a situation[9]. It is worth adding that in their explanatory statement, the authors of the bill unequivocally decided that legal services could be both payable and free of charge[10]. The quoted provision also recognizes the activity of collecting someone else's receivables (the collection service) as a legal service, provided that it forms the object of independent professional activity.

7 Explanatory statement of this bill – see *Gesetzentwurf der Bundesregierung – Entwurf eines Gesetzes zur Neuregelung des Rechtsberatungsrechts*, Deutscher Bundestag – 16. Wahlperiode, Drucksache 16/3655 vom 30.11.2006, p. 1.

8 Ibid.

9 Ch. Deckenbrock, M. Henssler, *Rechtsdienstleistungsgesetz*, München 2015, p. 101.

10 See. *Gesetzentwurf...*, p. 2.

On the other hand, by force of this provision, such activities as the following ones were excluded from the scope of legal services: preparation of scientific opinions, arbitration of arbitral courts and activities of magistrates' courts, proceedings undertaken by contingents of employees in the interest the employed, mediation and other alternative dispute resolution methods, analyses of legal issues of a universal dimension presented in the media and running legal affairs within the framework of enterprises covered by the provisions of the Act on Joint Stock Companies.

In turn, Section 5 includes the so-called incidental services (*Nebenleistungen*) in the scope of legal services, the content and subject matter of which are materially related to another activity being part of the professional activity of specific entities provided that such entities have appropriate legal knowledge. Such "incidental services" can also be performed in cooperation with attorneys-at-law[11]. As examples of such services, the above provision indicates the execution of wills, property management, and aid fund management consultancy.

Pursuant to the Act in question, legal services may be provided by two groups of entities. The first one is formed by unregistered entities. This category of services includes gratuitous legal services. This involves primarily legal services of a gratuitous nature provided as part of family and neighbour relations and other personal relations. Secondly, these are free services provided outside the above-defined circle of family, neighbourly and personal relationships by people who have professional qualifications to provide payable legal services and by people qualified to practice the profession of a judge or acting under their instructions. Moreover, free legal services may be provided by associations, societies, professional organizations, and other similar organizations as unregistered entities, within the framework of their statutory tasks and for the benefit of their members. The final group of unregistered entities that can provide free legal services includes selected public entities that provide legal assistance as part of their tasks and within their competence. These are people appointed by the court or public body, public authorities and legal persons of the public law (including enterprises established by them for the purposes of carrying out public tasks), entities competent under national laws and meeting the requirements provided for in Section 305(1) of the Consumer Bankruptcy Law, headquarters of consumer organizations and related entities using public funds, as well as free social welfare associations (Sections 6–8 of the Act on Legal Services).

---

11 Ibid.

The second group of legal services includes services provided by registered entities. Such entities may be natural and legal persons as well as organizations without legal personality entered in a relevant register. Such services can be provided in three areas: collection of someone else's receivables, social security, and foreign law. Such entities must simultaneously demonstrate specific professional qualifications in one of the said areas. An entry in the register is made upon request of the entity concerned within three months from the date of submitting an application in this regard. The proceedings for entry in the register are carried out according to the provisions on the administrative procedure by competent administration authorities of individual federal states. The condition for gaining entry in the register is that applicants should have appropriate personal predispositions and demonstrate credibility in life, should have appropriate theoretical and practical knowledge in the area of the services provided, and should hold a professional liability policy guaranteeing insurance in the amount of at least EUR 250,000 per case. The register of such entities is public, and it must include the most important details concerning the entity registered. Activities of such entities are supervised by the authority making entries in the register, which may decide to remove an entity from the register as part of the supervisory procedure in cases specified in the Act. Apart from entities entered in the register, activities consisting in providing legal services in the said areas may also be performed by entities that conduct the same activity in one of the EU Member States or Switzerland, provided that their activities in Germany are of an occasional nature. Such entities don't have to apply for entry in the register; they are only required to report their activities to the authorities keeping the register, and such a report is only valid for one year and must be repeated every time after this period (Sections 10–16 of the Act on Legal Services).

4. Assessment

An assessment of the legal solutions adopted in the Act on Legal Services is not uniform. Their supporters usually emphasize the social benefits of deformalization and deregulation of legal services. Until the provisions under discussion came into force, legal aid had been the domain of attorneys-at-law, which meant that it had been essentially corporate in nature. It significantly limited citizens' options of getting access to legal services, and the greatest barrier in this regard was the costs of services provided by attorneys-at-law. As a result, not only interests of many people seeking legal aid suffered, which adversely affected citizens' sense of legal security but many of them were even deprived of the right to legal aid. The phenomenon of concentration of legal services in the hands of attorneys-at-law also led to a far-reaching bureaucratization of legal services, which, in turn, practically exempted these services from social control. All this resulted in a limitation of the fundamental rights of individuals, including the right to a fair trial. Apart from the aspect of protection of an individual's rights, the supporters of the Act on Legal Services also evoke arguments of a systemic nature. Namely, it is about the legislative arrangement of the issue of legal services in line with standards applicable in this respect in other EU countries. Arguments relating to the economics of court proceedings are usually raised by the supporters of the adopted solutions as the final ones. Deformalization of legal assistance and facilitation of citizens' access to legal services are an opportunity to increase the application of amicable procedures of settling legal disputes. The work effectiveness of courts and other state bodies established to resolve legal disputes, which often have to take up cases suitable for resolution under mediation and conciliation procedures, may also benefit from it[12].

Opponents of the solutions contained in the analysed Act often question the very idea of deregulation and deformalization of legal services. The simplification of legal services must not deprive them of their professional and specialist nature. Citizens' welfare and concern for legal security require that such services be provided by people with high professional qualifications and high ethical standards. In the opinion of advocates of this view, instead of systemic changes, it was only necessary to make adjustments facilitating citizens' access to legal aid provided by people performing the profession of public trust. The allegation about the lack of social control over activities of attorneys-at-law is generally dismissed by defenders of their privileged position in the area of legal services by stating that the state has sufficient control instruments in this regard. On the other hand, a manifestation of social control is citizens' option of choosing an appropriate legal representative, as well as the possibility of initiating appropriate control proceedings with respect to specific attorneys-at-law under applicable procedures. What is interesting, the critics of the Act on Legal Services include not only circles representing attorneys-at-law but also some representatives of other legal professions and people from the circle of legal science[13].

As the review of the current practice shows, the solutions adopted in the Act on Legal Services have not revolutionized the market of legal services. There is still a belief in German society that legal services constitute a special type

---

12 M. Krenzler, *Rechtsdienstleistungsgesetz*, Baden-Baden 2017, p. 10–11.

13 H. Dreyer, Ch.P. Lamm, T. Müller, *Rechtsdienstleistungsgesetz. Kommentar*, Berlin 2009, pp. 31–33.

of services and should be entrusted to specialized and highly qualified entities. Hence, most citizens' cases relating to legal assistance are still handled by attorneys-at-law, and mediation has become an increasingly popular method of resolving legal disputes in recent years[14]. However, it does not mean that the Act on Legal Services is a collection of provisions devoid of any practical meaning. Like any legal instrument that has only found its way into legal circulation, it requires time and dissemination so that the solutions it contains could reach public awareness. The discussion on its content and form, which has been held since the moment the Act entered into force, is undoubtedly the best way for the concept of legal services it implements to take root in this awareness.

5. Conclusions

The remarks presented above lead to certain general reflections. First of all, it should be noted that the solutions applicable in the Federal Republic of Germany with respect to free legal aid were shaped as a result of many years of discussions in communities of legal practitioners. Secondly, it is worth emphasizing that the shape of the existing solutions is a consequence of the retrospective approach of German lawyers and results from a skilful combination of the existing tradition with reformative intentions. Thirdly, it should be stressed that these solutions are characterized by legislative complexity and systemness. Fourthly, it is impossible not to add that their characteristic features are also deregulation and deformalization of legal services. And fifthly, one can risk a statement that, contrary to the current practice of using the services with restraint, there is a chance they will become more common and will substantially contribute to increasing citizens' access to legal aid and, consequently, raising their legal awareness significantly.

Literature

Deckenbrock Ch., Henssler M., *Rechtsdienstleistungsgesetz*, München 2015 (C.H. Beck).

Dreyer H., Lamm Ch.P., Müller Th., *Rechtsdienstleistungsgesetz. Kommentar*, Berlin 2009.

Finzel D., *Kommentar zum Rechtsdienstleistungsgesetz*, Stuttgart 2008.

Kleine-Cosack M., *Rechtsdienstleistungsgesetz*, Heidelberg 2015.

14 https://de.statista.com/statistik/daten/studie/167532/umfrage/meinung-zu-den-erfolgsaussichten-von-mediation-in-deutschland/

Krenzler M., *Rechtsdienstleistungsgesetz*, Baden-Baden 2017.

Przywora B., *Normatywny model przedsądowej nieodpłatnej pomocy prawnej w Polsce*, Warszawa 2019.

Weber Th., *Die Ordnung der Rechtsberatung in Deutschland nach 1945*, Tübiungen 2010.

Grzegorz Krawiec

The System of Free Legal Aid in the Netherlands

Abstract: The study aims to present the legal provisions for free legal aid in the Federal Republic of Germany. The scope of the research will not only cover legal measures, but also the practices of law implementation, including the social and political environment. The core research question posed in the paper is the modeling of German solutions in this regard, as well as the issue of the reception of a possible German model in the legal systems of other European countries.

Keywords: legal aid, Federal Republic of Germany, constitutionalism

1. Introduction

The Netherlands is a democratic state, the organs of public authority operate on the basis of the law. The importance of the Dutch legal system also results from the fact that the Netherlands belongs to the countries of the Roman law, which brings it closer to many other countries, and the Dutch science of law (even mentioning Grotius) affects the whole world[1].

The Netherlands has developed a rich and autonomous legal culture, and the current legal picture of the state is the result of a blending of influences, ranging from the adoption of Roman law (in the form of Roman-Dutch law) to the actual impact of case law derived from the ECtHR in Strasbourg[2].

Therefore, Dutch legal solutions in various areas of public life can be a model for other countries, including Poland. It is particularly visible in the area of free legal aid. The basis of the system of free legal aid, both in the Netherlands and in Poland, are points of free legal aid. In the Netherlands, however, this system is more developed: if in a specific case the helpdesks themselves are not able to provide aid (due to, for example, the complexity of the case, or the necessity to "use" a professional lawyer resulting from legal provisions), then the applicant is referred to professional entity: lawyer or mediator. The legal regulations applicable in the Netherlands in this regard govern the procedure. Additionally, they

---

1 R. Pohyla, P. Szreniawski, *Edukacja prawnicza w Holandii*, „Studia Iuridica Lublinensia" 2003, vol. 2, p. 181.

2 J.F. Nijboer, *Prokuratura w Holandii*, „Prokuratura i Prawo" 1997, no. 11, p. 79.

provide financial support (from the state budget) for those professional lawyers who provide aid.

Thus, the Dutch legal aid system, on the one hand, is intended to help people who cannot afford a professional lawyer, and on the other hand, it is also to assist lawyers, which is particularly important nowadays: lawyers operate in conditions of high competition, there is also a pauperization of the legal profession; in addition, the pandemic has severely impoverished lawyers.

The basis of the Dutch free legal aid system are legal advice points (*juridisch loket*), where you can obtain, inter alia, free legal aid. The client can also be referred to a lawyer or mediator. In the Kingdom of the Netherlands, there is also the Legal Aid Council (*Raad voor Rechtsbijstand*) acting as an entity that supervises the quality of work of lawyers and mediators.

And the Polish system of free legal aid is not so developed. We only have legal aid points here. The generally outlined system of free legal aid in the Netherlands is – in my opinion – a good model for Poland. It would allow not only to provide effective aid (in Polish legal aid points you will not receive aid in particularly complex cases), and it could also be a form of aid for professional lawyers, legal advisers and attorneys at law. Pauperization is also visible in their environment, which can be seen in the number of law offices being closed, as well as in the number of legal advisers and attorneys-at-law who apply for judicial positions[3].

A comparative legal analysis concerning free legal aid has already been carried out in Polish literature, but it concerned international law and the law of selected countries[4]. So if only for this reason, it is worth analyzing the legal solutions related to free legal aid from other countries.

The benefits that result from the analysis of foreign regulations are the same as the benefits of comparative law. They are as follows[5]: (1) comparative law contributes to the unification and unity of law, (2) it can be extremely useful in the sphere of concrete practical activity, (3) educating the role of comparative law, (4) the comparative method is needed for the study of the history of law or the study of the philosophy of law. This method can give an idea of the full

3 On the website http://krs.pl, the National Council of the Judiciary lists the number of candidates for judicial positions, taking into account their current profession. There are especially many professional lawyers here: legal advisers and advocates.

4 cf. B. Przywora, *Normatywny model przedsądowej nieodpłatnej pomocy prawnej w Polsce*, Warszawa 2019, chapter entitled. *Nieodpłatna pomoc prawna – analiza prawnoporównawcza*.

5 Indicated after: M. Ancel, *Znaczenie i metody prawa porównawczego*, Warszawa 1979, pp. 18–20.

picture of the legal phenomenon, (5) knowledge of foreign law is important for the legislator.

Therefore, the cognitive value of solutions in other legal systems is undoubtedly. As reported in the literature, while the comparative legal method cannot be a remedy for the weaknesses of the Polish legal system, the knowledge of foreign solutions creates the basis for a reasonable policy[6]. Comparative research in the field of administration also serves as a means of understanding real social processes, and the results obtained are verifiable evidence of the possibility and usefulness of such research, regardless of differences in social and political systems between countries[7].

It should be particularly strongly emphasized that the mere existence of certain legal solutions in other countries does not mean that they are good and worth adopting on the domestic soil. Their introduction into Polish law, without knowing the circumstances in which they were introduced in other countries (and without taking into account the domestic context), may do more harm than good.

2. Building a legal aid system in the Netherlands

In general, it can be stated that the issue of human rights plays a very important role in the Netherlands, and – as it is reported in the literature[8] – has a long history; religious freedom; fundamental freedoms and rights were incorporated into the Constitution, inspired by the French Revolution. In 1815, 1840, and 1848, these rights were extended and modified[9]. The provisions regulating

6 Z. Kmieciak, *Sędziowie prawa administracyjnego w postępowaniu administracyjnym w USA*, PiP z. 3/2009, p. 89.

7 S. Rozmaryn, *O międzynarodowych badaniach porównawczych w dziedzinie administracji*, PiP z. 10/1965, p. 488.

8 The human rights literature in the Netherlands is quite extensive; see e.g. E.A. Alkema, *Mensenrechten*, Rotterdam 1990; D.F. Scheltens, *Mens en mensenrechten*, Samson 1981; P.H. Kooijmans, *Mensenrechten panacee voor alle kwalen?*, Haarlem 1990; *Geschiedenis van de mensenrechten bouwstenen voor een interdisciplinaire benadering*, red.: M. Kuitenbrouwer, M. Leenders, Hilversum 2000; E. Brems, P. V. Heede, *Bedrijven en mensenrechten. Verantwoordelijkheid en aansprakelijkheid*, Antwerpen, Apeldoorn 2003

9 E.A. Alkema, *Fundamental Human Rights and the Legal Order of the Netherlands*, w: *International Law in the Netherlands*, vol. III, ed. H. F: van Panhuys, New York 1980, p. 110.

fundamental rights are included in the first title of the Constitution, entitled Fundamental Rights (art. 1–23).

The importance of free legal aid is evidenced by the fact that in the Dutch Constitution (Constitution of the Kingdom of the Netherlands[10]) contains provisions relating to it. According to its art. 18 Everyone has the right to be represented in court and administrative proceedings (paragraph 1). The rules for providing legal aid to the less wealthy are laid down in the Act (Section 2). This provision is right behind the provision establishing the right to a fair trial (art. 17 of the Constitution of the Kingdom of the Netherlands, according to which no one may be deprived of the right to a court having jurisdiction under the Act against his will). The right to a professional lawyer who represents the individual in court is part of the right to a fair trial.

The issue of legal aid is an important element of human rights, and the limitation of this right cannot be arbitrary. Also, the law providing legal aid to less wealthy persons cannot contain any content, but only those that fall within the limits of the Constitution. The law regulating the issue of free legal aid in the Kingdom of the Netherlands is the Law of 23 December 1993 on legal aid (Dutch: *Wet op de rechtsbijstand*[11]).

As already indicated above, a feature of the Dutch free legal aid model is that there is a central supervisory body for the legal aid system; it is the Legal Aid Council (*Raad voor Rechtsbijstand*). The Legal Aid Council is an independent administrative body. It has legal personality and its seat – in accordance with the principle of relocation – is in Utrecht. Since the council is a legal person, it must act through its authorities. The executive body is the management board. The management board is responsible for the organization and provision of legal aid, as well as for the organization and implementation of mediation and the promotion of the use of mediation. The Management Board, as a body of the Council, acts on its behalf, which means that it supervises the activities of legal aid providers and mediators, concludes contracts with registered lawyers (see comments below), as well as mediators, decides on applications for granting allowances for professional lawyers (see the notes below). The management board also makes sure that no region of the state is deprived of legal aid and mediation.

In addition, there is an advisory board that oversees the general course of affairs in the board and has advisory functions. In performing its duties, the

10 Constitution of the Netherlands: *Grondwet voor het Koninkrijk der Nederlanden* of August 24, 1815 (Staatsblad 1815, No. 45).

11 Staatsblad 1993 r., no. 775.

advisory board focuses on the interests of the board, including the importance of the proper performance of the tasks entrusted to the management board by or under the law.

The "heart" of the law is Chapter III, which sets out the rules for granting legal aid. It is granted to both natural and legal persons. The aid is available to persons with an annual income of EUR 40,400 or less (this amount will apply from 1 January 2021). For singles, the amount is € 28,600 or less (effective from 1 January 2021). In 2006, the legal aid system was reformed: from then on, legal aid was made conditional on both the client's income and assets. The Council verifies data thanks to IT access to tax data. About 38 % of the Dutch population (which totals around 17 million people) qualifies for legal aid[12].

Legal aid is provided by employees of legal advisory points, registered lawyers, mediators and by notaries, bailiffs and by persons with whom the Council concluded a contract for the provision of legal aid in specific areas of law.

The cornerstone of the Dutch free legal aid system are legal advice centers (*juridisch loket*). At the beginning, the people employed there will look at the legal and factual situation together with the client. It will be determined whether a specialized person is needed at all to deal with the matter. The services provided at points are completely free of charge. They offer basic information on applicable substantive law and applicable procedures. Individuals can turn to points with virtually any matter. The first contact of a person with an employee of the point is to explain the nature of the problem and to find out whether the problem presented is really a legal problem and what kind of help is most appropriate for the client. The point employees cannot act on behalf of the client on their own – they cannot, for example, represent the client in court.

The Act specifies situations in which legal aid is not provided. It goes, among others about the situation when:

- the submitted application is manifestly unfounded;
- the costs related to the legal aid provided are not proportionate to the importance (importance) of the case;
- the application is submitted by an attorney appointed to conduct the court case;
- the application is submitted by a freelance or self-employed person.

Legal advice centers are generally considered to be easily accessible and are largely quite informal. The number of such points in the Netherlands is 30; their

12 https://www.rvr.org/binaries/content/assets/rvrorg/nieuws/2019/legal-aid-in-the-netherlands-a-broad-outline-may-2019.pdf.

employees are in uniform and the points look more like a store than an office, there is an open space inside, with a waiting room and a few desks[13]. However, their importance is much greater: point employees often get acquainted with the matter at an early stage and this helps to avoid escalation and minimize costs. There are several channels by which potential customers can request aid from the point: website, e-mail, telephone, contact point or referral for an hour of consultation (by appointment).

What is characteristic here is that legal advice points are customer-friendly and their services are completely free of charge. Contrary to Polish legal advisory points, employees of Dutch points of sale constitute a kind of "corps of employees of legal advisory points". In Poland, legal advice at points is provided by selected lawyers or representatives of social organizations – working at the point is an additional activity for them. Working at a Dutch legal advice point is of basic nature to you. This solution can be considered appropriate as it allows you to identify yourself more with your job.

If there is such a need, juridisch loket staff will refer the person to a registered lawyer or mediator. The choice of a particular professional depends on their availability, specialization, distance from home and the number of referrals they have recently received. A registered lawyer/mediator receives an e-mail with information about the client and his problem and any advice provided by an employee of the point. The customer receives a letter of recommendation (*diagnosedocument*). With such a letter you can get a discount from a registered lawyer/mediator. Part of the costs is covered by the state budget. A registered lawyer/mediator receives a cash allowance (*toevoeging*).

Legal aid costs are partially covered by the client himself. This personal fee, while typically covering only a small fraction of the actual expenses, is intended to encourage clients to carefully weigh the pros and cons of taking a case to court, thereby discouraging frivolous cases. Immediately after closing the case, the lawyer invoices the council for the service. As a rule, a lawyer receives a fixed fee due for a given type of case; some exceptions may be made where the lawyer has spent more time on a specific case.

A lawyer can provide legal aid upon registration with the Council. The council makes an entry in the register upon the lawyer's request. The Board of the Council may establish in detail the conditions to be met by the lawyer, and the Act stipulates that these rules may apply to the lawyer's knowledge in a specific

13 https://www.rvr.org/binaries/content/assets/rvrorg/nieuws/2019/legal-aid-in-the-netherlands-a-broad-outline-may-2019.pdf.

field of law, organization of the office where the lawyer work. For some cases – criminal, mental health, asylum and immigration law, youth, victims of crime – additional conditions apply. A lawyer must have the appropriate knowledge and sufficient experience in this specific field.

Removal from the register may occur when a given person has lost the status of a lawyer, and also when the lawyer no longer meets the conditions for entry in the register. However, the basis for deletion may be the lawyer's lack of due diligence in providing aid. As you can see, this premise for deletion is vague and requires extremely careful analysis by the Council.

Only exceptionally, with the consent of the Council, legal aid may be provided by an unregistered lawyer. It is about special cases. The Act specifies two such cases:

- clear and motivated wish of the client to get help from a specific lawyer;
- the need for a lawyer with specialist knowledge in a specific area of law.

In some cases (where there is a dispute between the parties, for example in the event of a divorce or a labor dispute), the legal aid agent may refer the applicant not to a lawyer but to a mediator. In the case of mediation, two parties try to find a solution with the help of a mediator. The difference from a lawyer is that a lawyer acts for the benefit of only one party and can defend it in proceedings before courts and authorities. The mediator will help both parties come to an agreement. No court proceedings are needed. Mediation is often faster and therefore cheaper. Finding a solution is not about who is legally right. Mediation only works when both parties want to solve the problem together.

Mediators are entered in the register kept by the Council. They must meet the conditions specified by the Council, which include professional competence, insurance, organization of the office where the mediator works.

This legal aid system is complemented by other elements. Among other things, the Rechtwijzer[14] website functions; this is an online legal advice site. It does not in any way replace personal legal advice. Rechtwijzer is a good starting point for beginners and those looking for basic information, e.g., on family law, consumer matters, rent, debt etc. Rechtwijzer allows and helps an individual to pre-assess their legal situation. In addition, it provides easy-to-understand information and guidance on possible solutions to the most common legal problems. Rechtwijzer

14 https://rechtwijzer.nl/

is constantly developed and improved through feedback from users and service providers. It should be emphasized that he cooperates with research centers[15].

Additionally, it can be pointed out that the Justice 42 platform offers the uitelkaar.nl divorce website, with public legal aid available to low-income clients.

The legal aid system is supplemented by the actions of notaries. The legal basis for this is art. 56 of the Act of 1 March 1999 on the Notary Public (*Wet op het notarisambt*)[16]. The president of the chamber of notaries may grant a discount to a given person, upon their request, for a given notarial act. It is, among others, for the drawing up of a will, prenuptial agreement, partnership agreement, establishment of guardianship.

3. Conclusions

Undoubtedly, the Dutch solutions should be considered extremely interesting. The Dutch legal aid system is firmly embedded in the Constitution of the Kingdom of the Netherlands and should be considered in the context of human rights. For this reason, the legal aid system should be extensive, very accessible to individuals, and fully professional. There is no equivalent of the Dutch art. 18 of the Constitution of the Kingdom of the Netherlands, but the right to legal aid can be derived from the right to a fair trial (art. 45 of the Constitution RP). So it is also a human right. In this context, it should be emphasized that legal aid in Poland is provided by not only legal advice points, but also ombudsman institutions, e.g., the Ombudsman. It seems that the services provided by legal advice points and the Ombudsman overlap; The Ombudsman acts only in the field of freedoms and rights violated by public authorities.

When trying to transfer the Dutch solutions to Poland, it can be indicated that the Polish legal aid system can, firstly, be modified and, secondly, extended. The modification may involve a change in the way Polish legal aid points operate – for example by introducing a "corps of employees of legal advisory points". The extension of the Polish legal aid system may consist in the extension of this system with the possibility of referring complex cases to a professional lawyer or mediator, with the help of such a professional being subsidized by the state. In such a case, professional lawyers would be "shifted" to the second line (currently lawyers can provide services in legal advice points – additionally). Taking care of the quality of the services of a lawyer/mediator, entry in the register may be

15 https://www.rvr.org/binaries/content/assets/rvrorg/nieuws/2019/legal-aid-in-the-netherlands-a-broad-outline-may-2019.pdf.

16 Staatsblad 1999, no. 190.

compulsory. However, it is necessary to consider who would keep such a register – a separate body (as in the Netherlands, the Legal Aid Council), or the existing central body (e.g., the Minister of Justice). It seems that the existence of the Dutch Legal Aid Council is related to the fact that legal aid is of a constitutional nature. It should be emphasized that if the Polish legislator decided to establish a separate body, then it should be provided with the attribute of independence.

Literature

Alkema E.A., Fundamental Human Rights and the Legal Order of the Netherlands, [in:] *International Law in the Netherlands*, Vol. III, red. H.F. van Panhuys, Nowy Jork 1980

Alkema E.A., *Mensenrechten*, Rotterdam 1990.

Ancel M., *Znaczenie i metody prawa porównawczego*, Warszawa 1979.

Brems E., Heede P. V, *Bedrijven en mensenrechten. Verantwoordelijkheid en aansprakelijkheid*, Antwerpen, Apeldoorn 2003.

Geschiedenis van de mensenrechten bouwstenen voor een interdisciplinaire benadering, M. Kuitenbrouwer, M. Leenders (eds.), Hilversum 2000.

Kmieciak Z., Sędziowie prawa administracyjnego w postępowaniu administracyjnym w USA, *Państwo i Prawo*, z. 3, 2009.

Kooijmans P.H., *Mensenrechten panacee voor alle kwalen?*, Haarlem 1990.

Nijboer J.F., Prokuratura w Holandii, *Prokuratura i Prawo*, nr 11, 1997.

Pohyla R., Szreniawski P., Edukacja prawnicza w Holandii, *Studia Iuridica Lublinensia*, t. 2, 2003.

Przywora B., *Normatywny model przedsądowej nieodpłatnej pomocy prawnej w Polsce*, Warszawa 2019.

Rozmaryn S., O międzynarodowych badaniach porównawczych w dziedzinie administracji, *Państwo i Prawo*, z. 10, 1956.

Scheltens D.F., *Mens en mensenrechten*, Samson 1981.

Bogusław Przywora, Aleksander Wróbel

The System of Free Legal Aid in the Kingdom of Sweden

Abstract: The chapter aims to submit the system of free legal aid in the Kingdom of Sweden from the historical, theoretical and practical perspective. The first part of the analysis will present the historical development of the institution of free legal help. It will provide the answer to several questions concerning contemporary solutions. Oftentimes, the Swedish system was once called as an exemplar of most expanded free legal help possibilities. The situation has changed in the late 90s. The current solutions adopted in Swedish legal realm lead to conclusions that there are no institutions of free legal aid since in the vast majority of cases the person seeking help participates in costs to a greater or lesser extent. At the same time, the Swedish system is perceived as one of the most economically efficient attitudes toward legal aid. It is Authors intent to present a whole picture of the legal acts regulating free legal help in the Kingdom of Sweden. The preliminary results of the research indicate that Swedish standpoint toward legal aid is unique and can be a valuable source of comparative work.

Keywords: free legal aid, legal aid in civil cases, legal aid in criminal cases.

1. Introduction

The legal system of the Kingdom of Sweden contains many interesting solutions that seem to be of particular interest from a comparative legal perspective. Undoubtedly, the solutions regarding legal aid at the stage of court proceedings in the Kingdom of Sweden are an example of a departure from the assumptions adopted, for example, in Polish legislation. The Swedish system is an example of an evolution from one of the most generous legal aid systems, which was ineffective[1], to the system of abandoning the concept of free legal aid in favor of the participation of the state in the costs of the trial and shifting the burden to the so-called legal insurance[2].

---

1 Regeringens proposition 1996/97:9, p. 83

2 See also: B. Przywora, A. Wróbel, *Formalised Access to Pre-jurisdictional Free Legal Aid. Analysis based on Example of Ukraine, Poland, Great Britain and Sweden*, Berlin 2023, p. 37–48.

2. History of the institution of legal aid

The legal aid institution has existed in the Swedish system for over a hundred years. The first regulations regarding this aid were adopted as early as 1919[3]. The first comprehensive law on legal aid was adopted on July 1, 1973 (orig. *Rättshjälpslagen*)[4] (RL 1973). The solutions contained therein coexisted with the instruments in the form of exemption from costs and the award of an ex officio defender in criminal proceedings under the Code of Court Proceedings (orig. *Rättegångsbalken*)[5]. The general basis for exemption from costs was the poor financial situation of the person applying for legal aid[6].

Legal aid could be provided at the local government level and at the state level as part of court proceedings. As part of legal aid at the local government level, the model adopted in the *Jämtland* poviat[7] was used. It was based on the assumption that legal aid was provided with financial support from the state and local governments on the basis of an agreement concluded between the Swedish Bar Association (orig. *Sveriges Advokatsamfund*) and a specific local government unit. Next, legal aid should be indicated in court proceedings, in particular in criminal proceedings, before a court at the national level[8].

RL 1973 assumed legal aid in four different forms. The first of these was the general legal aid (orig. *Allmän rättshjälp*) successively legal aid in criminal matters (orig. *Rättshjälp åt misstänkt and brottmål*), legal aid in matters of public (orig. *Rättshjälp genome offentligt bitrade*) and legal advice (orig. *Rådgivning*)[9]. The multitude of forms of legal aid made the system very costly and ineffective in practice[10].

General legal aid was provided to natural persons as well as in matters relating to property protection. However, this aid was not available in the case of marriage contracts, disputes over real estate and in cases where the person had taken out legal insurance[11]. Another type of legal aid is legal advice, which consisted

---

3 I. Schoultz, *Legal Aid in Sweden*, [in:] *Outsourcing Legal Aid in the Nordic Welfare States*, O. Halvorsen Rønning, O. Hammerslev (eds.), Lund 2018, p. 45.

4 Rättshjälpslagen (1972:429)

5 Rättegångsbalk (1942:740).

6 Regeringens proposition 1996/97:9, p. 7.

7 P. S. Muther, *Reform Oflegalaid In Sweden*, "International Lawyer", Vol. 9, No. 3, pp. 481–482.

8 P. S. Muther, Reform of Legal aid In Sweden…, pp. 482–484.

9 Regeringens proposition 1996/97:9, pp. 78–79.

10 Ibidem…p. 79.

11 Ibidem.

of a direct analysis of the case and not more than an hour. With this type of aid, the income of the person was not taken into account (each person was entitled to it)[12]. Further, in RL 1973 there was legal aid in the framework of criminal proceedings in the form of a legal aid lawyer in criminal cases under Chapter 21 of the RB[13]. The right to a public defense lawyer was not conditional on the perpetrator's income[14]. This aid was supplemented by regulations on legal aid for victims of specific crimes under the Act on Legal aid to Crime Victims (orig. *Lagen om målsägandebiträde*)[15]. This aid was also not dependent on the income of the person to whom a public defense lawyer was appointed[16].

Such a diverse system was criticized because it proved to be complex, making it difficult for citizens to access. It was also emphasized that the existing aid financing system was not very transparent and costly[17]. In practice, there were situations where different types of legal aid coincided and a person could be represented in the same case by different representatives under different types of legal aid[18].

The professional literature of that time indicated that the Swedish system was one of the most generous legal aid systems in the world[19]. It was emphasized that the Swedish solutions required deep thought and thorough reform. As a result of works on the amendments, a new legal act was adopted – the Legal Aid Act (orig. *Rättshjälpslagen*), which entered into force on 5 December 1997 (RL 1997)[20]. It contains a radically different approach to legal aid, which relocates the concept of free legal aid in favor of a system of co-financing proceedings by the state.

3. Central legal aid authorities

Central to RL 1997 are the bodies responsible for implementing the legal aid system. The Swedish system has a central body which is the highest authority for the granting of legal aid – the Legal Aid Council (*Rättshjälpsnämnden*) (RN). It is composed of persons having the citizenship of the Kingdom of Sweden. The

12 Prop. 1981/82: 28, p. 12.
13 Regeringens proposition 1996/97:9, p. 80.
14 Ibidem.
15 Lagen (1988:609) om målsägandebiträde.
16 Regeringens proposition 1996/97:9, p. 80.
17 Ibidem....p. 81.
18 Ibidem.
19 I. Schoultz, *Legal Aid in Sweden..*, p. 46.
20 Ibidem.

chairman of the Council is the chairman, who is a retired judge or an ordinary judge[21], two members with a university degree in law and two members of other specialties (§ 48 RL 1997).

The most important act from the point of view of the functioning of the Council is the Regulation on the Instructions for the Legal Aid Council of 22 November 2007 (orig. *Förordning med instruktion för Rättshjälpsnämnden*)[22] (Instruction I). RN is an appeal body under RL 1997 (§ 1 of Instruction I). The council is the second-instance body for appeals against decisions issued by the Legal Aid Authority (orig. *Rättshjälpsmyndigheten*) (§ 44 RL 1997). The Supervisory Board operates at the Court of Appeal for Nedre Norrland and also uses the administrative facilities of this Court (§ 5 of Instruction II).

Another body within legal aid is the Legal Aid Authority[23]. The basis of its operation is the regulation of 22 November 2007. Instruction for the Legal Aid Authority (orig. *Förordning med instruktion för Rättshjälpsmyndigheten*)[24] (Instruction II). The tan institution is competent, inter alia, in cases of reimbursement of costs for the provision of legal advice and legal aid, it deals with cases concerning the reimbursement of the remaining funds under RL 1997. It is also the body that actually determines the amount of the legal aid fee for the attorney of the person to whom the aid has been granted[25]. The Legal Aid Authority is also responsible for promoting legal aid and counseling institutions, informing citizens about their legal aid rights. The authority also prepares instructions on access to legal aid, forms for exemption from fees for legal aid, etc.[26].

The Legal Aid Authority is headed by the President of the District Court in Sundsvall (§ 2 of Instruction II), and some administrative or managerial tasks may be delegated to an employee of the court administration (§ 4 of Instruction II).

The third entity authorized under RL 1997 to supervise the granting of legal aid is the court in the course of court proceedings. In RB, the court has the power to control the performance of the lawyers' duties and, unanimously, the court

21 More about the division of the judge profession in Sweden: B. Przywora, A. Wróbel, *Status prawny sędziego w Królestwie Szwecji*, [in:] *Status prawny sędziego Państwa europejskie*. Tom I, B. Przywora (ed.), Warszawa 2019, pp. 405–427.

22 Förordning (2007:1079) med instruktion för Rättshjälpsnämnden.

23 B. Przywora, *Normatywny model przedsądowej nieodpłatnej pomocy prawnej*, Warszawa 2019, p. 318.

24 Förordning (2007:1078) med instruktion för Rättshjälpsmyndigheten.

25 Sveriges Domstolar årsredovisning 2019, p. 75.

26 Ibidem.

decides to increase the number of hours of legal aid in the proceedings before the court (§ 34 RL 1997).

The Swedish legislator decided to link the bodies responsible for granting legal aid with the judiciary. Such a solution seems to be logical, if only due to the fact that legal aid is supposed to foster the realization of citizens' rights and freedoms, and thus cases regarding the granting or refusal of legal aid interfere with the fundamental rights of an individual and ensuring the existence of an independent body is most favorable towards assumptions.

4. Legal insurance

Another element of the Swedish legal aid system is legal insurance. Legal aid in the Kingdom of Sweden is primarily based on legal insurance and therefore RL 1997 was intended only as a safety valve in the event that a person does not have legal insurance or if it does not cover a specific category of cases. In practice, legal insurance is offered as part of property insurance or as a separate instrument as part of the insurer's offer. Legal insurance has been operating in Swedish law since the 1960s and has evolved from an entirely optional instrument to a mandatory instrument[27]. Starting from 1997, i.e., with the adoption of the new act, having insurance practically excludes the possibility of receiving aid in civil cases, in land courts and before the Supreme Court[28].

Legal insurance comes in many forms and serves different purposes. As a rule, it is available in disputes related to real estate and other property. Legal insurance is regulated by the Act on Insurance Activity of 2 December 2010 (orig. *Försäkringsrörelselag*)[29] (FL) and in the Act on Certain Contractual Provisions for Legal Protection Insurance of 2 December 993 (orig. *Lag om vissa avtalsvillkor för rättsskyddsförsäkring*)[30] (LVR).

Legal insurance in its current form is an obligatory part of real estate insurance. It covers only the costs of proceedings in civil disputes. Legal aid in this case may only be granted in exceptional cases. Legal aid may not be available if the person has legal insurance or similar legal protection that covers the costs of the proceedings (§ 9 RL 1997). The word "may" used creates the possibility of receiving legal aid in cases where the person does have insurance, but due to the

27 Regeringens proposition 1996/97:9.
28 I. Schoultz, *Legal Aid in Sweden...*, pp. 48–49.
29 Försäkringsrörelselag (2010:2043).
30 Lag (1993:1303) om vissa avtalsvillkor för rättsskyddsförsäkring.

boundaries of legal insurance or financial and personal conditions, it requires state support (§ 9 (2) RL 1997).

Legal insurance covers the costs of legal representation, but not the court costs themselves. It is emphasized that the compulsory legal insurance actually contributed to the reduction of budgetary expenses for legal aid under RL 1997, however, the scope of insurance is quite narrow and therefore there may be situations where neither insurance nor legal aid will cover a specific case[31]. In principle, the introduction of universal legal insurance was to contribute to the creation of a system in which legal aid is still the main instrument supporting the exercise of citizens' rights and freedoms, and the insurance only complements it in civil matters[32], in practice, however, it seems that legal aid is the safety valve for legal insurance.

Legal insurance is dealt with in Chapter 12 § 11 of the FL. It contains an exhaustive list of the categories of cases in which insurance may be granted. In point 17 of this provision, one of the categories of matters covered by insurance is legal insurance. This provision is made more specific by the LVR, which regulates the conditions and the form of the legal insurance contract. Where the legal insurance contract is part of a general insurance contract, it shall in each case be a separate annex or a specific part of the insurance policy. This agreement must contain a written specification of the scope of protection (§ 2 LVR). Legal insurance entitles the insured person to appoint a lawyer or another person as representative (Section 3 LVR). The insurance company is to notify the person of such a possibility when reporting the insurance case[33].

5. Legal aid

The concept of legal aid sensu largo is regulated by RL 1997 in § 1, dividing it into two types: legal counseling and legal aid sensu stricto. These two types of legal aid form one coherent system which provides for the possibility of receiving legal aid in a narrow sense only after using legal counseling. Swedish legislation provides for exceptions to this obligation. They are defined by the introduction of general clauses, which allows the authorities responsible for legal aid to issue decisions tailored to the individual facts and individual needs of the individual[34].

---

31 F. Regan, *The Swedish Legal Services Policy Remix: The Shift from Public Legal Aid to Private Legal Expense Insurance*, "Journal of Law and Society", Vol. 30, No. 1, March 2003, p. 50.

32 F. Regan, *The Swedish Legal Services Policy Remix*...p. 56.

33 Prop. 2006/07:50, p. 44.

34 Utvärderingavrättshjälpslagen(1996:1619), Rapport, del A, p. 8.

For example, an exception is when legal advice is clearly unnecessary or there is another specific reason, such as urgent situation due to the approaching end of the deadlines for submitting a specific pleading. Legal advice is to be a barrier mechanism against abusing the costly structure of legal aid in the strict sense[35]. When examining the practice of the authorities authorized to be exempted from the need to obtain legal advice, it is often taken into account that the advice has already been preliminarily analyzed and the basic information is already known to the person requesting aid. The second type may be a quasi-preliminary ruling situation in which a civil case is a consequence of criminal or administrative proceedings. In the event of prior criminal proceedings, the ex officio defender, on the basis of RB, provides legal aid[36]. However, the analysis of decisions issued by the Supervisory Board exempting the person from the obligation to obtain legal advice shows that such consents are issued sporadically. Decisions issued in the first year of application of RL 1997 exempted from the need to obtain advice in the case of a paternity action or in cases related to benefits[37]. On the other hand, Supervisory Board's refusals concerned, for example, exemption from legal advice of a Swedish citizen residing in Germany who submitted an application for the possibility of omitting legal advice. The Council did not agree in this situation, on the grounds that the mere fact of being outside the Kingdom of Sweden does not constitute a serious ground for exemption from the obligation to obtain legal advice within the meaning of RL 1997, since legal advice can also be obtained by telephone[38]. This leads to the conclusion that the Supervisory Board is quite restrictive in its approach to deviations from this adopted system.

The Swedish legislator introduced conditions for granting legal aid *sensu stricto*. Legal aid is available to a natural person with an annual income not exceeding SEK 260,000 (§ 6 RL 1997)[39]. Interestingly, entrepreneurs and former entrepreneurs are excluded from the scope of legal aid in cases relating to matters arising during their conduct of business activity (§ 13 RL 1997). Despite these conditions being met, legal aid does not have to be granted. The Swedish legislature has provided for additional restrictions, namely the State's share of the costs, depending on the nature and importance of the case, the amount in dispute and the circumstances of the specific case (§ 6 RL 1997).

35 Utvärderingavrättshjälpslagen(1996:1619), Rapport, del A, p. 43.
36 Utvärderingavrättshjälpslagen(1996:1619), Rapport, del A, p. 41.
37 Utvärderingavrättshjälpslagen(1996:1619), Rapport, del A, p. 43.
38 RN 363/1998.
39 About PLN 114,400, NBP rate on 27 February 2021; Prop. 1998/99: 10, p. 17.

The Swedish system contains a general clause according to which legal aid in a narrow sense may be granted in any category of cases, except those expressly excluded in RL 1997. Under § 10 RL 1997, the possibility of granting legal aid is excluded in the following categories of cases:

1. preparation of a tax return, prenuptial agreement, will or donation;
2. administration of inheritance registers;
3. debt restructuring;
4. asset declarations;
5. regarding the valuation of property,
6. registry;
7. concerning the division of property other than as a result of allegations of the division of property;
8. dependent on previous judgments in pending proceedings, if the claim is based on substantially similar circumstances[40];
9. regarding compensation for road accidents.

On the other hand, at the second level, the Swedish legislator provided for categories of cases in which legal aid in a narrow sense could only be granted when specific circumstances warrant it (§ 11 RL 1997). These are matters of scope:

1. family law, including divorce cases, child support cases;
2. taxes, duties, fees or payment security in the field of taxes, duties and fees;
3. in cases conducted abroad.

As part of inheritance proceedings, a quite interesting solution is § 14 RL 1997, which assumes that in the event of the death of a person who has been granted legal aid, the heir is transferred to the heir if he or she requests it due to the

40 In relation to this category of cases, the term pilotfallen was used. At one point, this kind of thing generated very large budgetary expenses. It was a large number of cases, incl. on the illegal circulation of drugs and it was recognized that in order to introduce budget savings, the possibility of providing legal aid in such cases should be drastically limited. The introduced change assumed that legal aid could be postponed until the final ruling of the preliminary ruling, in which the circumstances of the case and the claim sought are essentially identical. If, in such a case, legal aid was granted in the original case, which will be of a preliminary ruling nature, that this aid will be withheld in the next case for the same person, which does not exclude that the state will cover the costs of legal aid at a later stage. Otherwise, the legal aid fee will be borne entirely by the person; L. Heuman, *Rättshjälp och pilotfall*, SvJT 1983, p. 223.

nature and importance of the case, financial situation and other circumstances of the case, which argue that the state should participate in the costs of the trial.

As already mentioned, the Swedish system does not know the concept of free legal aid. Accordingly, the best term for legal aid in the Kingdom of Sweden is legal aid for state co-financing. A person who has been granted legal aid must pay a legal aid fee (Section 23 RL 1997). The fee thresholds depend on the amount in dispute (§ 23 (1) RL 1997). These amounts are shown in the table below on the website of the Swedish courts[41]:

The value of the subject of the dispute	The share of a natural person in the costs as a percentage	Minimum participation amount
0–50 000 SEK	2 %	0 SEK
50 001–100 000 SEK	5 %	500 SEK
100 001–120 000 SEK	10 %	1 000 SEK
120 001–150 000 SEK	20 %	1 500 SEK
150 001–200 000 SEK	30 %	2 000 SEK
>200 000	40 %	5 000 SEK

It should be emphasized that a minor may each time be completely exempt from the costs of legal aid, if this is justified by his financial situation (§ 23 (4) of RL 1997). The percentage of the legal aid fees is calculated in accordance with § 24 RL 1997 at the time the legal aid was granted. However, if the financial basis for assessing the percentage share changes significantly before the closure of the proceedings, § 24 para. 4 RL 1997 provides for the possibility of adjusting the percentage. It can be either a change to a higher or a lower rate. In the case of the lower basis of § 24 sec. 3 RL 1997 assumes that the reduction of a person's participation is permissible only if the fee has not yet been paid.

Granting previously granted aid ceases pursuant to § 32 RL 1997, if:

1. the legal aid fee will not be paid to the attorney within the statutory periods;
2. the applicant provided false information, in the event of such information being provided, legal aid would not be granted;
3. the applicant intentionally or as a result of gross negligence provided incorrect information, which could have resulted in too low a legal aid fee;

41 Source: https://www.domstol.se/amnen/rattshjalp/for-dig-som-ar-rattshjalpsbitrade/regler-kring-rattshjalp/ access: 27.02.2021.

4. the applicant's financial situation has changed and he is no longer entitled to legal aid;
5. the representative under legal aid is released without appointing another representative;
6. due to the nature and importance of the case, the value of the subject matter of the dispute and the circumstances in general, the state's share of the plaintiff's costs is no longer justified,
7. The Consumer Ombudsman decides to provide the claimant with aid in a specific case.

Additionally, the Swedish legislator decided to define the hourly limits of legal aid. Pursuant to § 34 RL 1997, legal aid ceases if the number of working hours of the attorney under legal aid exceeds 100 hours, unless the specific conditions of the case require an extension of the number of hours. At the same time, the attorney should notify the court that the duration of the provided legal aid is 100 hours or is close to that number. Upon notification, the court should consider whether legal aid will cease or be continued within the additional hours. In the event that the representative does not submit the said information to the court, he risks not reimbursing the costs for working hours exceeding 100 hours.

The strict observance of hourly legal aid limits is emphasized by the practice of the courts. In the case heard by the Supreme Court of the Kingdom of Sweden, NJA 2007 p. 752, the attorney providing legal aid failed to notify the court that the legal aid exceeded 100 hours and then demanded reimbursement for 110 hours. The Supreme Court took the position that due to negligence in notifying the court about the upcoming hourly limit, the attorney would not be reimbursed for the additional 10 hours of legal aid[42].

6. Conclusions

The strict observance of hourly legal aid limits is emphasized by the practice of the courts. In the case heard by the Supreme Court of the Kingdom of Sweden, NJA 2007 p. 752, the attorney providing legal aid failed to notify the court that the legal aid exceeded 100 hours and then demanded reimbursement for 110 hours. The Supreme Court took the position that due to negligence in notifying the court about the upcoming hourly limit, the attorney would not be reimbursed for the additional 10 hours of legal aid. This had a negative impact on the protection of citizens' legal interests, especially in minor cases. The literature on

42 NJA 2007 p. 752.

the subject indicates that a large number of cases do not go to court. This can be explained by the fact that the parties, wanting to avoid significant costs related to legal representation (especially in family law cases), agree to solutions that generate greater difficulties. In the long run, this leads in turn to the opposite results in the form of lengthy and even more costly court proceedings[43].

Analyzing the Swedish solutions, it may seem that legal aid in this system is a "kind of reward" after meeting subsequent levels of requirements. The first level is the receipt of legal advice and, after being admitted by the person providing this advice, goes to the second level, which is legal aid in the strict sense. However, an additional challenge unexpectedly arises – determining whether the participant has legal insurance and whether it covers a given category of cases, and only then is the possibility of granting legal aid as a reward for passing the additional challenge considered. At the same time, as already mentioned, the award in the form of legal aid only provides for state aid in costs, since the concept of free legal aid is practically absent in Swedish law.

The participation of the beneficiary in legal aid seems to be an appropriate solution, which, however, requires careful implementation, because overly onerous financial thresholds and restrictive interpretation policy of the terms allowing for complete exemption from costs may discourage people from using legal aid. When analyzing the practice of applying RL 1997, it is undoubtedly the fact that the Swedish legislator is slowly expanding the scope of cases in which a person may obtain state support under legal aid, thus the institution of legal aid is constantly improving.

The experience of Swedish legislation can be used on the basis of Polish considerations in the process of improving the institution of legal aid. The starting conclusion as part of the juxtaposition of the two systems is a thorough analysis of the possibility of introducing mandatory legal insurance in the Polish system. It is pointed out that in Sweden it is too narrow and many matters are beyond the scope of both legal insurance and broadly understood legal aid, which should be a valuable hint for the Polish system.

On the other hand, a unique feature of the Swedish system is the lack of a structure for free legal aid. In fact, the state co-finances the defense of citizens' rights, and it is the participation of individuals in the costs that has made legal aid a more structured and cheaper tool. According to the authors, such a solution can be successfully introduced into Polish legislation by introducing an initially uniform "block" fee in all categories of cases. At the first level of introducing

---

43 F. Regan, *The Swedish Legal Services Policy Remix*…p. 63.

small fees for legal aid, the amounts of citizen participation should be symbolic. Gradually, as the economy develops, the share of citizens should be calculated in proportion to the income of the person. An important supplement to the system of citizen participation in the costs of legal aid should be to consider exceptional cases in which the aid should be completely free of charge.

The comparison of Polish solutions with the Swedish ones leads to the conclusion that the institution of legal aid and civic counseling adopted in Polish law resembles the Swedish solutions from before 1997. Consequently, this system may turn out to be too expensive and will not lead to the achievement of the assumed goals. RL 1997 is an example of introducing savings in response to significant expenses.

Literature

Heuman L., Rättshjälp och pilotfall, *SvJT*, 1983, s. 223.

Muther P.S., Reform of Legal aid In Sweden, *International Lawyer*, Vol. 9, No. 3.

Przywora B., *Normatywny model przedsądowej nieodpłatnej pomocy prawnej*, Warszawa 2019.

Przywora B., Wróbel A., Status prawny sędziego w Królestwie Szwecji, [in:] *Status prawny sędziego Państwa europejskie.* Tom I, red. B. Przywora Warszawa 2019.

Przywora B., Wróbel A., *Formalised Access to Pre- jurisdictional Free Legal Aid. Analysis based on Example of Ukraine, Poland, Great Britain and Sweden*, Berlin 2023.

Regan F., The Swedish Legal Services Policy Remix: The Shift from Public Legal Aid to Private Legal Expense Insurance, *Journal of Law and Society*, Vol. 30, No. 1, March 2003, s. 50.

Schoultz I., Legal Aid in Sweden, [in:] *Outsourcing Legal Aid in the Nordic Welfare States*, O. Halvorsen Rønning, O. Hammerslev (eds.), Lund 2018.

Marcin Grzybowski, Marian Grzybowski

Free Legal Aid in Denmark and Norway

Abstract: The intended study is meant to be a concise, comparative overview of the legal conditions and practice of providing free legal aid at the prejudicial stage in Denmark (Marcin Grzybowski) and Norway (Marian Grzybowski). The fact of taking note of two indicated countries is justified by the close relationship between their legal systems and cultures, a similar demographic potential and the level of socio-economic development, as well as the interpenetration of practical solutions with similar problems to be solved (such as – for example – legal aid for economic immigrants and refugees). In the paper we used the dogmatic and the comparative methods.

The core focus of the authors is legal aid, provided free of charge or for partial payment, the costs of which are compensated by the state according to legally defined rules. In Denmark, the rules for granting this assistance are set out in Articles 323 and 330 of the Judicial Act (*Retpjejeloven*) and in (Ministerial) Order No. 637 of 2014. In Norway, the basic regulations are contained in the Special Legal Aid Act of 1981.

Keywords: free legal aid, Denmark, Norway.

1. Introduction

The study illustrates the assumptions of the regulation on legal aid that is refinanced from state funds and provided in the pretrial phase in Denmark and Norway. Taking account of both countries is justified by the kinship of their legal cultures, comparable potential and level of development, and the permeation of best practices.

In Denmark, the granting of free legal aid, the costs of which are reimbursed by the state, is initially regulated by art. 323 and art. 330 of the Courts Act (*Retplejeloven*), the Social Help Act (*Bistandsloven*) of 1974 and Regulation No. 637 of the Minister of Justice of 2014. In Norway, the basic regulations are contained in the Legal Aid Act of June 13, 1980 (*Lov om rettshjelp*), which has been in force since 1981 and amended 27 times (until the end of 2020).

Free legal aid at the pretrial phase (as well as during court proceedings) serves to equalize the opportunities of citizens in the application of law. It constitutes an element of the Scandinavian concept of a welfare state (*velferdsstaten*)[1]. Free legal

---

1 S. Kuhnle, N. Kildal, *Velferdsstatens idégrunnlag i perspektiv*, [in:] *Den norske verferdsstaten*, A. Hatland, S. Kuhnle, T.I. Rømoren (ed.), Oslo 2011, pp. 19,30.

aid envisages that equality in the exercise of freedoms and rights requires knowledge of their content and familiarity with mechanisms of their enforcement. In particular, this applies to eliminating the legal exclusion of economically or socially marginalized people. This is the main purpose of legal aid available regardless of the ability of paid usage[2].

Denmark and Norway have similar (though not identical) traditions of legal aid in regards to people who are unable to afford the costs involved. In Norway, the beginnings of the regulation date from the years 1274 and 1276, when the obligation to assist those who, due to lack of resources, were unable to assert their rights, was introduced in national and municipal law. This obligation was perpetuated by Christian IV (1577–1648) in the so-called judicial compositions in the jointly managed Denmark and Norway. In Denmark, codification of the *Danske lov* from 1683 obliged the lawyers entered the lists kept by the courts with the duty to provide aid.[3]

Legal circles accepted this obligation with skepticism, mainly due to the lack of financial compensation for providing aid. In the light of the above, the obligation was treated as marginal and neglected. The remedy was the departure from the model of aid provided without compensation and the assumption by the state of obligations to reimburse the costs of aid granted free of charge. This required clarification of the group of persons entitled to aid and explication of the situation(s) which the legislator considered as justifying the application for free legal aid.

In Denmark, from 1827 justification for the need for providing legal aid was the intention to issue a claim to the court with the simultaneous insufficient funds to cover costs. The Act of 1916 guaranteed the right to free legal aid in court proceedings. From 1966, people at poverty obtained guarantees of access to free legal aid, also at the pretrial stage[4]. At present, the fundamental regulation is the Social Assistance Act of 1974 (*Bistandloven*)[5]. It obliges local authorities to offer their assistance, while providing them with state subsidies. The functioning of the legal aid system and refinancing of its costs is supervised by the Department of Civil Affairs (*Civil-styrelsen*) at the Danish Ministry of Justice.

In Denmark, legal aid, whose costs are covered from public funds, rests on two unequal pillars. The former is represented by "first line" aid, available to everyone,

2 K. Andænes, *Rettshjelp til norske sigøynere*, [in:] *Rettshjelp til samfunnstruktur*, A. Eidsen, S. Eskeland, T. Mathiesen, Oslo 1975, pp. 118–152

3 *Danske lov*, D.L. 1-9-12

4 Cf. *Betænkning 404/1966*, pp. 8–13.

5 *Lov om bistand* 1974:333 (*Bistandloven*).

while the second pillar represents advanced aid, provided free of charge only to some people, i.e., on condition that the amount of annual income specified by the law is not exceeded.

"First line" aid is provided to every natural person who applies for it. It is limited to simple oral advice, informing the beneficiary about his rights and the means of enforcing claims. The second pillar of free legal aid exists in two forms: (a) pretrial (out-of-court) aid, (b) aid provided in court proceedings.

In Norway, the 1980 law guarantees: (a) rudimentary assistance to every applicant, and (b) qualified assistance, subject to financial and economic conditions. Matters of considerable direct significance to the status of the person applying for aid or of substantial social meaning (e.g., the matters of child custody, protection of the rights of persons with mental disabilities) were included in the scope of free legal aid without applying the income and property criteria.

2. Types and criteria for providing free extrajudicial aid in Denmark and Norway

Since the 1970s, in Denmark free legal aid is rendered in three isolated spectrums. The first spectrum, open to everyone, comes down to the provision of rudimentary oral legal advice by an attorney practicing in a law office or by an employee of a legal aid office, who informs the beneficiary about the rights (freedoms) he or she is entitled to, possible claims and the procedure for pursuing them. The second spectrum has a specialized dimension. An attorney at the law office or a lawyer (employee) at a legal aid office determines – based on the materials – the status of the case and suggests the settlement procedure. In divorce matters, he determines the consequences of marriage contracts. He amends notices to adopt a stance, subpoenas and pretrial pleadings. He indicates evidence necessary to pursue claims. By the third spectrum, the attorney provides assistance in the settlement proceedings. If the proceedings fail, he helps to redact the claim (application) to a competent court (without participating in the proceedings himself). The free out-of-court assistance program excludes criminal areas. The second and third spectrum of aid also does not concern matters related to economic activity, trade and debt restructuring. Since the entry into force of Ordinance No. 637 of the Minister of Justice of 2014, cases concerning administrative decisions have also been excluded[6].

---

6 Pursuant to the regulations of the administrative procedure (*Forvaltningsloven*), the obligation to inform citizens about their legal remedies was imposed on the competent public administration bodies.

In Norway, after the period where free legal aid (representation before courts in civil and employment law cases) was guaranteed in 1973, work on a comprehensive law on legal aid was initiated. A special committee prepared the assumptions of this regulation. These assumptions were put forward for discussion as a submission of NOU 1976:38. Following consultations, the Law on Legal Aid was passed on June 13, 1980. The law entered into force at the beginning of 1981.

In Denmark, since 1974, obtaining oral legal advice does not require verification of the applicant's annual income, seen as a ceiling which, if exceeded, deprives of the chance to obtain free legal aid. Such counselling does not require the beneficiary's own contribution. The regulations for the second and third aid spectrum show different development. In such case, the applicants are obliged to participate in the costs of the aid: at the level of 25 % in the second spectrum and 50 % in the third spectrum (which makes the aid only "partially free"). In Norway, advanced aid involves the payment of own contribution (within 5–40 % of costs). The following cases are exempt from co-payment: child custody, certain matrimonial matters, employment protection and related social benefits. As in Denmark, the Norwegian law on aid does not cover the institution of legal aid in criminal proceedings. Free legal aid may be provided only to natural persons who, due to their life or financial situation, do not have the capacity to cope with the costs of paid aid. The Act deviates from this principle in listed cases, where aid is essential for the living situation of people.

The Norwegian Act of 1980 emphasizes two groups of cases in which free legal aid may be requested. The first group concerns art. 11 (1) of the Act. These are cases: where the subject of protection is the wellbeing of children (in terms of protection against violence and their livelihood), and in addition: divorce and related family matters associated with rental accommodation, safeguarding employment and social rights. In this area, the state guarantees access to free legal aid, regardless of the yearly income or the value of assets. As a result of the amendment to the Basic Law, the catalog of cases has been enriched with health care and issues with immigration to Norway.[7] Application forms for free legal aid are available on the website of the district governor's office; information on the conditions for obtaining free legal aid is also available there.

The catalog of cases where free legal aid is provided regardless of the fulfillment of income and financial conditions is clarified by the Legal Aid Amendment

7 The largest proportion includes cases related to childcare. In 2018, expenditure on compensation by the state of granted legal aid in the indicated scope absorbed 46 % of expenditure on the costs of aid granted regardless of the income and property criterion.

Act of 2004 and the related executive regulation of the Norwegian Minister of Justice and Public Security. The list includes: (a) immigration, (b) child custody, (c) compensation on account of groundless accusations, (d) domestic violence, (e) forced marriage, (f) degrading treatment of people with mental disabilities, (g) conflict between the obligation to service in the army and a person's beliefs. The act also provides for cases where free legal aid is possible granted that a certain amount of annual income is not exceeded or that property is owned with a value lower than indicated. This particular group includes the following cases: (a) matrimonial (other than divorce), (b) claims for unjustified deprivation of liberty, (c) unjustifiable dismissal, (d) tenant rights, (e) compensation for victims of criminal violence, (f) social security. The 1980 law, as amended, gives county governors (*fylke*) the right to increase the income and wealth ceiling in concrete situations (although restraint is recommended).[8]

In Denmark, free legal aid, dependent on the amount of annual income, is granted under the condition that a single person earns an annual income of no more than DKK 336,000 or DKK 427,000 for married persons, partnerships or people who live in shared housing. When a dependent child's age is below 18, the income ceiling is increased by DKK 58,000 for each child. In view of the statistics, such income conditions were met by 85 % of the Danish population in 1966, in 1988 – 60 %, and in 1995 – 50 %[9].

In Norway, aid is provided free of charge, as long as the beneficiary does not exceed the annual income and does not own assets of more than NOK 100,000 (approx. € 11,400). The income ceiling is NOK 246,000 (approx. € 27,300 in 2018) for single persons and NOK 369,000 (approx. € 40,750) for marriages and other relationships. The law does not provide for an increase in the income limit for people with children. Therefore, the income threshold in Norway is significantly lower: both for the single and married people. This testifies to the wider – taking into account the income limit – availability of free legal aid in Denmark.

3. Free legal aid entities and compensation principles

The entities providing free legal aid are lawyers practicing in private law firms and legal aid offices. In Denmark, there are two types of free legal aid entities: lawyer-based legal aid offices (*Advokatvagter*) and private legal aid offices

8 Legal literature and journalism criticized the omission of deportation cases from Norway (for breaking the law or exceeding the permitted length of stay) as well as eviction cases and rentals for dwellings.

9 *Betænkninger*: 404/1966, 1341/1997, 1436/2004.

(*retshjaelpkontorer*), in numbers circulating around seventy/eighty. The former pursue this activity in parallel with other legal services, often on the sidelines. Denmark also has, yet less numerous, public legal offices specializing in providing free legal aid, to which the state provides financial aid from funds obtained after the introduction of VAT on legal services in 1978. Further to this financial arrangement, more than a dozen (free) legal aid offices have emerged in a number of larger Danish cities. Following the reform of court processes and the introduction of a special procedure for handling small claims of low value, the demand for legal aid in the second and third areas of granting it has plummeted significantly, and thus also the expenditure related to it[10]. In Norway, out of the few previously operating public offices only one office of this type has remained (in the capital city of Oslo). It provides nationwide legal assistance thanks to electronic means of communication.

Where costs of assistance are compensated by the state, the hourly rate for providing legal aid is determined by executive acts of the Ministry of Justice, and also the maximum number of hours assigned to individual types of cases. In Denmark, it was (in 2020) DKK 1,140 (approx. € 151) for aid in the second phase of assistance and DKK 2,600 (approx. € 346) in the third phase. In Norway, the rate for a lawyer who provides free legal aid was initially NOK 995 (approx. € 110). Following the order of the Minister of Justice of 2015, it was increased to NOK 1,403 for lawyers (approx. € 155) and NOK 1,254 (approx. € 140) if the lawyer is not an attorney.[11] The time limits for dedicated legal assistance in individual categories of cases are determined by a publicly declared ordinance of the Minister of Justice.[12]

The applicant should prove his/her predisposition to obtain free legal aid. They are subject to verification by the attorney providing assistance, the councilor (his assistant) or the legal aid office employee. Own contribution paid before providing assistance at the chancellery or at the office is transferred to the fund, from which the state co-finances free-of-charge assistance points and gives support to organizations that provide *pro bono* assistance. In Norway, the calculation of aid costs is submitted to the county governor's office (*fylke*), who verifies its correctness. The governor has the right, with the help of his services, to correct the calculations in the documentation prepared by the chancellery (office); here, the appellate jurisdiction remains the Court of Appeals.

---

10 B. Lemann Kristiansen, *Legal Aid in Denmark*, as above, p. 113.

11 Cf. *Den Norske Advokatforening 2014*, Oslo 2015, p. 21.

12 It is acknowledged that in highly complex cases, the upper time limit may be exceeded, which requires additional documentation.

Offices that provide free legal aid are active in more than ten larger cities of Denmark. The compensation of lawyers and office workers for the costs of provided assistance (except for *pro bono* activities) involves county offices benefiting from state subsidies. They are responsible for protecting the facilities and equipment of assistance points (most often located in local libraries). The activities of law firms and offices benefiting from state refinancing of aid costs are complemented by the work of counseling and legal aid centers run by social organizations, trade unions, and the Danish Evangelical Church. An original way of reaching marginalized groups with legal aid is the Copenhagen experiment of counselling with "Street Lawyers" (*Gade-juristen*)[13], which was also imitated in Oslo in the aftermath.

The Norwegian specificity is – with the territory of: 397 thous. sq. km – the lack of an evenly developed network of stationary aid points. Broadening access to aid is supported by the so-called *Juss-Buss* – a unique center bringing together thirty students and doctoral students of law, operating with the support of the state under the auspices and care of the Faculty of Law of the University of Oslo[14]. The only public aid office in Oslo is currently dominated by the affairs of immigrants and asylum seekers. Norway is distinguished by the fact that it allocates considerable funds to financing free legal aid. With an average annual expenditure of EUR 50–55 *per capita* Norway is well in advance of 46 countries in the Council of Europe system.

As in Denmark, alongside aid financed from state funds, *pro bono* assistance is provided by volunteer lawyers (under the auspices of the Norwegian Bar Association, university (student) law clinics and – assuming the models from

---

13 C. Lied, *Irriterende till stede? Om gatejurister i Oslo og København*, Oslo 2011, p. 7 et seq.; S.P.Porner Nielsen, O. Hammerslev, *Gadejuristen (The Street Lawyers) Offering Legal Aid to Socially Marginalised People*, [in:] Outscourcing Legal Aid…, as above p. 170 et seq.

14 *Juss-Buss*, operating since the late 1960s, was based on integrating the students' activity at the center into the reformed course of legal studies. There is a year-long transition to work at *Juss-Buss* by an interested group of students that takes place in a rotational design. *Juss-Buss* combines the provision of legal aid and legal education by stationary, phone and *on-line* means while reaching groups with a high degree of social marginalization. This refers among others to immigrant communities, people awaiting deportation, persons serving prison sentences. *Juss-Buss* is co-financed by the Ministry of Justice, the Municipality of Oslo and several charity foundations. More in: T. Mathiesen, *Juss-Buss 30år* [in:] Juss-Buss (ed.) *Tvers ingennom lov til seir*, Oslo 2001, p. et seq.; J. T. Johnsen, *Juss-Buss – arbeidsprincipper og efaringer: veiledning for medarbeidere i Juss-Buss*, Oslo 2003, p. 11 et al., 21 et al.

Denmark in 2005 – the Evangelical Augsburg Church of Norway) in the form of advice in church institutions and supporting legal services provided by "Street Lawyers" (*gatejuristen*).

4. Aspirations of the reform of the free legal aid system in Norway

The commission for the new law on legal aid and executive acts, set up in 2018, submitted a study report, published and – as a governmental document NOU 2020:5 – brought forward for consultations. From 23 November 2020, work has been pending on the results of this consultation at the Norwegian Ministry of Justice.

According to the project, free legal aid shall be granted only in the case of the lack of entitlement to it under other programs, including: legal liability coverage. The principle of providing aid by lawyers practicing their profession in accordance with the Courts Act or by employees of public legal aid offices was preserved. Assistance would be allocated only to natural persons. The Commission consequently proposes linking the income limit for entitlement to aid to five times the social security contribution base. It is suggested, moreover, that the property criterion for the value of the house occupied by the applicant for assistance be excluded. It is assumed to maintain the increased income limit for married couples and unions forming a joint household and for people with dependent children up to 18 years of age. Beneficiaries whose annual income exceeds 5 times the basis of the insurance premium are to be covered by the obligation of own contribution in the scale of 5–75 % of the costs of the aid provided (according to a unified algorithm). The aim was to extend the circle of people eligible for aid: in the optimum policy option, from 9 % in 2017 to 25 % of the population (with an increase in government expenditures by 22 %), in the minimum variant – up to 17 % (at the current level of support). The utmost priority is shifting the emphasis on pretrial aid, covering the total costs of providing assistance with the beneficiary's own contribution, putting a definite value on fees for legal aid in relation to other legal services, establishing the upper time limit for oral advice at 15 hours.

The Committee calls for emphasizing free legal aid from public funds in the name of the act on financing free legal aid from public funds, adjusting the regulation of entitlements to apply for legal information in relation to acts regulating situations where such a right is granted. The Commission proposes to establish a separate administration of a legal aid system with powers to collect and process data using digital tools.

The work underway in the Ministry of Justice, and subsequently – in the Norwegian parliament, will determine the future and final form of the bill.

Literature

Andænes K., Rettshjelp til norske sigøynere, [in:] *Rettshjelp til samfunnstruktur*, A. Eidsen, S. Eskeland, T. Mathiesen (eds.), Oslo 1975.

Johnsen J.T., *Juss-Buss – arbeidsprincipper og efaringer: veiledning for medarbeidere i Juss-Buss*, Oslo 2003.

Kuhnle S., Kildal N., Velferdsstatens idégrunnlag i perspektiv, [in:] *Den norske verferds-staten*, A. Hatland, S. Kuhnle, T.I. Rømoren (eds.), Oslo 2011.

Lemann Kristiansen B., *Legal Aid in Denmark*.

Lied C., *Irriterende till stede? Om gatejurister i Oslo og København*, Oslo 2011.

Mathiesen T., Juss-Buss 30år [in:] *Tvers ingennom lov til seir*, Juss-Buss (ed.), Oslo 2001.

Porner Nielsen S.P., Hammerslev O., Gadejuristen (The Street Lawyers) Offering Legal Aid to Socially Marginalised People, [in:] *Outscourcing Legal Aid…*

Ksenia Kakareko

Legal Aid in the Republic of Belarus

Abstract: The study aims to present the issues of legal aid in Belarus. In the study we used the dogmatic and the comparative methods. The Republic of Belarus has kept its approach to the concept of providing legal aid to citizens unchanged since the times of the Soviet Union. Belarus actually does not provide free legal aid to citizens in need, neither at the level of the provisions of normative acts, nor real actions. The obligation to carry out such activities was entrusted to lawyers at their expense. The cost of an ex officio lawyer provided by the state must be settled by the person at the end of the trial, which means that it cannot count as legal aid. Information, advice and mediation activities are carried out by attorneys, notaries and non-governmental organizations as one-off actions.

Keywords: legal aid, Belarus, human rights, equality before the law, right to a fair trial

1. Introduction

To understand the creation and operation of legal mechanisms of free legal aid in Belarus, it is worth realizing that the territory of this state used to be part of the Grand Duchy of Lithuania, which was part of the Polish–Lithuanian Commonwealth. As a result of the partitions, it became part of the territory of the Russian Empire[1]. However, this area was included in the judicial districts of Vilnius (Grodno and Minsk Oblasts), Kiev (Mogilev Oblast), and Petrograd (Vitebsk Oblast)[2]. An attempt to regulate the problem of free legal aid was made in Belarus during the judiciary reform in 1864[3], which provided for a single judicial system for all citizen classes and a uniform form of proceedings, among other things. Crown courts and magistrates' court were established then. The crown courts consisted of district courts and judicial chambers, with jurisdiction

1 In the mid-nineteenth century, the term "Belarus" included the former Mstislaw, Smolensk, Połock, Vitebsk and Minsk Voivodships.

2 This kind of fragmentation of the territory of Belarus may seem surprising given that it become part of the Vilnius educational district (including Vitebsk, Grodno, Minsk, and Mogilev).

3 On 20 November 1864, four significant documents were issued: *Establishment of the Judiciary System, Charter of Civil Procedure, Charter of Criminal Procedure, Charter of Penalties Imposed by Magistrates*, which radically changed the judicial system of the Russian Empire. See http://constitution.garant.ru/history/act1600-1918/3450/

over several districts[4]. As a result of the introduced reforms, two corporations were established, consisting of people authorized to act as legal advisers and represent clients in court[5]. The first of these corporations consisted of sworn attorneys; the second included private attorneys. It resulted in the development of the self-government of sworn attorneys, the structure of which was based on the territorial division of the state and related to the division of its territory into judicial districts. An internal body of the self-government was a council, which also acted as a disciplinary body towards the said attorneys. Both the Belarusian and Russian bars derive their origins from these institutions.

Sworn attorneys were obliged to provide legal assistance to the poor. Cases of this type in criminal proceedings were assigned by court presidents. On the other hand, a territorially competent council appointed individual attorneys to conduct civil cases of people exercising the law of the poor. A sworn attorney could not refuse to perform the task assigned to them. The council of sworn attorneys laid down higher requirements for sworn attorneys who carried out cases of people who exercised the law of the poor than those required from attorneys working based on a commission given by their principals. With regard to people exercising the law of the poor, an attorney could only refuse to provide legal assistance if their claims were evidently groundlessness or immoral[6]. However, a sworn attorney executing a commission could refuse to accept the commission in the event of doubts as to the legitimacy of the plea. The duty of sworn attorneys representing people benefiting from the law of the poor was to participate in hearings before crown courts. They didn't have to take part in cases pending in magistrates' courts, as well as in private prosecution cases and cassation proceedings[7]. Neither were they obliged to travel outside their place of residence unless they received funds to finance such a trip[8].

---

4 D. A. Solodov, *Reformy procesu karnego w Rosji: zarys historyczno-prawny*, Łomża 2015, p. 42; С. Н. Трегубов, *Самостоятельность суда*, Петербург 1905, p. 6; И. Михайловский, *Основные принципы организации уголовного суда*, Томск 1905, p. 89.

5 А. П. Галоганов, *Российская адвокатура: история и современность*, Москва 2003, p. 38.

6 *Правила адвокатской профессии в России. Опыт систематизации постановлений Советов присяжных поверенных по вопросам профессиональной этики. Составил член Совета присяжных поверенных округа Московской судебной палаты Александр Николаевич Марков*, Москва 1913, p. 168.

7 Н. Н. Курова, *Оказание бесплатной юридической помощи в России: развитие института*, „Адвокат" 2014, No. 8, p. 40.

8 *Правила адвокатской профессии…*, p. 185.

The councils of sworn attorneys financed cases of people exercising the law of the poor carried out by those attorneys from funds obtained from contributions of those councils' members who were required to pay part of their fees to the council. Cases of people exercising the law of the poor were assigned according to a specific order. Failure to comply with this order resulted in disciplinary liability. The number of such cases, as proved by the source study, was quite significant. Carrying out cases commissioned to a sworn attorney by the council under the law of the poor had the nature of the public duty of such an attorney, thus, being a public service[9].

The so-called counter-reforms of Tsar Alexander III, followed by the actions of Piotr Stolypin undertaken in 1912, resulted in an increase in the influence of courts over the bar, although the system of evidence law was not affected[10].

After the October Revolution, the "bourgeois" bar was abolished, as a result of which free legal assistance was not provided by professional lawyers in the 1917–1922 period. Pursuant to the provisions of Decree No. 1 of 22 November 1917 on the judiciary[11], counsels in courts could be all unblemished citizens of both sexes who enjoyed civil rights. Under Decree No. 2 of 7 March 1918 on the judiciary[12], special colleges of legal deputies authorized to act in courts as social defenders and social prosecutors were established. They could also defend individual citizens. Based on the Law on the People's Court of the RSFSR of 30 November 1918, colleges of legal deputies assigned with both official and social functions were organized. They existed for a very short time, as they were abolished in 1922. From that moment on, the functions of attorneys and defenders in court proceedings could be performed by people employed under an employment contract registered by territorially competent councils.

In 1922, the bar law was adopted, which established colleges of counsels, which were social self-government organizations existing at governorate courts. However, in practice, attorneys-at-law who were members of a college worked outside the college, which was contrary to the assumed objectives and tasks of

9 *Правила адвокатской профессии...*, p. 185.

10 А. А. Козявин, *Судьба судебных реформ в России: век XIX и век XXI*, „Актуальные проблемы российского права", 2014, No. 4, p. 639.

11 Декрет Совета Народных Комиссаров Российской Советской Федеративной Социалистической Республики «О суде», Распубликован в № 17 „Газеты. Временного Рабочего и Крестьянского Правительства" от 7 декабря (24 ноября) 1917 г., СУ РСФСР, 1917. № 4. ст.50.

12 Декрет о суде № 2 от 7 марта 1918 г., «Свод Указов РСФСР», 1918, No. 26, item 420

the bar. On 5 July 1922[13], the rules and regulations for colleges of counsels were established and approved by the People's Commissariat of Justice. Pursuant to this document, colleges for criminal and civil matters were established at the governorate departments of justice. The general assembly of counsels elected the presidium responsible for overseeing the college's activities. This presidium's competence included providing free legal aid to people recognized as entitled to exercise the law of the poor. In 1932, the bar's organizational structure was changed, obliging attorneys-at-law to work in collectives.

At the constitutional level, the right to free legal aid was first expressed in art. 111 of the Constitution of the Soviet Union of 1936[14]. It stated that "cases in all USSR courts shall be heard in public as the law does not provide for exceptions while providing the accused with the right to defence". However, it is worth noting that the wording of the said provision, which was commonly treated in the Soviet doctrine as a text authorizing the use of free legal aid, may also be interpreted as a provision that only ensures the right to defence rather than the right to free legal aid in the course of proceedings. Simultaneously, it should be emphasized that in normative instruments from the Soviet period regulating the operation of courts and legal professions, the problem of free legal aid was not regulated more precisely. In 1939, the republic-wide Act on the Bar introduced organizations of bar associations (colleges) based on the territorial principle, and legal consultations became the basic form of the colleges' work[15].

The Constitution of the Soviet Union[16] adopted in 1977 provided in art. 161 that bar colleges operate to provide legal assistance to citizens and legal persons. It was added that in cases provided for by law, legal aid was free of charge. Two years later, on 30 November 1979, the USSR Act on the Bar[17] was passed, and then the Rules and Regulations of the RSFSR Bar were adopted on 20 November 1980.[18]. Similar regulations developed a little later in the Byelorussian Soviet

---

13 „Положение о коллегии защитников" (утв. Наркомюстом РСФСР 05.07.1922), ГАЧО ф. Р – 11, оп. 3, д. 57, л. 3 – 6.

14 Конституция (Основной закон) Союза Советских Социалистических республик, approved by Постановлением Чрезвычайн. VIII Съезда Советов СССР от 05.12.1936, „Изв. ЦИК СССР и ВЦИК", 1936, No.r 283.

15 G. Szafir, *50 lat adwokatury radzieckiej*, "Palestra" 1967, No. 10–11 (118–119), p. 3–8

16 Конституция (Основной закон) Союза Советских Социалистических республик (принята ВС СССР 07.10.1977), „Ведомости ВС СССР", 1977, No. 41, item 617.

17 Закон СССР от 30.11.1979 «Об адвокатуре в СССР», „Ведомости ВС СССР" 1979, No. 49, item 846.

18 Закон РСФСР от 20.11.1980 «Об утверждении Положения об адвокатуре РСФСР», „Ведомости ВС РСФСР", 1980, No. 48, item 1596.

Socialist Republic[19]. The cited normative instruments defined the rights and obligations of attorneys-at-law, being of particular importance for the institution of free legal aid[20].

According to the regulation, the head of the bar college, the presidium of the council, the investigating body, the prosecutor, and the court in which circuit the case was pending had the right, based on the financial situation of a citizen, to exempt them from costs of legal aid in whole or in part. If a citizen was exempted from legal aid fees based on a decision of the team leader or the college presidium, the lawyer's remuneration came from the college funds. In the event of exemption from the fee for legal aid by the investigating body, the prosecutor's office, or the court, costs of the attorney-at-law were borne by the State Treasury.

2. Constitution of Belarus

The right to legal aid is enshrined in art. 62 of the Constitution of the Republic of Belarus[21], which states that everyone has the right to legal aid when it comes to exercising and protecting rights and freedoms. The law enshrined in the Belarusian Constitution is described in sufficient detail and also includes "the right to use the assistance of lawyers and other representatives at any time in court, before other state bodies, local government bodies, in enterprises, institutions, organizations, associations, and relations with officials and citizens"[22].

---

19 Положение об адвокатуре БССР (21.05.1981г.), „СЗ БССР", 1981, No. 15, item 296.

20 The content of the rules and regulations indicated that the obligation to provide free legal assistance applied to the following categories of citizens: plaintiffs before courts of first instance in cases of claims for alimony and in labour cases; in cases of collective claims of farmers against kolkhozes for remuneration, for compensation for damage or injury related to work, for compensation for damage caused by the death of the family's sole provider in connection with work and in the situation of drawing up citizens' applications for pensions and benefits. Moreover, such an obligation existed with respect to complaints concerning incorrect entries in an electoral roll and in respect of deputies to Boards of People's Deputies when advising them on legislative matters and those related to exercising their mandate, and, finally, members of peer tribunals and people's voluntary teams for the protection of the public order through counselling in the field related to their public activity.

21 Конституция Республики Беларусь 24 ноября 1996, „Национальный реестр правовых актов Республики Беларусь, 1999, No. 1.

22 In Russian legal writings, it is emphasized that the authors of the Belarusian Constitution defined the object of legal assistance very broadly, with an indication of specific subjects of such aid. On this issue, see С. А. Казарян, *Сравнительный анализ законодательства, регулирующего оказание бесплатной юридической помощи*

Moreover, it emphasizes that in cases stipulated by law, legal aid is provided from public funds.

On 5 October 2000, the Constitutional Court of Belarus ruled on the practice of applying decisions of the Constitutional Court of the Republic of Belarus of 2 July 1999 on certain issues of representation in civil proceedings and of 13 December 1999 on certain issues related to granting legal aid to convicted persons in terms of implementation of the provisions of art. 62 of the Constitution. The ruling stated that the right to legal aid provided for in art. 62 of the Constitution was based on generally accepted principles of international law. Striving to exercise and protect citizens' rights and freedoms, this right was guaranteed by the state providing access to qualified legal assistance of professional lawyers or people entitled to provide such services. It was emphasized that the right to receive legal aid "at any time" – as it was stated in the judgment – should be guaranteed not only to any accused but also to a suspect remanded in provisional custody[23]. The ruling states that the accused and the suspect may benefit from legal assistance, also free of charge, provided by attorneys-at-law and other people authorized under specific provisions to perform activities of attorneys-at-law, as well as defence provided by immediate family members or legal representatives. The latter solution may raise certain doubts not only because the term "immediate family member" is not defined more precisely in the ruling, but mainly due to the fact that the status of an attorney-at-law, who is a professional lawyer, is equated with that of an immediate family member, who is not required to have any education, especially in law, in this case. It may be a mechanism to limit the use of free legal aid.

A characteristic feature of the Belarusian legal system in the area of free legal aid is that the constitutional solutions, which are further detailed with respect to civil and criminal proceedings, are based on the fact that these cases are treated differently in respect of reimbursement for costs of such assistance. The Act on the Bar clearly applies to proceedings in civil cases and cases of labour and social security law, regulating both the issue of entities entitled to free legal aid and the issue of reimbursement for costs of such assistance due to the attorney who

на территории Республики Беларусь, Республики Казахстан и Российской Федерации, «Новый Юридический Вестник», 2018, № 1, с. 6-10; Т. Н. Вязовская, Л. А. Евсеева, Д. В. Змиевский, Г. В. Галиева, *Конституционное право на получение бесплатной юридической помощи в Российской Федерации и Республике Беларусь*, „Вестник Российского университета кооперации", 2019, No. 4 (38), pp. 104–109.

23 Ruling of the Constitutional Court

has provided the aid. In cases relating to criminal proceedings, these issues are autonomously governed only by the Criminal Procedure Code.

3. Act on the Bar

Pursuant to art. 28 of the Bar Act[24], free legal assistance is provided to citizens, foreigners, and stateless persons at the expense of bar colleges. It is available to people filing an action before courts of first instance in cases relating to employment relationships and claims for alimony, as well as to veterans of the Great Patriotic War[25] in cases not related to economic activity; however, this is limited to oral advice. Moreover, free legal aid is available to all citizens in connection with preparing applications for pensions and other benefits, and people with disabilities of the first and second categories, but only in cases of oral counselling that doesn't require reading documents, as well as minors and their parents (guardians) acting in the children's (charges') interests. It can also be provided during the preparation of a statement of claim for deprivation of parental rights in cases provided for by law. Moreover, this right is available to people who disagree with a decision of an election commission on irregularities in electoral rolls. Other categories of citizens may also receive free legal aid based on a decision of the bar college.

Free legal aid provided from funds of the State Treasury (from the republican budget) in the field of social welfare and rehabilitation of victims of trafficking in human beings is available to these persons and, if they are under the age of fourteen, to their legal representatives. It can also be used by people who have suffered as a result of an act of terrorism. Furthermore, free legal aid may be provided at the expense of the local budget in the case where the lawyer who provides it is involved in the investigation, pre-trial, and trial proceedings, being appointed by a territorially competent bar college upon request of the authority conducting the criminal proceedings. Simultaneously, it is indicated in art. 28 of the Bar Act that a territorially competent bar collage determines the procedure for granting free legal aid provided at the expense of that collage and also

24 Закона Республики Беларусь от 15 июня 1993 года «Об адвокатуре», „Ведамасці Вярхоўнага Савета Рэспублікі Беларусь", 1993 г., № 20, ст. 242, as amended.

25 It is worth noting that, from the point of view of the Belarusian authorities, a citizen of Belarus who was a partisan of the Home Army, People's Army or Peasants' Battalions during World War II or who took part in the war fighting in the British, French or US army is not a veteran of the Great Patriotic War. Neither is, obviously, a person who served in formations collaborating with the Nazi occupiers during the war.

divides costs of providing the same among attorneys-at-law who run their own law offices and teams of attorneys-at-law. The procedure for transferring remuneration costs from the State Treasury (republican budget) or local government funds is determined by the Council of Ministers of Belarus.

4. Criminal Procedure Code and free legal aid

In criminal cases, free legal aid may be used by suspects and those accused of committing a crime before the first questioning and in the case of detention or applying a preventive measure. Pursuant to art. 43(2)(4) of the Criminal Procedure Code[26], the suspect has the right, immediately after the arrest or announcement of a decision on applying a preventive measure, to receive a written notice of their rights from the prosecuting authority that made the arrest or issued the decision on applying a preventive measure. On the other hand, the accused is entitled to use the free assistance of a lawyer in the case of applying a preventive measure in the form of temporary detention.

The head of a law firm, the presidium of a bar college, or the body conducting the criminal proceedings in a pending criminal case has the right to exempt the suspect or accused, in whole or in part, from the payment for legal aid in the manner provided for in the laws of the Republic of Belarus, In the event of such an exemption, the head of the law firm or the presidium of the bar college receives remuneration for work of the counsel at the expense of the bar college; in other cases – at the expense of the state (art. 46(8) of the Criminal Procedure Code).

Pursuant to art. 163(5) of the Criminal Procedure Code, amended in 2020[27], if the accused is acquitted or criminal proceedings are terminated according to art. 29(1)(1), (2), (7) and (10) and art. 29(2) of the CPC, namely in the case of minimal social harm of an act and an indictment lacking *corpus delicti*; with respect to the deceased, except for cases where criminal proceedings are necessary to vindicate the deceased; in the event where a statute abolishing the punishability of an act comes into force. In such cases, pursuant to art. 29(2) of the

26 Уголовно-процессуальный кодекс Республики Беларусь от 16 июля 1999 года № 295-З (с изменениями и дополнениями по состоянию на 17.07.2020 г.), «Ведамасці Нацыянальнага сходу Рэспублікі Беларусь» от 25 августа 1999 г., № 28–29, ст. 433; „Национальный реестр правовых актов Республики Беларусь“ 20 августа 1999 г., № 77–78, item 2/71.

27 Закон Республики Беларусь от 17 июля 2020 года № 45-З об изменении кодексов, «Национальный правовой Интернет-портал Республики Беларусь» от 23.07.2020 г., № 2/2764.

CPC, the proceedings should end with the acquittal of the accused, and at the stage of preparatory proceedings, in accordance with art. 250 of the CPC, with discontinuation of the proceedings. In other situations where the accused has used free legal assistance of a public defender, they should reimburse costs of legal assistance provided to them to the institution which paid these costs during the proceedings, namely to the State Treasury or a local government unit. As a side note, it should be added that this also applies to interpreters who provide assistance in the course of proceedings.

5. Conclusions

The analysis of the principles of providing free legal aid in the legal system of Belarus proves that, on the one hand, it assimilated the model applicable in the Russian Empire, but on the other hand, it adopted the solutions functioning in this respect in the legislation of the Soviet Union. The guarantees of access to free legal aid are so minimal that, in practice, such legal aid is completely illusory. This is related to the problem of the status of attorneys-at-law, which is extremely low in the practice of the Belarusian administration of justice. It has more in common with the function of a state official soliciting for the state's interest than with a representative of the profession of public trust caring for the client's interest.

The Polish reader may conclude with some surprise that Belarus has absolutely not applied the current Russian model, which, at least from a formal point of view, seems to meet all the requirements of international law[28]. The perceived differences in regulations on free legal aid applicable in Belarus and the Russian Federation prove the unequal treatment of citizens of the Eurasian Economic Union Member States and indicate imperfections of the declared process of law harmonization.

28 Федеральный закон № 324-ФЗ «О бесплатной юридической помощи в Российской Федерации», Собрание законодательства Российской Федерации от 2011 г., N 48, ст. 6725; *Бесплатная юридическая помощь*, „Министерство юстиции Российской Федерации“, https://minjust.gov.ru/ru/pages/pravovaya-informaciya/besplatnaya-yuridicheskaya-pomosh/. See also А. Н. Борисов, Комментарий к Федеральному закону от 21 ноября 2011 г. №324-ФЗ «О бесплатной юридической помощи в Российской Федерации» (постатейный), Москва 2014, passim.

Literature

Борисов А.Н., *Комментарий к Федеральному закону от 21 ноября 2011 г. №324-ФЗ «О бесплатной юридической помощи в Российской Федерации» (постатейный)*, Москва 2014

Вязовская Т.Н., Евсеева Л.А., Змиевский Д.В., Галиева Г.В., Конституционное право на получение бесплатной юридической помощи в Российской Федерации и Республике Беларусь, *Вестник Российского университета кооперации*, nr 4 (38), s. 104–109, 2019.

Галоганов А.П., *Российская адвокатура: история и современность*, Москва 2003.

Казарян С.А., Сравнительный анализ законодательства, регулирующего оказание бесплатной юридической помощи на территории Республики Беларусь, Республики Казахстан и Российской Федерации, *Новый Юридический Вестник*, № 1, с. 6–10, 2018.

Козявин А.А., Судьба судебных реформ в России: век XIX и век XXI, *Актуальные проблемы российского права*, 2014, Nr 4.

Курова Н.Н., Оказание бесплатной юридической помощи в России: развитие института, *Адвокат*, Nr 8, 2014.

Михайловский И., *Основные принципы организации уголовного суда*, Томск 1905.

Правила адвокатской профессии в России. Опыт систематизации постановлений Советов присяжных поверенных по вопросам профессиональной этики. Составил член Совета присяжных поверенных округа Московской судебной палаты Александр Николаевич Марков, Москва 1913.

Solodov D.A., *Reformy procesu karnego w Rosji: zarys historyczno-prawny*, Łomża 2015, s. 42; С.Н. Трегубов, *Самостоятельность суда*, Петербург 1905

Szafir G., 50 lat adwokatury radzieckiej, *Palestra*, nr. 10–11 (118–119), s. 3–8, 1967.

Бесплатная юридическая помощь, *Министерство юстиции Российской Федерации*, https://minjust.gov.ru/ru/pages/pravovaya-informaciya/besplatnaya-yuridicheskaya-pomosh/.

Dávid Tóth

Legal Aid and Cooperation in Criminal Matters in Hungary

Abstract: The purpose of my study is to give an overview and analyze the legal aids used in the legal cases where an international element is present. Since the last century and since the rise of the internet crime groups and criminal conducts are becoming more and more international. The subject of my research is to review the current legal tools available for the Hungarian law enforcement. In addition, the chapter evaluates not just the Hungarian legislation but the situation of the European Union on this topic as well. My hypotheses is that the current regulations of the EU and Hungary need improvements to combat international organized crime and cybercrime. The aim of the research is to give recommendations for lawmaker for the future (*de lege ferenda*).

Keywords: legal aids, international cooperation, EU law.

1. Introduction

Since the last century and especially since the rise of the internet crime groups and criminal conducts are becoming more and more international. Crimes cannot be dealt with by individual countries effectively and cooperation became necessary. For example, if a perpetrator escaped from a country where he committed a crime, the state of the place of commission can not exercise his criminal power (sovereignty) outside its territory to punish the offender. Legal aids are required to issue an international arrest warrant and extradition if the offender is caught in another country. These legal institutions have to be regulated in international conventions or in domestic law. In Hungary two laws are regulation the cooperation and legal aids in criminal matters. On one hand, we have the Act on International Mutual Assistance in Criminal Matters (Act XXXVIII of 1996) which gives provisions how to coordinate these legal institutions with most of the countries worldwide. On the other hand, there is a regional regulation the Act on cooperation in criminal matters with the Member States of the European Union (Act No CLXXX of 2012).

In my current paper I will analyse these regulations with a theoretical, practical and descriptive approach. My hypothesis is, that the current regulations of the EU and Hungary need improvements to combat international organized crime and cybercrime. The aim of the research is to give recommendations for the lawmaker for the future (de lege ferenda).

2. International Mutual Assistance in Criminal Matters

2.1. Scope of law and general rules

According to the Act on International Mutual Assistance in Criminal Matters (IMAC Act) international treaties have priority compared to the application of the domestic regulation. Hungary has plentiful bi- and multilateral convention related to cooperation in criminal matters with other countries[1]. The IMAC Act applies unless an international treaty provides otherwise. This provision gives possibility to answer problematic cases when some an international legal source did not regulate certain questions (e.g., extradition) and the domestic law can fill in this legal gap if necessary.

It is also important to mention that the background norms of the IMAC Act are the Criminal Code and the Criminal Procedure Code[2].

The aim of the regulation is:

- to regulate cooperation with other states in criminal matters.
- Create the possibility to use legal aids in these criminal proceedings.
- Prevent international crimes by cooperation.
- Especially if there is no international convention.

The IMAC sets out two general positive conditions for the provision of legal aid in criminal matters: double criminality and reciprocity or in other words mutuality.

Double criminality means that the act is punishable under both the law of Hungary and the law of the foreign state. When examining double criminality, the obstacles to criminality do not have to be examined under either Hungarian or foreign criminal law. (IMAC art. 5) The requirement of double criminality is justified by the fact that from a constitutional and human rights point of view there would be concerns about the "mobilization" of the Hungarian penal power in connection with acts that are not ordered to be punished by Hungarian law[3].

1 L. Kőhalmi, *A Nemzetközi Bűnügyi Együttműködés*, [in:] *Magyar Büntetőjog Általános Rész*, M. Tóth, Á. Balogh (eds.), Budapest 2010, pp. 375–386, 376.

2 Á. Budaházi, *A Nemzetközi Bűnügyi Jogsegély*, [in:] *A Nemzetközi Bűnügyi Együttműködés Joga*, B. Blaskó, Á. Budaházi (eds.), Budapest 2019, pp. 85–118, 87.

3 L. Kőhalmi, op. cit., p. 377.

Mutuality is part of the international customary law and used in international co-operations and in the use of legal aids. In accordance with this the competent minister may request a statement of reciprocity from the foreign state and may, upon the initiative of the foreign state, make such a statement of reciprocity. (IMAC art. 5).

The Act. gives a general obstacle to international criminal legal assistance the so-called public policy clause. Pursuant to this Requests for mutual assistance shall not be executed nor made if they impair the sovereignty, endanger the security, or violate the public order of Hungary.[4] The purpose of this clause is to protect national sovereignty.[5] If the legal aid request is against Hungarian constitutional principles or would violate human rights, (e.g., extradition for the purpose of death penalty) than the authorities have to deny the request or stipulate conditions before granting it.

Pursuant to the art. 5 of the IMAC Act, requests for mutual assistance shall be executed or made where mutual assistance is requested not in respect of a political offence or an offence connected with a political offence or a military offence. This means that in the cases of military and political offenses usually the request for legal aid needs to be denied. This is in accordance with the international regulations. The first legal source in Europe that excluded political crimes from extradition for Belgian Extradition Act from 1833 and since than more and more country followed this regulation. Later in history was the reason why Lajos Kossuth survived. After the defeat of the Hungarian Revolution and the Independence war against the Habsburgs in 1849, many refugees went to Turkey. With British support Turkey refused to extradite more than 5,000 rebels, including the extradition of Lajos Kossuth. Lord Palmerston stated that *"the ban on the extradition of political offenders has become an institutionalized international rule, a violation of which would be detrimental to humanitarian considerations."*[6].

It is important to mention another obstacle international criminal cooperation is the *ne bis in idem* principle, also known as the prohibition of double jeopardy[7].

There is no legal definition for political crimes in Hungary but it includes conducts that are political in nature and purpose. For example offenses against

4 K. Ligeti, *A Nemzetközi Bűnügyi Együttműködés Általános Feltételei*, [in:] *Az Európai Büntetőjog Kézikönyve*, F. Kondorosi, K. Ligeti (eds.), Budapest 2008, pp. 59–85, 75.

5 Ibid.

6 P.M. Nyitrai, *Nemzetközi- És Európai Büntetőjog*, Budapest, 2006, pp. 35–37.

7 Ibid.

the state like attempt to overturn constitutional order by force (Section 254 of the Criminal Code), conspiracy against constitutional order (Section 255 of the Criminal Code), high treason (Section 256 of the Criminal Code) are typical political crimes. Besides these according the crime of human trafficking can have a political nature as well according to the Hungarian extradition practice.[8]

The IMAC Act states that an offence shall not be considered a political offence if in the course of its perpetration – taking into account all the circumstances, including the purpose, motive, modus operandi and the instrumentalities used or intended to be used – the ordinary criminal law related aspects of the offence outweigh the political ones. With regard to this regulation, courts have to value every aspect of the crime respectively. In the case of homicide or an offence involving homicide (e.g., the act of terrorism), the ordinary criminal law-related aspects shall always outweigh the political ones of the crime[9].

The IMAC Act. it does not contain a general obstacle to cooperation on the nature of the penalty. However, provisions on certain forms of international criminal assistance (such as extradition) allow for the refusal of legal assistance in the case of the death penalty as well as corporal punishment. These provisions are described in the relevant chapter of the book.

The ne bis in idem principle cannot be applied in connection with political and military crimes.

Lastly in the general conditions I would like to highlight section 47 which regulates the "Recognition of the Validity of Foreign Judgments." Pursuant to the IMAC Act the final judgment of a foreign court shall be regarded as having equal validity with the judgment of a Hungarian court if the proceedings conducted against the offender in the foreign state and the penalty imposed or measure applied are not contrary to the Hungarian legal order. An unrecognized foreign judgment cannot be considered in criminal proceedings. If the validity of the foreign judgment has been recognized by the Hungarian court the offence shall be regarded as having been finally adjudicated by a Hungarian court. By "judgment of a foreign court" the final judgment of an international criminal court set up under an international treaty or agreement promulgated by an Act of Parliament or under a mandatory resolution of the United Nations' Security Council shall also be meant.

8 K. Ligeti, op. cit., p. 76.

9 E. Kussbach, *Nemzetközi És Európai Büntetőjog*, Budapest 2005, p. 325.

2.2. Forms of legal aid

For many centuries extradition was the main form of international criminal justice assistance. This started the change slowly 19th century, other, newer forms of co-operation appeared[10].

Today we have the following forms of legal assistance in criminal matters in the IMAC Act

- extradition,
- surrender and acceptance of criminal proceedings,
- acceptance and surrender of the enforcement of sentences of imprisonment and measures involving deprivation of liberty,
- acceptance and surrender of the enforcement of confiscation or forfeiture, or of a penalty or measure having equivalent effect (henceforth: confiscation or forfeiture),
- acceptance and surrender of the enforcement of irreversibly rendering electronic data inaccessible, or of a penalty or measure having equivalent effect (henceforth: irreversibly rendering electronic data inaccessible)
- procedural legal assistance,
- laying of information before a foreign state. (IMAC Act art. 4).

2.3. Extradition

Under the definition of Bassiouni extradition is a formal process by which a person is surrendered by one state to another based on a treaty, reciprocity, or comity, or on the basis of national legislation[11].

---

10 Á. Budaházi, *A Nemzetközi Bűnügyi Jogsegély És Az Európai Elfogatóparancs*, [in:] *A Nemzetközi Bűnügyi Együttműködés Jogi Alapjai*, B. Blaskó, Á. Budaházi (eds.), Budapest 2018, pp. 33–56, 34.

11 Bassiouni, M. Cherif, *International Extradition: United States Law and Practice*, Oxford, USA 2014, p. 2.

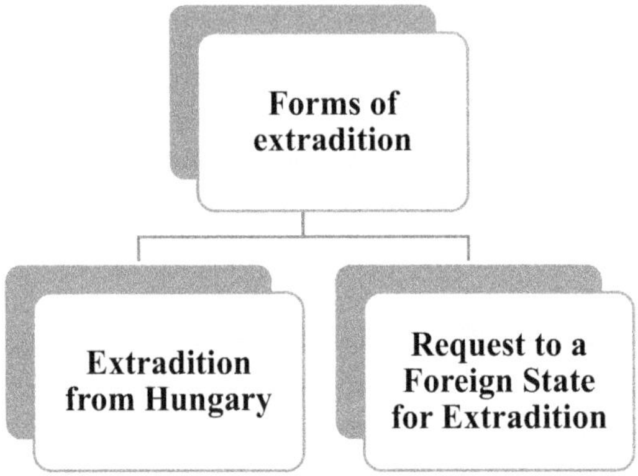

The Hungarian legislation allows extradition only in connection with a crime or punishment that reaches a certain degree of seriousness. Therefore, according to the law – following the solution applied by most extradition contracts concluded by Hungary – extradition is allowed where the act for which extradition is requested is punishable under both the law of Hungary and the law of the Requesting State by imprisonment of at least one year; extradition for the purposes of enforcement of a sentence of imprisonment or a measure involving deprivation of liberty shall be granted where at least six months from the sentence or measure imposed are still to be served[12].

The IMAC Act contains so-called absolute obstacles on extradition in the following cases:

- the offence or penalty for which extradition is requested has become barred by lapse of time under the law of either the Requesting State or Hungary,
- the person claimed has been granted a pardon or amnesty in respect of the offence or punishment,
- in the Requesting State the private bill of indictment or other motion having equivalent effect, or the consent required for the institution of criminal proceedings has not been submitted or granted,
- a Hungarian court has already finally adjudicated the offence for which extradition is requested.
- the State that requests the extradition of a person for the purpose of enforcing a custodial sentence or measure involving deprivation of liberty imposed on

12 L. Kőhalmi, op. cit., p. 379.

him in a decision rendered in absentia and the rights of the defense were not ensured in the pre-trial proceedings.

The request for extradition shall contain information as to whether there are any obstacles in the case like private or res judicata. Even if there is no procedural obstacle in the foreign country, the Hungarian authorities must also be examined whether there are any grounds for refusal in Hungary[13].

Pursuant to Section 14/A of the IMAC Act extradition shall be refused if its execution would be against an international convention.

The extradition of a Hungarian citizen is only possible if the person requested to be extradited is also a citizen of another state and does not have a residence in the territory of Hungary. This is one of the examples of the so-called relative extradition obstacle just like in the cases of refugees. Usually, the Hungarian State has to deny the refugees edition of unless it requested from a safe third country under the Act on Asylum[14].

Where the offence for which extradition is requested is punishable by death under the law of the Requesting State, extradition shall not be granted by the Minister unless the Requesting State furnishes sufficient assurances that the death penalty, if imposed, shall not be executed. This rule is in accordance with that the Hungarian Constitutional Court abolished the death penalty in 1990 and Hungary is a signing party of the ECHR[15].

Under Section 17 of the IMAC Act if several country request the extradition of the same perpetrator (for example in the case of high-risk international terrorist criminals), the decision on extradition shall take into account in particular the place of commission, the nationality of the person claimed, the respective dates of the requests and, if the requests pertain to different offences, the relative seriousness of the offences.

The IMAC Act also contains an institution called simplified extradition. This makes the whole procedure faster if the requested person declares that he or she wants to take part in the simplified extradition procedure.

Pursuant to Section 24 of the IMAC Act the requests for provisional extradition arrest may be filed through the International Criminal Cooperation Centre (in Hungarian abbreviated as: NEBEK). NEBEK shall take measures to ensure that the person claimed is taken into custody and brought before the

---

13 A. Budaházi, *A Nemzetközi Bűnügyi Jogsegély*, 2019, p. 89.

14 L. Kőhalmi, op. cit., p. 379.

15 L. Kőhalmi, op. cit., p. 379–380.

Budapest-Capital Regional Court with a view to being extradited. Custody shall not last longer than seventy-two hours.

3. European cooperation in criminal matters

3.1. Scope of law

The Act CLXXX of 2012 on Criminal Cooperation with the Member States of the European Union (CCMSEU Act) regulates regional aspects of the legal aids. The background norms of the CCMSEU Act are the Criminal Code, the Criminal Procedure Code and the previously analysed IMAC Act. This Act complies with many EU norms like the Council Framework Decision of 13 June 2002 on the European arrest warrant and the surrender procedures between Member States

It is important to note that neither reciprocity nor double criminality is a general condition for criminal cooperation with EU Member States. The Act however, applies the principle of double discrimination to some extent to certain forms of cooperation with other EU Member States[16].

3.2. Legal aids

There are several legal aids in the CCMSEU Act; one of the most significant is the European Arrest Warrant (EAW). Other legal aids are the following:

- Legal aid for the execution of the European Investigation Order. This includes Certain forms of procedural acts, in particular:
  - an interim measure,
  - the temporary transfer of a detained person to the Member State which issued the EIO,
  - interrogation by telecommunications,
  - use of covert devices.
- Establishment of a joint investigation team;
- Legal aid for the enforcement of a decision ordering a supervision measure;
- Procedural legal aid for the enforcement of a means of proof, a confiscated property and a decision to preserve property confiscated;
- Prevention and settlement of conflicts in the exercise of jurisdiction by Member States in criminal proceedings;
- Transmission and receipt of the report;
- Executive legal aids like assistance;

16 Ligeti, "A Nemzetközi Bűnügyi Együttműködés Általános Feltételei" 76.

- o the enforcement of judgments in criminal matters imposing a custodial sentence or measure involving deprivation of liberty,
- o the enforcement of probation measures and other alternative sanctions,
- o to enforce a fine or other financial obligation; and
- o legal aid for the execution of confiscation and confiscation of property.

3.3. Main rules of the European Arrest Warrant

There was a need in the European Union to replace the extradition and give reform to this institution. For these reasons, the EU did not differentiate between legal aids for the purpose of conducting criminal procedures or executing a punishment[17].

The European Arrest Warrant (EAW) is a new, simplified system for surrender for the purpose of serving a custodial sentence or measure involving deprivation of liberty or criminal proceedings. An arrest warrant issued by an EU Member State is valid throughout the EU.

The European Arrest Warrant has been in force since 1 January 2004 and has replaced the lengthy extradition procedures that previously existed between EU Member States.

The procedure is based on the principle of mutual recognition of judicial decisions and in all EU Member States. It operates through direct contact between judicial authorities.

In applying the EAW, the authorities must respect the procedural rights of accused and suspected persons, including the right to information, the right to legal assistance, and the right to legal aid.

It is similar to the traditional institution of extradition but there are many differences as well:

- The limits are stricter. The state of arrest must be dedicated to the execution of the European arrest warrant no later than 60 days after the arrest of the person concerned. If the person consents to the transfer, the decision on this must be made within ten days. The requested person shall be surrendered as soon as possible, at a time agreed by the authorities concerned, but no later than ten days after the final decision on the execution of the European arrest warrant has been taken.

---

17 A. Nagy, *Az Európai Elfogatóparancs*, [in:] *Fejezetek Az Európai Büntetőjogból*, Á. Farkas (ed.), Miskolc 2017, pp. 191–204, 192.

- It is not necessary to check double criminality. For 32 categories of offenses, it is not required to examine whether the act constitutes a criminal offense in both Member States. The only requirement is that the maximum sentence in the issuing Member State be at least 3 years of imprisonment. In the case of other offenses, the transfer of persons may be made subject to the condition that the act constitutes a criminal offense in the Member State of enforcement.
- Immunity from politics. Judicial authorities make their decisions independently, without political influence.
- Surrender of own nationals. Member States may no longer refuse to surrender their own nationals unless they are serving a custodial sentence imposed on the requested person.
- Guarantees. The Member State implementing the EEP may require guarantees for:
  - o after a certain period of time, the person concerned is entitled to request a review if the sentence imposed is life imprisonment.
  - o The requested person may also serve the custodial sentence imposed at the end of the proceedings in the Member State of enforcement if he is a national of that Member State or has his habitual residence there.
- There are limited grounds for refusal. A Member State may refuse only to surrender the wanted person, if one of the mandatory or optional grounds for refusal applies[18].

Under the CCMSEU Act a person residing in the territory of Hungary may be admitted and transferred for the purpose of conducting criminal proceedings, imprisonment or a measure involving deprivation of liberty on the basis of a European arrest warrant issued by a judicial authority of a Member State, where, under the law of the issuing Member State, the sentence is limited to at least twelve months imprisonment or a custodial sentence, or if it has been finally imposed for a custodial sentence of at least four months.

Pursuant to the Act there are cases where the court must deny the request. For example if:

- the criminal offense on which the European arrest warrant is based is under Hungarian jurisdiction and the offense is covered by pardon under Hungarian law.

18 "Európai Elfogatóparancs," Európai igazságügyi portál, 7 September 2020, https://e-justice.europa.eu/content_european_arrest_warrant-90-hu.do.

- If in certain crimes double criminality must be examined, and the act on which the European Arrest Warrant is based is not a criminal offense under Hungarian law,
- If the accused is a Hungarian national residing in the territory of Hungary and the judicial authority of the issuing Member State does not provide an adequate legal guarantee that, in the event of a final custodial sentence or measure involving deprivation of liberty, the sentence or return to the territory of Hungary, or
- If the execution of the European arrest warrant would seriously infringe the fundamental rights of the accused as enshrined in an international treaty or an act of the European Union.

The court may refuse to execute the European arrest warrant if:

- criminal proceedings are pending against the accused in Hungary for the act on which the European arrest warrant is based.
- If the court, the public prosecutor's office or the investigating authority has rejected the report due to the criminal offense on which the European arrest warrant is based or has terminated the investigation or proceedings.
- If the criminal offense on which the European arrest warrant is based falls under Hungarian jurisdiction and the criminal offense or sentence is time-barred under Hungarian law.
- If the European arrest warrant applies to a criminal offense committed in whole or in part in the territory of Hungary.

The person who is detained in the territory of Hungary shall be ordered and brought before a court if a European arrest warrant has been issued against him or her or if a Member State has ordered an international detention against him. Detention can last for the maximum of seventy-two hours.

Similar to the simplified extradition the CCMSEU Act also contains a simplified transfer. If the accused agrees to the surrender and the conditions for the surrender are met, the court shall order the arrest and simplified surrender of the surrendered person. The court may order the arrest of surrender and simplified surrender before the European arrest warrant is received. If the accused agrees to the surrender, the court shall decide on the arrest and surrender of the surrender within ten days of the accused's consent.

3.4. The Tobin case

I would like to give a summary of the infamous Tobin case to show the practical side of criminal cooperation in the EU. Petra Bárd has written a lot of publication[19] in this topic and who is interested in more depth of the case should look up her work. Francis Tobin caused a fatal accident in Hungary in the village of Leányfalu in 2000. The Hungarian court sentenced him to three years in prison in his absence for causing a road accident through negligence that resulted in death. According to the decision, he can be released on parole after 18 months at the earliest[20].

Tobin's travel documents were confiscated during the proceedings, but the Hungarian court allowed him to return his passport and at the same time ordered him to deposit a security deposit of HUF 500,000. Tobin got his passport back during the lawsuit and left the country. At the end of 2000, Tobin's fixed-term employment contract expired and he returned to Ireland with his family. By the way, the man had a residence permit until 31 December 2000, so he could not have stayed in Hungary after that. This was assessed by the Hungarian authorities as an escape, but according to the Irish Supreme Court, after recovering his passport, Tobin could rightly think that he could travel home. However, Tobin did not appear in Hungary to serve his sentence, and the Hungarian state could not do anything, as extradition was regulated between Hungary and Ireland at the time by a 1957 Council of Europe convention that stated that states could refuse to extradite their own nationals[21].

This situation changed in May 2004, and it became possible to apply for the transfer of Tobin based on EU law and Hungary has issued a European arrest warrant. The Irish Supreme Court denies the legal aid two times. In the first round the Irish legislator failed to correctly the EU Law. According to this the custodial sentence may be surrendered for enforcement if a person has escaped from the issuing country. However, this technically was not the case with Tobin who had a passport to leave the country. In 2009 the Irish lawmaker has fixed the loophole and the word "escaped" has been abolished from the law. After this Hungary has issued arrest warrant (this was the fourth one) in 2009. After a long procedure in 2012 the Supreme Court decided to refuse to extradite Tobin. The

19 P. Bárd, *The Rough Road of EU Criminal Cooperation: The Tobin Case," Ügyészek Lapja* "21, no. 6 (2014): pp. 157–168; P. Bárd, *A Rocky Road: European Arrest Warrants and Tobin Case*, "Law Society Gazette Ireland" 108, no. 8 (2014): pp. 38–41; P. Bárd, *Traps of Judicial Cooperation in Criminal Matters*, " Hungarian Yearbook of International Law and European Law" 2014, pp. 469–505; P. Bárd, *Az Európai Elfogatóparancs Magyarországon: The European Arrest Warrant in Hungary*; Budapest 2015.

20 P. Bárd, *Az Ír Gázoló És Az Európai Büntetőjog*, Szuverén: A liberális demokrácia oldalai, 7 March 2014, http://szuveren.hu/jog/az-ir-gazolo-es-az-europai-buntetojog.

21 Ibidem..

court has examined the amending law and concluded that its purpose was to ensure that Irish law complied with EU law, not to change the 2007 Tobin judgment. After this the legal options for Hungary have been exhausted. The transfer was diverted to the diplomatic level[22].

After diplomatic negotiations, finally Tobin spent five days in Hungary in January 2014, with special conditions, like he had an individual prison cell, and his wife could also visit him daily. Meanwhile, he applied for his transfer to Ireland, which was approved by both the Hungarian and Irish ministers and the Irish Supreme Court. He was returned to Ireland on the fifth day of his detention to serve the remainder of his sentence there.[23]

4. Conclusions

In my study, I examined the institutions and legal aid related to international criminal legal aid. Due to its historical significance, I paid special attention to extradition, and due to its topicality, to the European Arrest Warrant. In addition to these, there are many other legal aids in Hungarian law, such as the transfer or receipt of criminal proceedings, a report to a foreign state, or legal aid for the execution of a European investigation decision in European dimensions, the establishment of a joint investigation team, etc.

The institution of the European Arrest Warrant has been a major reform from a regional point of view, as it has replaced the institution of previously slow and not entirely politically free extradition. We have also seen through a practical example, the Tobin case, that this legal aid is not without problems either. Nevertheless, it has created the opportunity to speed up and in many cases even create the possibility of criminal cooperation between Member States that did not exist before.

It is important that EU rules are properly transposed by Member States and then interpreted by law enforcement bodies in line with their objectives. Legislative expectation that provisions are clear and well-defined and unambiguous[24].

Besides this I would like to highlight another problematic area which are not dealt entirely dealt with in these legal sources that I analysed in my paper. International cybercrime poses new jurisdictional challenges for states and in many cases it can lead to negative collision of jurisdiction. While some

22 Ibidem.

23 Ibidem.

24 László Kőhalmi, *A Büntetőjog Alapproblémái (Basic Problems of the Criminal Law)* (Pécs, Hungary: Kódex Nyomda, 2012), 37.

jurisdictions have adopted cybercrime-specific jurisdiction rules, the principles underlying fair enforcement of criminal jurisdiction may also justify the enforcement of jurisdiction against internal and external criminals. In my opinion it would be necessary to renew existing international legislations or to adopt the new convention that emphasizes the principle of citizenship or passive personality rather than the traditionally used territorial principle.

Literature

Bárd P., A Rocky Road: European Arrest Warrants and Tobin Case, *Law Society Gazette Ireland*, Vol. 108, No. 8, 2014.

Bárd P., *Az Ír Gázoló És Az Európai Büntetőjog*, Szuverén: A liberális demokrácia oldalai, 7 March 2014, http://szuveren.hu/jog/az-ir-gazolo-es-az-europai-buntetojog.

Bárd P., The Rough Road of EU Criminal Cooperation: The Tobin Case, *Ügyészek Lapja*, Vol. 21, No. 6, 2014.

Bárd P., Traps of Judicial Cooperation in Criminal Matters, *Hungarian Yearbook of International Law and European Law*, 2014.

Bárd P., *Az Európai Elfogatóparancs Magyarországon: The European Arrest Warrant in Hungary*, Budapest 2015.

Bassiouni, Cherif M., *International Extradition: United States Law and Practice*, Oxford, USA 2014.

Budaházi Á., A Nemzetközi Bűnügyi Jogsegély És Az Európai Elfogatóparancs, [in:] *A Nemzetközi Bűnügyi Együttműködés Jogi Alapjai*, B. Blaskó, Á. Budaházi (eds.), Budapest 2018.

Budaházi Á., A Nemzetközi Bűnügyi Jogsegély, [in:] *A Nemzetközi Bűnügyi Együttműködés Joga*, B. Blaskó, Á. Budaházi (eds.), Budapest 2019.

Európai Elfogatóparancs, *Európai igazságügyi portál*, 7 September 2020, https://e-justice.europa.eu/content_european_arrest_warrant-90-hu.do.

Kőhalmi L., A Nemzetközi Bűnügyi Együttműködés, [in:] *Magyar Büntetőjog Általános Rész*, M. Tóth, Á. Balogh (eds.), Budapest 2010.

Kussbach E., *Nemzetközi És Európai Büntetőjog*, Budapest 2005.

Ligeti K., A Nemzetközi Bűnügyi Együttműködés Általános Feltételei, [in:] *Az Európai Büntetőjog Kézikönyve*, F. Kondorosi, K. Ligeti (eds.), Budapest 2008.

Nagy A., Az Európai Elfogatóparancs, [in:] *Fejezetek Az Európai Büntetőjogból*, Á. Farkas (ed.), Miskolc 2017.

Nyitrai P.M., *Nemzetközi- És Európai Büntetőjog*, Budapest, 2006.

Marta Osuchowska

Free Legal Aid in Spain

Abstract: The study aims to analyze the issue of free legal aid in Spain, with particular emphasis on the material and personal scope. The extent of the research covers normative acts on the subject, with special attention paid to the constitutional foundations and acts to which it refers directly. Due to the fact that Spain is a unitary but decentralized state, the subject of analysis is also specific legal regulations for autonomous regions and cities. The core research hypothesis concerns the actual legal aid provided under a free guarantee, i.e., the effectiveness of normative solutions in this regard. The research questions relate to the possibilities and conditions of using free legal aid, also in the context of Spain's presence in the structures of the European Union. Within the research, it was assumed that there is an institution of free legal aid in Spain.

Keywords: Spain, free legal aid, the Constitution

1. Introduction

The Constitution of the Kingdom of Spain[1] guarantees gratuitous distribution of justice. According to its provisions and pursuant to art. 119, the right to free legal aid has also been introduced for people who have insufficient resources to carry out court proceedings to defend their rights[2].

Therefore, it must be concluded that in Spain, there is a constitutionally guaranteed procedure by which a number of benefits are granted to all those who can prove that they don't have sufficient economic resources, consisting mainly in the exemption from fees of attorneys-at-law and legal advisers, as well as expenses relating to court proceedings, including gathering evidence.

The legal basis for providing free legal aid services is the Free Legal Aid Act (*Ley de Asistencia Jurídica Gratuita*) of 1996.[3] Because of the guarantees of rights in individual autonomous communities, the administration of justice lies with different bodies, depending on the community regulations. However, free legal

---

1 *Constitución Española*, BOE núm. 311 de 29/12/1978, BOE-A-1978-31229; https://www.boe.es/eli/es/c/1978/12/27/(1)/con (accessed: 20.02.2021).

2 Art. 119 of the Constitution of Spain: "La justicia será gratuita cuando así lo disponga la ley y, en todo caso, respecto de quienes acrediten insuficiencia de recursos para litigar".

3 Ley 1/1996 of 10 January 1996 BOE núm. 11 de 12/01/1996, BOE-A-1996-750; https://www.boe.es/eli/es/l/1996/01/10/1/con [access: 20.02.2021].

aid services financed from public funds are most often provided by attorneys-at-law or prosecutors through various bar associations (*colegio de abogados*). All these activities are coordinated by the General Council of Spanish Bar Associations (*Consejo General de la Abogacía Española*), which acts as an intermediary between a citizen and a relevant agency of the administration[4].

The constitutional provision forms the legal basis for the functioning of the public defender institution (*turno de officio*) and the establishment of the Legal Guidance Service (*Servicio de Orientación Jurídica, SOJ*), as well as the introduction of exemptions from particular court and administrative fees. The Legal Guidance Service is a public service consisting in free legal aid provided through 83 different bar associations in Spain. Thus, depending on the particular association that provides the service, it may concern general proceedings or involve expertise in a specific field, such as violence against women.

A decision to grant or refuse legal assistance is in principle made by the Legal Aid Commission operating within a given territorial jurisdiction.

2. Objective scope

The right to free legal aid in Spain includes the following services:

- free pre-trial information and advice for people who intend to seek judicial protection for their rights and interests when they want to avoid a procedural conflict or analyse the legitimacy of their claim;
- the assistance of an attorney-at-law for a detained person or a prisoner who has not appointed that attorney with respect to any police action not resulting from pending criminal proceedings or during the first appearance before the court;
- free defence and representation by an attorney-at-law or a counsel in court proceedings, when their intervention is required by law or when it is ordered by the court or tribunal, considering the need to guarantee the equality of parties during a trial;
- posting announcements in official publications in the course of a trial;
- an exemption from the obligation to pay bail and court fees required when lodging an appeal;
- free expert assistance in the proceedings by technical staff assigned to jurisdictional authorities or, in the absence thereof, officials, bodies, or technical

4 For example, the Autonomous Community of Madrid https://www.comunidad.madrid/servicios/justicia/asistencia-juridica-gratuita (accessed: 21.02.2021).

services subordinate to the public administration. In exceptional cases, also by experts appointed from among relevant private experts according to the provisions of procedural law acts;

- obtaining free copies, certificates, documents, and notarial deeds on the terms as provided for in the notarial law;
- a reduction by 80 % in relevant fees for the execution of public deeds and obtaining notarial copies and certificates if they are directly related to a trial and are required by the judicial authority during such a trial or if they substantiate a claim of a person benefiting from the free legal aid service;
- a reduction by 80 % in relevant fees for obtaining notes, certificates, annotations, entries in real property registers and commercial registers if they are directly related to the proceedings and required by the judicial authority during the proceedings or if they substantiate a claim of a person benefiting from the free legal aid service;

However, no fees are charged if the party concerned proves an income below the minimum wage (*salario mínimo interprofesional, SMI*)

As a legal aid fee is paid in the form of grant aid, it must be included as income in a tax return.

3. Subjective scope

The Free Legal Aid Act defines who may benefit from such aid and how to receive it. According to its provisions and obligations resulting from signed international treaties and conventions, the right to free legal aid is available to citizens of Spain and other European Union Member States as well as foreigners residing in Spain if they show they have insufficient funds to bring a case to court. Moreover, such a service is available to institutions and services of the social welfare sector (*Entidades Gestoras y Servicios Comunes de la Seguridad Social*) as well as designated legal persons, namely public benefit organizations and foundations[5].

5 Art. 2 pkt. (a)–(c): "En los términos y con el alcance previstos en esta ley y en los tratados y convenios internacionales sobre la materia en los que España sea parte, tendrán derecho a la asistencia jurídica gratuita: (a) Los ciudadanos españoles, los nacionales de los demás Estados miembros de la Unión Europea y los extranjeros que se encuentren en España, cuando acrediten insuficiencia de recursos para litigar; (b) Las Entidades Gestoras y Servicios Comunes de la Seguridad Social, en todo caso; (c) Las siguientes personas jurídicas cuando acrediten insuficiencia de recursos para litigar: 1.º Asociaciones de utilidad pública, previstas en el artículo 32 de la Ley Orgánica 1/2002,

4. Conditions for obtaining

The right to free legal aid is granted to those natural persons who have insufficient assets and whose financial resources and gross income, calculated annually from all sources in total and broken down by family members, don't exceed statutory thresholds.

For a single person, the indicator calculated based on resources and income from all sources in total is not more than twice the IPREM (*Indicador Público de Renta de Efectos Múltiples*[6]) applicable at the time of filing the application. If a family consists of fewer members than four, this indicator must not exceed two and a half times the IPREM. In a situation where there are more family members, it is increased to three times the IPREM[7]. In turn, when the resources and income are higher but do not exceed five times the IPREM, the Free Legal Aid Commission (*Comisión de Asistencia Jurídica Gratuita*) may decide to grant the right to free legal aid considering the applicant's family situation, health, disability, and financial obligations, the number of dependent children or relatives and costs of initiating a trial or other circumstances, especially where the applicant is an ascendant of a multi-child family that belongs to a special category[8].

---

de 22 de marzo, reguladora del Derecho de Asociación; 2.º Fundaciones inscritas en el Registro Público correspondiente (...)".

6 The reference indicator for awarding benefits and grant aid related to income, updated at the beginning of each year in the Budget Act, was introduced on 1 July 2004 to replace the SMI.

7 Art. 3 ust. 1: „Se reconocerá el derecho de asistencia jurídica gratuita a aquellas personas físicas que careciendo de patrimonio suficiente cuenten con unos recursos e ingresos económicos brutos, computados anualmente por todos los conceptos y por unidad familiar, que no superen los siguientes umbrales: (a) Dos veces el indicador público de renta de efectos múltiples vigente en el momento de efectuar la solicitud cuando se trate de personas no integradas en ninguna unidad familiar; (b) Dos veces y media el indicador público de renta de efectos múltiples vigente en el momento de efectuar la solicitud cuando se trate de personas integradas en alguna de las modalidades de unidad familiar con menos de cuatro miembros; (c) El triple de dicho indicador cuando se trate de unidades familiares integradas por cuatro o más miembros o que tengan reconocida su condición de familia numerosa de acuerdo con la normativa vigente".

8 Art. 6 ust. 1 i 2: "En atención a las circunstancias de familia del solicitante, número de hijos o familiares a su cargo, las tasas judiciales y otros costes derivados de la iniciación del proceso, u otras de análoga naturaleza, objetivamente evaluadas y, en todo caso, cuando el solicitante ostente la condición de ascendiente de una familia numerosa de categoría especial, la Comisión de Asistencia Jurídica Gratuita ante la que se presente la solicitud podrá conceder excepcionalmente, mediante resolución motivada, el

It should be emphasized that people who are in informal relationships are treated on an equal footing with spouses except for those who are legally separated. The right to free legal aid may only be granted to those people who defend their own rights and interests or the rights and interests of people on whose behalf they act as a legal representative[9].

In the case of legal persons, the free assistance is provided to associations with the status of public benefit organizations (*asociaciones declaradas de Utilidad Pública*) or registered foundations. Furthermore, their tax base for corporate income taxation is lower than an amount corresponding to three times the IPREM per annum[10]. Entities engaged in social security receive such assistance unconditionally and in any situation.

Free legal aid limited to a specific jurisdiction area is also available to special groups of people who may be deprived of protection in a given situation. Thus, with regard to social security, it is available to employees and beneficiaries of

---

reconocimiento del derecho a las personas cuyos recursos e ingresos, aun superando los límites previstos en el artículo 3, no excedan del quíntuplo del indicador público de renta de efectos múltiples, teniendo en cuenta además la carencia de patrimonio suficiente. (…) En las mismas condiciones señaladas en el párrafo anterior, se podrá reconocer el derecho a la asistencia jurídica gratuita atendiendo a las circunstancias de salud del solicitante y a las personas con discapacidad señaladas en el apartado 2 artículo 1 de la Ley 51/2003, de 2 de diciembre, de igualdad de oportunidades, no discriminación y accesibilidad universal de las personas con discapacidad, así como a las personas que los tengan a su cargo cuando actúen en un proceso en su nombre e interés, siempre que se trate de procedimientos que guarden relación con las circunstancias de salud o discapacidad que motivan este reconocimiento excepcional. En tales casos, la Comisión de Asistencia Jurídica Gratuita correspondiente determinará expresamente qué prestaciones de las contempladas en el artículo 6 son de aplicación al solicitante".

9 Art. 3 ust. 2, 4: „Para la determinación del concepto de unidad familiar en sus diversas modalidades se estará a lo establecido en la Ley del Impuesto sobre la Renta de las Personas Físicas, equiparándose a los cónyuges no separados legalmente las parejas de hecho constituidas de conformidad con los requisitos que les fueran exigibles. (…) El derecho a la asistencia jurídica gratuita solo podrá reconocerse a quienes litiguen en defensa de derechos o intereses propios, o ajenos cuando tengan fundamento en una representación legal. En este último caso, los requisitos para la obtención del beneficio vendrán referidos al representado".

10 Art. 3 ust. 5: „Se reconocerá el derecho de asistencia jurídica gratuita a las personas jurídicas mencionadas en el apartado c) del artículo anterior, cuando careciendo de patrimonio suficiente el resultado contable de la entidad en cómputo anual fuese inferior a la cantidad equivalente al triple del indicador público de renta de efectos múltiples".

the social security system. In the area of criminal law, assistance is available to all citizens, as well as foreigners who will prove insufficient funds for a trial, even if they are not legally residents in Spain. They are entitled to legal aid and free defence representation. In the area of court administrative proceedings, the situation is similar with respect to foreigners as regards all asylum application procedures and the rights under the Law on Foreigners (*Ley de Extranjería*).

Regardless of funds for litigation, the right to free legal aid is available and immediately provided to victims of gender-based violence, terrorism, and trafficking in human beings in trials relating to their victim status, as well as minors and mentally disabled people who are victims of abuse or mistreatment. It also applies to people who have suffered, as a result of an accident, from permanent after-effects that prevent them completely from performing their job and who require the help of other people in performing vital activities of everyday life in a situation where the subject matter of a court dispute is a claim for compensation for personal injury or a claim for punitive damages[11].

5. Procedure

To apply for free legal aid, the person concerned has to complete a relevant application form available in printed and electronic versions as well as on websites of bar associations and the Free Legal Aid Commission and attach documents that confirm the lack of funds for litigation. The claims that are the subject of the application should also be indicated.

Applications for free legal aid, along with relevant documents, have to be submitted with the Legal Advice Office of the Bar Association at the location of the court or tribunal hearing the primary case, or with a court at the applicant's place of residence if the proceedings have not started yet.

11 Art. 2 pkt. h) i i): „Con independencia de la existencia de recursos para litigar, se reconoce el derecho de asistencia jurídica gratuita a quienes a causa de un accidente acrediten secuelas permanentes que les impidan totalmente la realización de las tareas de su ocupación laboral o profesional habitual y requieran la ayuda de otras personas para realizar las actividades más esenciales de la vida diaria, cuando el objeto del litigio sea la reclamación de indemnización por los daños personales y morales sufridos. (...) Con independencia de la existencia de recursos para litigar, se reconoce el derecho de asistencia jurídica gratuita a las asociaciones que tengan como fin la promoción y defensa de los derechos de las víctimas del terrorismo, señaladas en la Ley 29/2011, de 22 de septiembre, de reconocimiento y protección integral a las víctimas del terrorismo".

The General Council of Spanish Bar Associations has made available a website where it is also possible to fill in an application form for free legal aid or check whether the financial requirements for benefiting from the right to fee assistance are met[12].

6. Conclusions

When analysing the basis of the free legal aid institution in the Kingdom of Spain, it should be concluded that it's both objective and subjective scopes guarantee extensive rights in this area of justice. It should be stressed that the identification of specific groups of sufferers and people at risk and the introduction of flexible conditions guaranteeing free legal aid in their situation is a good example of the authorities' effective response to society's needs. Moreover, it is worth drawing attention to the wide range of entities providing free legal aid, including professional institutions operating throughout the country. Detailed information is provided by websites and Internet portals dedicated to the free legal aid institution, which not only provide basic data but also make it possible to carry out the entire procedure in electronic form. In turn, the possibility of verifying documentation and data sent to the system guarantees higher efficiency of the system.

Literature

https://www.mjusticia.gob.es/es/ciudadania/tramites/asistencia-juridica-gratuita (accessed: 21.02.2021).

12 See https://www.mjusticia.gob.es/es/ciudadanos/tramites/asistencia-juridica-gratuita [access: 21.02.2021].

Dorota Kottmann, Grażyna Szpor

Access to Information About Law in Switzerland

Abstract: The term "access to information about law" is sometimes understood broadly, but also distinguished from "access to law" or treated as its element, or just one of the stages of legal aid. The reason behind attributing such a broad meaning to it is understanding information as a good that reduces uncertainty or, in other words, entropy. Information about law is obtained as a benefit or as a service. In the benefit model, it is passed on by the public authorities free of charge, as well as under non-profit activities of other organizations.

The aim of the chapter is to analyze the issue concerning access to information about law in Switzerland.

Keywords: information, law, Switzerland

1. Introduction

The term "access to information about law" is sometimes understood broadly, but also distinguished from "access to law" or treated as its element, or just one of the stages of legal aid. The reason behind attributing such a broad meaning to it is understanding information as a good that reduces uncertainty or, in other words, entropy. This interdisciplinary definition that combines non-contradictory elements of various definitions coined in multiple fields, leads to a framing of information about law as "the reduction of uncertainty relating to law." Information about law *sensu largo* encompasses legal and law-related information, as well as facts connected with the two. Thus, reduction of uncertainty applies not only to provisions of law, but also to judicial decisions and opinions expressed in scholarly publications[1].

The political system of a given country affects how access to information about law is regulated there. The specificity of Switzerland stems from the federal structure of this state[2] and the fact that it has four official

---

1 *Modele dostępu do informacji o prawie*, G. Szpor (ed.), Warsaw 2014; G. Szpor, *Jawność i jej ograniczenia*, Vol. 1 *Idee i pojęcia*, Warsaw 2016.

2 Switzerland is a federal state comprising 26 cantons and 3000 municipalities with broad autonomy. State authority is exercised by the Bund, the Cantons and the Municipalities. Not only the Bund, but also each Canton, has its own constitution that lays down their organization. Each of the units mentioned has its own legislative and executive power; the Bund and the Cantons also hold judiciary power. The federal constitution of

languages[3], which makes providing information about law more difficult. Yet it also deals with the universal dilemmas associated with old and new access channels, charges, search options and comprehensibility. In this chapter we analyze the solutions to these dilemmas and verify the thesis according to which they affect the citizens' ability to satisfy their own information needs in the area of law, and the legal aid needs.

2. Development of electronic access to information about law in Switzerland

The preservation of data comprising information about law on traditional and IT carriers has become the basis for distinguishing the old model of access from the new one, in which the use of electronic communication has gradually come to the fore.

Switzerland began to create electronic legal databases in the 1980s[4]. In 1985, the implementation of the Federal Government's Plan for the Establishment of a Swiss Legal Database (*Konzept des Bundes für den Aufbau einer Schweizerischen Juristischen Datenbank*) was transferred to the private entity SWISSLEX AG. Owing to the advancing computerization and development of the information society, after a decade the strategy for dissemination of law and facilitation of access to law via electronic means[5] was changed, based on the assumption[6] that the state should ensure universal access to the law in force and judicial decisions

---

Switzerland strictly defines the powers resting with the Bund. Cantons are responsible, among other things, for ensuring access to information about the law in effect in their territories via their own legal databases. In reality, the level of access to information about law differs in individual cantons.

3 There are four official languages in Switzerland: French, German, Italian and Romansh. Legal acts at the federal level must be promulgated and available in at least three of them: French, Italian, and German. The publication of legislation and of judicial decisions in all the different official languages naturally entails additional work, but it also functions as a link between the different cultural and linguistic areas within Switzerland.

4 Holenstein, *Alles gratis?*, Ak. 1.

5 Studie für ein Konzept des Bundes zur Verbreitung des Rechts und dessen Zugänglichkeit über den Informatikweg (Konzeptstudie Schweiz. Rechtsinformationssystem); available at: https://www.bj.admin.ch/bj/de/home/staat/rechtsinformatik/copiur.html.

6 Entry: "Grundversorgung durch den Bund, Veredelung durch Private"; Cf. HOLENSTEIN, Alles gratis?, Ak. 10.
H. Müller Muralt,, Grundversorgung durch den Bund, Veredelung durch Private, [in:] copiur 1999, edition Februar 1999.

in all official languages[7]. Meanwhile, private entities should instead take care of publishing more specialized legal materials, such as commentaries, monographs, law journals, as well as create search engines for legal provisions and judicial decisions[8]. The Swiss Ministry of Justice (*Bundesamt für Justiz*) established a department responsible for legal informatics (*Rechtsinformatik*), that is for making federal legislation and judicial decisions available through electronic means[9]. Specialized publications, referred to as "enhanced products" in Switzerland, were subjected to the rules of the free market and SWISSLEX AG lost its privileged position.

At the beginning of the second decade of the 21st century, federal legislation was published both in traditional, printed form, and in digital form, but pursuant to art. 9 of the Law on Promulgation of Legislation, only the printed version was binding. In 2013, a draft law was presented with the objective of giving precedence to digital version over the printed one (the so-called *Primatwechsel*)[10]. The need to change the law was justified with the argument that technological advancement makes it possible to publish laws in digital form in a way that ensures their authenticity and integrity, thus eliminating the risk of their modification by unauthorized parties[11]. Moreover, it was argued that electronic access to law is much easier and cheaper, and that other European states had opted to recognize digitally published legal acts as binding[12]. According to the official commentary on the discussed reform, its purpose was also to create an Internet platform that would enable all those seeking information about law free of charge and secure access to legislation of federal level[13].

The discussed reform took effect on 01.01.2016. It introduced a new provision, 1a, pursuant to which publication of laws takes place at a central level, via a publicly accessible Internet platform. In principle, legal acts must also be drafted

7 The most important laws can now be found also in English at the Bund website, www.admin.ch.

8 The so-called *Veredelungsprodukte* literally translate into *enhanced* or *improved products*. The opinions on what the process of "enhancing" legal information consists of are very much divided; Cf. Tschümperlin, p. 271.

9 www.bj.admin.ch//bj/de/home/themen/staat_und_buerger/rechtsinformatik.html.

10 Cf: Botschaft zur Änderung des Publikationsgesetzes (Primatwechsel von der gedruckten zur elektronischen Version der amtlichen Veröffentlichungen) dated 28 August 2013, BBl 2013 7057.

11 Cf: Botschaft zur Änderung des Publikationsgesetzes, p. 7063 and p. 7070 et seq.

12 Such as Austria, Belgium or the Netherlands.

13 Cf: Botschaft zur Änderung des Publikationsgesetzes, p. 7062.

in a form that can be machine read and that allows for the retrieval of all prior versions of legislation. The art. 9, pursuant to which printed version was the only one with binding force, was repealed.

Legal informatics has been supported since the 1980s by the Swiss Association of Legal Informatics (*Schweizerischer Verein für Rechtsinformatik*)[14], which initially was involved in the creation of a legal database that could be accessed free of charge. In the 21st century its main objectives became, on the one hand, to promote the use of IT technologies to raise the work efficiency of public authority bodies at the federal and cantonal levels, and on the other hand to bring public administration closer to citizens in areas of legislation, public registers, electronic contact with public administration tasked with identification of persons, electronic signatures, science and scholarly publications, and archiving of documents[15].

The Association groups both public entities (chancellery of the government, cantons, Federal Supreme Court, law faculties of public universities) and private ones (law publishers, law offices, Swiss Post and others), which finance its activities[16].

This initiative demonstrates that many entities contribute to increasing the availability of information about law. It is yet another manifestation of active participation in public life, characteristic of the Swiss society, but it is also a confirmation that awareness of the benefits brought by computerization in the public law sector is widespread. These benefits include, among others: transparency of the public administration structures, universal access to the law in force, facilitation of contacts between citizens and public administration bodies, as well as reduction of costs on the part of the citizens, public entities and entrepreneurs thanks to time savings, electronic communication channels and simplified procedures.

3. Provision of access to information about law by the state

Access to information about law is considered a condition of the rule of law in Switzerland. The Swiss constitution does not provide for the obligation to publish laws (as does art. 88 of the Constitution RP). The doctrine explains the absence of a relevant provision by the fact that the obligation to publish laws

---

14 www.svri.ch/de/index.html.

15 Cf. Art. 1 of the Association's statute, available at: www.svri.ch/de/pdf/Statuten_eJustice_2011_de.pdf.

16 Cf. Art. 20 and Art. 21 of the Association's statute.

derives from the very idea of a democratic state. A state in which effective laws are not duly promulgated is not a state under the rule of law, but an authoritarian one[17]. One of the state's obligations resulting from the principle of the rule of law is to disseminate information about the law in force in such a way as to enable citizens to access this information without undue effort[18].

The *principle of equality before the law* also calls for ensuring access to the binding law[19]. Within the context of the law on electronic access to information, the principle of equality calls for this access to be *easy* and *universal*. In order for these conditions to be fulfilled, each interested person must be technically and economically able to obtain information of interest to them. Hence, the postulate of equal access to information about law also requires information to be comprehensible to users, as well as free of charge, in principle[20].

Therefore, the duty to publish effective legislation stems from the constitutional principles of the rule of law and of equality before the law. The method and scope of disseminating information by the state is, in turn, regulated by statute.

In Switzerland, the rules of promulgating acts legislation are governed by the Law on Compilations of Federal Law and on the Federal Gazette, in short referred to as the Law on Promulgation of Legislation[21]. Based on this, two compilations of law are issued on the federal level: Official Compilation[22] (*Amtliche Sammlung*, AS) and Systematic Compilation (*Systematische Sammlung*, SR)[23].

---

17 ROTH, Die Veröffentlichung von Rechtsnormen, 21; Cf. also Poledna, p. 96; Hangartner, [in:] Ehrenzeller et al. (eds.), Die schweizerische Bundesverfassung – Kommentar, Art. 5 Ak. 8.

18 Roth, Die Veröffentlichung von Rechtsnormen, p. 1.

19 Forstmoser/Vogt, p. 665 et seq.

20 Poledna, p. 93. The state's obligation to inform its citizens about law is also reflected in Art. 16 of the Constitution, which addresses freedom of opinion and access to information (own translation):

[1] The freedom of opinion and of obtaining and disseminating information is guaranteed.

[2] Everyone has the right to freely form, express, and disseminate their opinions.

[3] Everyone has the right to receive information freely, to gather it from generally accessible sources and to disseminate it.

21 Bundesgesetz über die Sammlungen des Bundesrechts und das Bundesblatt (Publikationsgesetz, PublG), SR 170.512 of 18 June 2004.

22 It has been pointed out in the doctrine that the term *official compilation* is misleading, as all legislation issued by state organs is official, including those laws that have been published in the consolidated (systematic) compilation; Cf. Roth M., Aktuelle Anforderungen, p. 34.

23 Database address: www.admin.ch/bundesrecht.

All federal legislation is published in the official compilation in chronological order. It also includes laws that are no longer in effect. The official compilation makes it possible to trace the process of creation and amendment of a given law in a historical perspective[24].

Laws that have been previously consolidated are published in the systematic compilation. It is possible to search for legislation that was in force on a given date, as well as to view previous versions of a given law[25]. The electronic systematic compilation of legislation is very user-friendly. Laws are divided into two categories: national and international. National law is in turn divided into further sub-categories[26].

Users also have at their disposal an alphabetical index to search for legislation, which is a practical solution, because anyone is able to quickly find a law concerning a given area even if they do not know its name.

Each law is marked with an SR number (short for *Sachregister*), which, on the one hand, indicates the position of a given piece of legislation within the Swiss legal system, and on the other hand makes it easier to cite laws[27].

Art. 14 of the Law on Promulgation of Legislation provides for the publication of the so-called Federal Gazette (*Bundesblatt*), in which all federal laws and official texts of the federal public administration can be found. The Bund's website offers access to all the issues of the Federal Gazette ever published, going back to 1849.

Access to all the foregoing electronic compilations of laws is universal and free of charge. It is easy enough for any citizen to find the laws of interest to them.

Cantons are responsible, among other things, for ensuring access to information about the law in effect on their territories via their own legal databases. In reality, the ease of access to information about law differs in individual cantons[28].

---

24 Roth, Aktuelle Anforderungen, p. 32 et seq.

25 If needed, the systematic compilation is updated daily. The standard procedure is for an amended version of a given law to be published in the electronic database on the date of its enactment, Cf. Roth, Aktuelle Anforderungen, p. 44.

26 Such as: "State- Society- Authorities", "Private Law - Civil Proceedings - Recognition and Enforcement of Judicial Decisions", "Criminal Law - Criminal Proceedings - Enforcement of Criminal Judgements", "Education- Science- Culture", "State Defense and Security", "Public Finances, Public Tasks - Energy- Public Transport", "Health- Work- Safety", "Economy- Technical Cooperation".

27 E.g. Bundesgesetz über die Gleichstellung von Man und Frau (Gleichstellungsgesetz, GlG) vom 24. März 1995, SR 151.1.

28 Owing to space constraints of this chapter, it only addresses access to databases containing laws and judicial decisions of the federal level.

Access to the judicial decisions of common courts stems from the fact that court proceedings must be public. In light of art. 30 par. 3 of the Swiss Federal Constitution, court hearings are in principle public, unless a relevant statute provides otherwise[29]. Scholars have emphasized that there are no reasons for anonymized judicial decisions not to be made available to all those who have an interest in them[30].

The largest database of judicial decisions on the federal level is maintained by the Federal Supreme Court (*Bundesgericht*)[31]. It publishes rulings rendered by the civil, criminal, public affairs and social insurance chambers. The database contains both judicial decisions with binding effect, that is so-called landmark rulings (*Leitentscheide*) from 1875 (!)[32], and all the other rulings; the latter category from 2000. The individual rulings of the Federal Supreme Court are usually published within a month from their delivery. Each day, the *Bundesgericht* publishes on average 20–30 judicial decisions.

Rulings of the Federal Supreme Court are published in the same language in which the proceedings were conducted: German, French or Italian. This may pose a difficulty for the users who are not fluent in all the official languages. Although a part of rulings with binding effect is translated into the other official languages, such translations are published almost exclusively in commercial legal databases.

The Federal Supreme Court website offers a search engine that can be used to find rulings by reference number, keyword or date of issuance. Moreover, there is an option to search for information only in the database of rulings with binding effect or in the database containing all rulings.

4. Commercial access to information about law

Besides public legal databases, there also exist many private (commercial) ones, which offer mainly what is called "enhanced products" in Switzerland, such as commentaries to legislation and to rulings, scholarly journals or monographs.

The Swisslex database is available against a payment in German and French. It contains publications of the main legal publishers, that is Schulthess Verlag,

29 Cf. Art. 30 par. 3 of BV.

30 Tschümperlin, p. 266.

31 Website at: www.bger.ch.

32 It is worth mentioning that rulings from the period between 1875 to 1953 can be accessed through the website of the University of Bern Faculty of Law (in cooperation with the Federal Supreme Court).

Stämpfli Verlag and DIKE Verlag, including numerous commentaries, ca. 60 law journals and databases with judicial decisions of all federal and cantonal courts[33].

The recht.ch portal offers publications issued by the Stämpfli publishing house. Among them are both law journals and monographs. The materials available are divided into modules devoted to specific branches of law, such as labour law, family law, private international law, insurance law, criminal law, etc., which facilitates the search.[34]

Legalis is a legal database of the Helbing & Lichtenhahn publishing house. It offers access to numerous law journals, including Die Praxis (PRA), which contains the most important rulings of the Federal Supreme Court delivered in Italian and French, subsequently translated into German[35].

Weblaw is a legal platform, parts of which are accessible without payment, but given the development of profiling, this does not necessarily mean that access is free. Users can find there legal publications, newest developments in legislation and in court rulings, job offers for lawyers, among other things[36]. Weblaw also publishes *Jusletter*, Switzerland's most popular law journal available in digital form only[37].

5. Conclusions

Information about law is obtained as a benefit or as a service. In the benefit model, it is passed on by the public authorities free of charge, as well as under non-profit activities of other organizations. The scope of tasks of the legislative, executive and judicial branches, as well as their collaboration with other entities in connection with the advancement or electronic communication, are changing. The service model is heterogeneous: the structures of service providers and service recipients as regards law information differs from that regarding legal information or the facts related to them. Moreover, processing personal data of portal users is becoming an increasingly frequent equivalent to payment within the service model.

Direct, indirect and integrated knowledge about law is determined by strategies of reducing uncertainty in this regard. Large databases that employ artificial intelligence facilitate it for users to find and understand information about

33 www.swisslex.ch.
34 www.recht.ch.
35 www.legalis.ch.
36 www.weblaw.ch.
37 See: www.weblaw.ch/de/services/linkliste/erlaeuterungen.asp.Künzle/Holenstein/Münst/Schäuble, Die Erneuerung der Rechtsdatenbanken, p. 147.

law on their own. Comprehensive action is needed to shape a strategy that will be adjusted to the contemporary requirements, cohesive, in line with the public interest and satisfying needs that do not collide with it. In Europe, such action is taken up both by European Union bodies[38] and by individual member states. This transformation may be made more effective by legal comparative research.

Literature

Adjust Fn. 17 as: Schindler, [in] Ehrenzeller et al., *Die schweizerische Bundesverfassung*, Art. 5 Ak. 44 et seq.

Ehrenzeller B. et al. (Ed.), *Die schweizerische Bundesverfassung*, St. Galler Kommentar. 4. Ed., Zurich/St. Gallen 2023

Forstmoser Peter/Vogt Hans-Ueli, Einführung in das Recht, Ed. 5, Berno 2012

Holenstein Urs Paul, Alles gratis? Grund- und Mehrwertrechtsinformation im Netz, JurPC Web-Dok. 67/2001, Abs. 1 - 30

Künzle Hans Rainer/Holenstein Urs Paul/Münst Hubert/Schäuble Peter, Die Erneuerung der Rechtsdatenbanken in der Schweiz, AJP 2007, pp. 147–155

Müller Muralt Hanna, Grundversorgung durch den Bund, Veredelung durch Private, [in:] copiur 1999, edition Februar 1999 (compare footnote 6)

Poledna, Hangartner, [in:] *Die schweizerische Bundesverfassung - Kommentar*, Ehrenzeller et al. (eds.), Art. 5 Ak. 8, p. 96.

Poledna Tomas, Staatliche Informationspflichten (Grundversorgung mit elektronischen Daten), [in:] Koller Thomas/Koller Heinrich, Tagung 2003 für Informatik und Recht vom 29. August 2003 in Bern, Recht und Rechtsdaten – Anspruch und Wirklichkeit, Bern 2004, pp. 69–104

Roth Marius, Aktuelle Anforderungen an amtliche Sammlungen, LeGes 2013, pp. 33-62 (cit. Aktuelle Anforderungen)

Roth Marius, Die Veröffentlichung von Rechtsnormen in der Schweiz, Zurich/St. Gallen 2011 (cit. Die Veröffentlichung von Rechtsnormen)

Roth, *Die Veröffentlichung von Rechtsnormen.*

Szpor G. (ed.), *Jawność i jej ograniczenia*, Vol. 1, *Idee i pojęcia*, Warsaw 2016.

Tschümperlin Paul, Öffentlichkeit der Entscheidungen und Publikationspraxis des Schweizerischen Bundesgerichts, SJZ 99/2003, pp. 265–272

---

38 The European e-Justice Portal is conceived as a future electronic one-stop-shop in the area of justice. As a first step it strives to make your life easier by providing information on justice systems and improving access to justice throughout the EU, in 23 languages. [https://e-justice.europa.eu]

Beata Nuzzo

The System of Free Legal Aid in the Italian Republic

Abstract: The aim of the chapter is to describe the system of free legal aid in the Italian Republic from the historical, theoretical, and practical perspectives. The first part presents the historical development of the institution of free legal aid, which sheds light on the strong and weak points of contemporary legal and institutional solutions. The Author's intention is to present all legal solutions that constitute the Italian model of free legal aid. The Italian model described here belongs to a group which in the Anglo-Saxon doctrine is called coordinated assigned counsel programs, i.e., programs of legal aid based on the intervention of free professionals who must meet certain professional requirements and whose activity is monitored through supervision, which in Italy is provided by the Council of the Order of Lawyers. The second part analyses impediments and inefficiencies of the Italian legislation, which were indicated by the ECHR and offers their explanation from the historical perspective of legal aid in Italy.

Keywords: free legal aid, legal aid in civil cases, legal aid in criminal cases

1. Introduction

The term legal aid refers to the provision of legal assistance to people who cannot afford it. The concept of "legal aid" is inseparable from its function as a vital means of access to justice. Access to justice is defined as "the ability of people to seek and obtain a remedy through formal or informal institutions of justice, and in conformity with human rights standards," and it is also seen as fundamental to the protection of human rights[1]. The right to legal aid has been recognised for many years as a fundamental right of the individual by numerous international regulations, including art. 6(3)(c) of the ECHR and the New York International Covenant on Civil and Political Rights of 19 December 1966, art. 14(3)(d). The Charter of Fundamental Rights of the European Union also recognises the right to an effective remedy and to a fair trial.

---

1 Cf. *United Nations Development Programme, Access to Justice Practice Note* (2004). *United Nations Office on Drugs and Crime, Access to Justice: Legal Defence and Legal Aid* (2006).

The Italian legal system recognises and guarantees the right to proper representation in court as a fundamental human right. Art. 24 of the Constitution, in fact, defines the right to defense as an inviolable right of the individual, and states that "The indigents are entitled by law to proper means for action or defense in all courts." This protection is an extension of the fundamental right of every person to have access to the courts to initiate legal proceedings to protect his or her rights. This article therefore introduces a real obligation on the state to effectively guarantee the exercise of the right of defense to everyone. In the Italian legal system, the right to legal aid is a social right in that its exercise guarantees its beneficiary effective participation in the political, economic, and social organisation of the state, as provided in art. 3(2) of the Constitution. The provisions stated in art. 24 of the Constitution, in paragraphs 1 and 3, thus implement the principle of equality enshrined in art. 3 of the Constitution. In fact, guaranteeing effective legal aid for the indigents is one of the state's obligations which is aimed at removing economic and social obstacles which, by limiting the freedom and equality of citizens, prevent the full development of the human person[2].

2. Legal aid – The Italian experience

2.1. History of legal aid

Over the centuries, the Italian legal systems developed different systems which guaranteed legal aid to the poor. The right to legal aid was traditionally exercised in one of two models: one based on public legal offices, in which the states covered legal costs, and the other based almost exclusively on the services of lawyers who were responsible for assisting those entitled to legal aid.

In 1861, after the unification of Italy, the "Advocacy of the poor" (*Avvocatura dei poveri*) was extended to the whole Kingdom, which entrusted the defence of the poor to state legal offices made up of lawyers appointed and paid for by the state[3]. Advocacy of the poor was created in the Savoyard-Piedmontese state, but in the unitary state it did not last long. With the law of 1865, the government, justifying it with the need to reduce public spending, abolished the public offices of assistance to the poor and introduced the system of legal aid as an honorary

2 Cf. G. Cascini, *L'assistenza legale ai meno abbienti: una riforma che non può più attendere*, "Questione Giustizia" 1998, p. 668.

3 Earlier, the lawyer of the poor as an official paid by the state, was established for the first time in 1233 in Parma. Cf. Pasini, *Il gratuito patrocinio nel diritto giudiziario civile*, Milano, 1906, p. 9.

and compulsory office of the legal profession. This solution, at that time, was also adopted by other European countries (Austria, France, Germany) and had previously been introduced in some Italian pre-unitary states: the Kingdom of the Two Sicilies, the Grand Duchy of Tuscany, and Lombardy-Venetia[4].

Next, with the Royal Decree of 1923, legal aid for the poor was regulated in an organic manner[5]. This marked the definitive transition from a system of public assistance to a system based exclusively on the services of lawyers. According to the Royal Decree of 1923, the conditions for the granting of legal aid to a person included their being poor and high likelihood that the case would be won[6]. Legal aid was granted for all stages of the trial cases with high likelihood of winning, to anyone – citizens, foreigners, natural persons, and legal person – whose financial situation that did not allow them to meet legal expenses. Legal aid excluded situations in which certain natural or legal persons were granted tax concessions or were exempted from any payments by means of other legal regulations[7]. In order to obtain legal aid, applicants had to prove not only that they was poor but also that their reasons were well-founded and that the case was likely to be won.

Over time, the granting of legal aid to the indigents evolved: from an original conception in which it was regarded as a favour to those who were worthy of it, it came to be treated as a mandatory act of social solidarity towards the poor. Consequently, the notion of "poverty" in this context no longer indicated the condition of a person who were deprived of the means of subsistence but rather the state in which this person was unable to bear the costs of the trial. The consequence of this conceptual evolution was the extension of legal aid to legal persons and, in addition, the fact that, in order for it to be granted, no consideration was given to whether the applicant was responsible for the causes that led to his needing it. For this reason, legal aid could also be granted to those who were directly responsible for their poverty. The notion of poverty thus referred not only to those who possessed nothing but also to those who were unable, even temporarily, to bear the costs of a trial[8].

---

4 Denti, *Avvocatura dei poveri*, [in:] "Novissimo digesto", Torino, 1958, I, 2, p. 1683.

5 Cf. Royal Decree (R.D.) no. 3282 of 30 December 1923.

6 Cf. V. Vigoriti, *Fumus boni iuris' e diritto d'azione e di difesa*, "Journal of Procedural Law" 1966, p. 284.

7 This was the case, for example, with the benefits enjoyed by those injured at work. The same was true when, as an act of national solidarity, war orphans were exempted from taxes and court fees, limited to cases concerning their custody. In these and other similar cases, it was not a question of applying the law of 1923. Cf. P. Brandi, *Gratuito patrocinio*(voce), [in:] "Enciclopedia del diritto", XIX, Milan, 1970, p. 734.

8 Cf. P. Brandi, *op. cit.*, p. 735.

The idea of legal aid, which was inspired by charity towards the poor and social solidarity towards the less well-off, meant that it was also granted to charities whose aim was to assist and defend the poor. Therefore, the law granted legal aid to public charity institutions and, amending previous legal regulations, to institutions whose aim was "charity or education of the poor", and whose aim was verified by specific authorities in order to avoid misuse. Granting legal aid was decided by a legal aid commission[9]. If this commission issued a positive opinion and granted legal aid to an applicant, a lawyer was appointed, the beneficiary was exempted from advance payment of court costs and fees and was also offered certain other services free of charge. In addition, the decision of granting legal aid entailed providing assistance not only for the legal action for which the application was made but also for potential appeal.

2.2. Critique of the "pre-Republican" model of legal aid and the first reforms

With time, the weak points and limitations of legal aid for the indigents, as an "honorary and compulsory duty of lawyers" were increasingly emphasised[10]. It was observed that "the social burden of legal defence of the poor has been shifted, because of this old law, from its natural recipient, the state, to lawyers, who had some prospects of compensation only if their clients won the case". The natural consequence was that, apart from rare exceptions, and apart from those groups of the population whose defence could be provided by various patronage bodies and some legal offices paid for by e.g., trade unions, the poor were defended in courts by less experienced, less skilled, and less committed lawyers. "The poor person is like a sick person who, by not paying for his doctor and treatment, serves the youngest and most inexperienced lawyers to practice their profession or unsuccessful lawyers to stay in touch with the courts"[11].

9 These commissions are to be considered administrative bodies, both because of the task they perform (providing for the poor, while protecting the financial interests of the state) and because of the essentially administrative nature of decisions they issue. However, some authors consider them to be an integral part of the judiciary due to their composition and function. Cf. N. Ambrosone, *I provvedimenti delle commissioni pel gratuito patrocinio sono soggetti a ricorso per cassazione?*, "Journal of Procedural Law" 1956, pp. 112.

10 This harsh criticism was expressed, for example, by M. Cappelletti, who stated: "One of the most shameful wounds in current Italian legislation, and one that most urgently calls for attention and care, is that of the law on legal aid: the law, or rather the fascist royal decree, of 30 December 1923, no. 3282". Cf. M. Cappelletti, *Gratuito patrocinio, le cavie della giustizia*, "L'astrolabio", 12 May 1968, p. 31.

11 Cf. M. Cappelletti, *op.cit.*, p. 33.

Another weakness of the Italian law on legal aid was concerned the lack of preliminary advice. The Italian law, unlike law in England, France and other countries, did not provide, not even minimally, for the establishment of free out-of-court legal advice offices, located throughout the country, "to which the poor could confidently turn for advice". This lack was criticised because "legal advice is the first and most basic form of legal assistance." It was emphasised that citizens primarily need a lawyer to advise them on whether or not to pursue a dispute or to establish a case rather than to assist them in court. The greatest difficulty that the poor face when dealing with legal matters is that they do not know what to do or where to turn for explanations. For this reason, as several authors pointed out, "depriving the poor of any form of preliminary advice would make legal aid itself useless"[12].

Moreover, after the promulgation of the Republican Constitution of 1948, the provisions of the Royal Decree which entrusted granting legal aid to a mixed commission of an administrative and not judicial nature were also harshly criticised. It was argued that making the exercise of the right to bring a case before a court of law dependent on the assessment of an administrative body violated the principle stated in art. 24 and 25 of the Constitution[13].

With time, the legal protection of the indigenes, which was initially based on legal aid founded on the obligation imposed on lawyers and prosecutors to defend the indigenes (who were assigned to them by special commissions or – in criminal cases – by the judge) free of charge, took other forms. In 1973 this system was abrogated and replaced by a new system of state-funded legal aid (*patrocinio a spese dello stato*) which at that time covered only disputes in the area of labour law and social security. In 1983 it was extended to cover adoption and child custody proceedings, in 1988 to cover the liability of judges, and in 1990 to cover criminal and civil proceedings for damages and restitution for crimes. Between 1973 and the 1990s the scope of the old legal aid was increasingly reduced, because it was considered "obsolete and inadequate"[14], whereas the scope of the "new" legal aid was increasingly expanded[15].

12 Cf. M. Cappelletti, *Processo e ideologie*, Bologna 1969, p. 550.

13 Gallo, *Assistenza giudiziaria ai non abbienti*, [in:] "Enciclopedia Giuridica Treccani", III, Rome, 1991, p. 4.

14 Varano, *Recent trends in the organization of legal services in Italy*, [in:] *Studi senesi*, 1984, p. 273.

15 It is no coincidence that in 1973, when the legislator made provision for this in the labour law proceedings and social security proceedings, he stated the relevant rules

2.3. The present model of state-funded legal aid (*patrocinio a spese dello stato*)

The reforms of 1973 and 1990 concerning labour law proceedings and criminal proceedings were not enough to compensate for the shortcomings of the Italian system of protecting the indigenes. That is why a reform covering all areas of justice became necessary, and it introduced the system of "legal aid financed by the state"[16]. Within this system, a person who can prove that their annual income is below a fixed threshold (determined by biennial adjustments on the basis of particular indices) may apply for legal aid in the chancellor's office of the court before which the case is pending (in criminal proceedings) or at the Bar Association in the district of the competent Court (in civil, administrative, accounting, and tax proceedings)[17]. If legal aid is granted, it is free for the beneficiary, and the Treasury will preliminarily cover the costs of proceedings. The beneficiary can choose a lawyer from the list of lawyers who volunteer to be placed on it and have been accepted by the Bar Association after being positively evaluated. The state will be able to recover its advanced payment only if the beneficiary wins the case (because the losing party is obliged to cover all the costs)[18].

On 1 July 2002 the consolidated Act on legal costs, passed by the Council of Ministers on 24 May 2002 and approved by Presidential Decree No. 115 of 30 May 2002[19], came into force. The Presidential Decree ordered the regulations scattered in several Acts and other sources of law and introduced some significant novelties in the matters regulated. For the first time, legal aid became extended to all types of proceedings: criminal, civil, administrative, tax, labour, etc., and to all: citizens, stateless persons, foreigners with a residence permit, and non-profit organizations. In addition, the high quality of legal aid was ensured

---

would remain in force until the approval of "the legal provisions that will ensure legal aid to the poor in disputes before all courts" Cf. Legge 11 August 1973 no. 533, *Disciplina delle controversie individuali di lavoro e delle controversie in materia di previdenza e di assistenza obbligatorie*. (GU n.237 del 13-09-1973).

16 Cfr. G. Cascini, *L'assistenza legale ai meno abbienti…*, *op. cit.*, p. 669.

17 For a commentary on current legislation in civil and administrative proceedings see G. Scarselli, *Il nuovo patrocinio a spese dello Stato nei processi civili ed amministrativi*, Padova 2003; in criminal proceedings see P. Sechi, *Il patrocinio dei non abbienti nei procedimenti penali*, Milan 2006; A. Buzzoni, *Il gratuito patrocinio*, Milano 2010; S. Bologna, *Guida al patrocinio alle spese delo Stato*, Milano 2018.

18 A.Vigani, *Guida Breve al Gratuito Patrocinio*, Segrate 2021.

19 Presidential Decree No. 115, 30 May 2002 *Consolidated Act on legal costs* (*Testo Unico in materia di spese di giustizia*) (Gazzetta ufficiale, General Series no. 39, of 15 June 2002).

thanks to, firstly, providing lawyers with fair remuneration for their work and, secondly creating new mechanisms, such as lists of lawyers characterised by honesty and high level of professionalism[20].

The consolidated Act eliminated one of the previous conditions of access to legal aid in civil and administrative proceedings, namely "the likelihood of winning the case"[21] and was replaced by a new condition, that of "not manifestly unfounded reasons", to be deduced solely from the documents provided by the applicant[22]. In criminal proceedings, legal aid is provided to all poor applicants, including suspects, defendants, convicted criminals, victims who want to take civil action, persons civilly liable, or civilly obliged to pay a fine. The difference between this Act and the old Act lies in the fact that the latter excluded suspects, defendants, and convicted criminals from legal aid[23].

Art. 74 of the consolidated Act on Legal Aid specifies the temporal frames of access to legal aid, stating that it is available at all levels of jurisdiction, including all further connected incidental and/or contingent proceedings. Legal aid is granted only for court proceedings and cannot be granted for out-of-court assistance (e.g., it cannot be granted for legal advice nor a lawyer's activities before the trial). The only exception is advice in case of cross-border litigation in the civil pre-litigation stage. This refers to advice with a view to achieving a non-judicial settlement of cross-border disputes in civil and commercial matters, i.e., disputes in which the party applying for legal aid is domiciled or resides lawfully in a European Union Member State other than the one where the trial would take place.

Legal aid is granted to those who – at the time the application is made and throughout the trial – are considered to be indigenes, that is their income declared in the latest income tax return, does not exceed € 11,493.82 per year[24], but that aid is subject to withdrawal if that condition ceases to exist. This limit is higher in criminal proceedings and in cross-border out-of-court disputes. The income limit is updated every two years on the basis of data provided by the Italian National Institute of Statistics[25]. The consolidated Act takes into consideration only the economic capacity of the party seeking legal aid, without

20 Article 81, Consolidated Act on legal costs (C.A.), Legislative Decree no. 115 of 30 May 2002.

21 Cf. art. 20, R.D. 3282, op. cit.

22 Cf. art. 74 (2), C.A., op. cit.

23 Cf. art. 74(1), C.A., op. cit.

24 Cf. art. 76, C.A., op. cit.

25 Cf. art. 77, C.A., op. cit.

considering the procedural costs, which may significantly differ depending on the proceedings to be instituted[26].

When a legal aid is granted, some legal costs are free of charge, others are paid in advance by the Treasury.

Legal costs that are free of charge:

(a) copies of necessary procedural documents.
Legal costs that are paid by the Treasury in advance:
(b) travel expenses payable to magistrates, clerks, and judicial officers for their trips related to the performance of procedural acts outside the place where the trial is held;
(c) travel expenses payable to witnesses;
(d) postage for the service of documents by judicial officers at the request of the court or of a party;
(e) travel expenses and expenses incurred in carrying out the assignment, and the fees of court-appointed assistants, expert witnesses, and authorised private investigators;
(f) custody;
(g) fees and expenses for lawyers;
(h) costs of court publications[27].

If the beneficiary of legal aid loses the case and is convicted by the court, they have to cover the expenses born by the winning party and pay them compensation.

Finally, this Act introduced easy procedural means of accessing legal aid, strengthened the role of lawyers providing this aid, and abolished all those mechanisms whereby the professional conduct of lawyers was subject to the control and discipline of the state authorities. Art. 81 of the consolidated Act specifies the requirements that lawyers providing legal aid to the poor must meet in order to be included in the special list[28]. Such list is kept by the Bar Association and includes only those lawyers who have applied for it and who possess the qualities

---

26 The concept of non-subsistence, as expressed in the Consolidated Act on Social Security, had been harshly criticised in the past. Some authors even thought more highly of the concept of "state of poverty" proposed by the legislator in 1923. Under that system, in fact, non-subsistence referred to persons "unable to meet the costs of litigation". Cf. Gallo, *Assistenza giudiziaria ai non abbienti*, [in:] "Enc. Giur. Treccani", 1991, p. 2.

27 Cf. art. 107, C.A., op. cit.

28 E. Sacchettini, *Scelta dei difensori solo dall'elenco degli ordini*, in "Guida al diritto", Dossier n. 7/2000, p. 114.

set out in art. 81(2) of the consolidated Act, namely: professional aptitude and experience; absence of disciplinary sanctions[29]; professional seniority of not less than six years.

3. Conclusions

For the last century the Italian legal system has experimented with various legal solutions aimed at guaranteeing legal protection to the indigenes. This allowed to develop the system that truly guarantees the removal of "the obstacles of economic and social order" ensuring the "freedom of access to justice", provided by the Constitution of the Republic.

The principles of the Constitution of 1948 are reflected in the current Italian model of state-funded legal aid – developed on the basis of the 2002 consolidated Act on Legal Costs. In the Anglo-Saxon doctrine this is called *coordinated assigned counsel programs*, i.e., legal aid programs implemented by private lawyers, who are required to meet certain professional requirements and whose activity is monitored through supervision, in the Italian case ensured by the Bar Association. Although the introduction of this new model has removed certain old interpretative problems and imperfections, it is not perfect. For example, doubts may be raised regarding constitutional legitimacy of certain provisions of the consolidated Act, such as differentiating between granting legal aid in civil and administrative proceedings and criminal proceedings. In the latter case, in order to have access to legal aid, it is necessary to prove that one does not have income sufficient to cover the costs of litigation, whereas in the former, together with the income requirement, an additional element is required, as already stated, of "not manifestly unfounded reasons".

Other doubts of unconstitutionality may arise from the comparison of art. 82 of the consolidated Act with art. 130 of the consolidated Act, both of which refer to fees due to lawyers who offer their services to the poor. These two articles contain provisions that are in conflict with each other, which violates the principle of equality. While in criminal proceedings, lawyers' fees are covered by the judiciary, and these fees "do not exceed the average sums of the professional tariffs", in civil and administrative proceedings these average sums are further "reduced by half". The same Act thus provides for two different ways of calculating fees for the same professional service.

29 Paragraph 3 of art. 81 of the Consolidated Act states that lawyers towards whom disciplinary measures have been taken are removed from the list, regardless of the type, nature, and effects of sanctions.

The solutions adopted in Italy for almost a century can be valuable also for other countries, since they demonstrate how two different models (which can be called the private model and the public model) of legal aid offered to the indigenes function in practice. These models reflect two different visions, which are often in contradiction with each other. The first is totally opposed to any intervention of a state into the judiciary system, as such intervention is considered undue interference and a symptom of the executive's desire to control the judiciary, while the other, which is more attentive to communal and social issues, considers public action to be a neutral and supreme instrument of protection. Both models have advantages and disadvantages: the public model, for example, meets the needs of the indigenes to a greater extent, thanks to the existence of lawyers who specialise in legal aid (and are employed by the state) and thanks to their authority, which is guaranteed by the fact that they are generally perceived as members of the judiciary. The private model, on the other hand, offers the poor greater independence in access to legal aid, thanks to, among others, the fact that they can choose a lawyer themselves. Disadvantages of the public model include, for example: a lawyer's possible lack of motivation to work well caused by the certainty of salary, which is typical of all public offices; excessive bureaucracy; the risk of a lawyer's lack of autonomy in his work; and excessive burden on the state budget. Disadvantages of the private model include the risk of abuse on the part of the "greedy" lawyers and, above all, their lack of commitment, which results from lower earnings in legal aid cases (financed by the state) than in other cases (financed by private clients). All these point to the need to search for such a model of legal aid which will lead to creating a fair and effective system of legal protection of the poor, in which the exchange of experiences between European states may prove useful.

Literature

Ambrosone N., I provvedimenti delle commissioni pel gratuito patrocinio sono soggetti a ricorso per cassazione?, *Journal of Procedural Law*, 1956.

Bologna S., *Guida al patrocinio alle spese delo Stato*, Milano 2018.

Brandi P., Gratuito patrocinio (voce), [in:] *Enciclopedia del diritto*, Vol. XIX, Milano 1970.

Buzzoni, A., *Il gratuito patrocinio*, Milano 2010.

Cappelletti M., Gratuito patrocinio, le cavie della giustizia, *i"L'astrolabio*, 12 May 1968.

Cascini G., L'assistenza legale ai meno abbienti: una riforma che non può più attendere, *Questione Giustizia*, 1998.

Denti V., Avvocatura dei poveri, [in:] *Novissimo digesto*, Vol. I, Torino 1958, 2.

Gallo E., Assistenza giudiziaria ai non abbienti, [in:] *Enciclopedia Giuridica Treccani*, Vol. III, Roma 1991.

Sacchettini E., Scelta dei difensori solo dall'elenco degli ordini, *Guida al diritto*, Dossier n. 7/2000.

Scarselli G., *Il nuovo patrocinio a spese dello Stato nei processi civili ed amministrativi*, Padova 2003.

Sechi, P., *Il patrocinio dei non abbienti nei procedimenti penali*, Milano 2006.

Varano V., Recent Trends in the Organization of Legal Services in Italy, in *Studi senesi*, 1984.

Vigani A., *Guida Breve al Gratuito Patrocinio*, Segrate, 2021.

Małgorzata Augustyniak

Forms of Free Legal Aid in France

Abstract: This text explores the concept of free legal aid in France from a historical and contemporary perspective. It examines the axiological framework of legal aid, emphasizing the principles of liberty, equality, and fraternity. The text traces the evolution of legal aid in France, from a practice of charity to a state-funded public service. It discusses the current model of state-funded legal aid, including its provisions for financial assistance, access to legal advice, and assistance in court proceedings. The criteria for granting legal aid and the challenges faced by middle-class individuals are also addressed. The text concludes by highlighting recent reforms aimed at improving the accessibility and effectiveness of the legal aid system, including the use of modern technology.

Keywords: Free legal aid, France, state-funded legal aid, financial assistance, access to justice, legal advice, criteria for granting assistance

1. Introduction

The question of free legal aid is worth considering from an axiological perspective, particularly in light of the normative provisions of a given system. They define the legal model and the associated value system prevailing in a given country. They define rights and obligations both between individuals and between individuals and the community, which is closely linked to the question of the scope of action of state institutions in seeking a harmonious arrangement in these relationships. From this point of view, the question of the legal capacity of citizens, an important element of which is access to justice in the broad sense, proves to be essential. In considering normative regulation from this perspective, the constitutional question should first be examined. In France, since 1971, this has been constituted by the so-called constitutional block. It includes the Constitution of the Fifth Republic, adopted on 4 October 1958, of which the 1789 Declaration of the Rights of Man and of the Citizen is an integral part, in accordance with the tradition to date. The 1958 Constitution also recognised the Preamble to the Constitution of the Fourth Republic of 19 April 1946 as an integral part and, since 2004, has included the Charter on the Protection of the Environment[1].

---

1 J. Wawrzyniak, *On some peculiarities of the Constitution of the Fifth Republic of France*, "Studia Iuridica Lublinensia" 2014, no. 22, p. 153.

None of the regulations indicated directly establish a right to justice[2]. They do, however, call for the respect of civic equality, which should be considered vital in the context of access to legal aid. The importance of this value is highlighted in art. 1 of the Declaration of the Rights of Man and of the Citizen: *Men are born free and equal in their rights. Social distinctions may be based only on considerations of the common good.* The meaning of this provision is reinforced by art. 16 of the Declaration, which speaks of the need for the guarantee of respect for the law to function in society. In light of these provisions, it must be recognised that the right of access to justice and an effective judicial review is one of the conditions for realising civic equality. The realisation of this value is primarily the responsibility of state institutions, which should assist those who cannot meet the costs of professional legal services. Organising such assistance also involves respecting the principle of equality before the law, which prohibits discrimination on any ground. This approach is essential to combat exclusion from access to justice, mainly due to lack of financial resources or ignorance of the specificities of the judicial system. From this perspective, the modern basis of legal aid is the financial support provided by the State, under certain conditions, to those who wish to appear in Court, defend themselves in Court or reach an out-of-court settlement.

2. Legal aid in France

2.1. Historical background

In monarchical France, the administration of justice to all subjects was one of the primary attributes of the king's power and the clerical apparatus under his authority. Both the drafting and the application of the law were primarily conditioned by particularisms resulting from state affiliation. It is, therefore, difficult to speak of universal access to justice and equal treatment before the courts. While there were some forms of support in this area, they were marginal. For example, in the 7th century, royal law ordered judges to adjudicate the cases of the poor free of charge. It is also worth mentioning that medieval councils authorised monks to assist the poor before the courts free of charge. This was a manifestation of the Christian idea of mercy and related charity. French kings, too, sometimes issued acts aimed at giving access to justice and legal aid to all those who could not cover the costs of a trial. For example, the Edict of 6 May

2 The exception to this is art. of the Draft Constitution of 19 April 1946, which guarantees free access to public affairs and the law.

1610 appointed lawyers and prosecutors in each jurisdiction to defend the plaintiffs and to receive appropriate funds from the king for this purpose. In practice, however, such assistance was not particularly developed, and, for the most part, the initiative to provide it depended on the goodwill of the legal profession[3]. The omission of this issue in the famous *Ordonnance civile touchant la réformation de la justice of* 1667 is symptomatic of the lack of interest of the state authorities of the time in the development of assistance in access to justice.

A breakthrough in attitudes to legal aid came with the events leading up to the overthrow of the *ansien régime of* 1789. By affirming the slogans of liberty, equality and fraternity, the Revolution changed the perception of justice, treating it as one of the fundamental goods from which no one should be excluded. Justice thus began to be approached as a public service – subject to impartial rules of operation and equally accessible to all citizens. The decree of 16–24 August 1790 on the judiciary's organisation stated that elected judges would administer justice free of charge[4]. Thus, the revolutionary reorganisation was aimed at democratising access to justice. One means to this end was to be simplifying the civil procedure by eliminating various elements from it, each of which had hitherto entailed separate costs. Napoleon introduced a new codification and reorganised the legal profession, changing how these intentions were put into practice[5]. One of the most significant consequences of these changes was reducing a considerable part of the functions previously performed by lawyers. This was guided by the assumption that the unification of the sources of law, their systematisation, the clarity and precision of norms, would contribute to a better understanding of the law by all, and not only by those with relevant training[6]. Legal aid then began to be seen again as a private charity, voluntarily provided by the local bar[7]. Charities also assisted people experiencing poverty in civil matters, focusing in

3 M. H. Renaut, *L'accès à la justce dans la perspective de l'histoire du droit*, "Revue historique de droit français et étranger", 2000, vol. 78, no. 3, p. 474.

4 Décret des 16–24 août 1790 sur l'organisation judiciaire, titre II, articles 1 and 2.

5 The French Civil Code was not only intended to consolidate several legal systems, but also to reinforce its immutable authority by overcoming the uncertainty and arbitrariness of the law, as its authors had intended.. B. Lewaszkiewicz-Petrykowska, *Współczesne prawo cywilne a Code civil Napoleona jako dziedzictwo wielowiekowej kultury prawnej*, "Czasopismo Prawno-Historyczne" 2005, vol. 57, z. 2, p. 122.

6 The legal community, especially judges, was experiencing a certain identity crisis. J.-L. Halpérin, *L'impossible Code civil*, Paris 1992, p. 293; K. Sójka-Zielińska, *Great civil codifications. History and contemporaneity*, Warsaw 2009, p. 243.

7 A. Blandin, *L'avocat des pauvres à Pau*, 'Annales de la Charité', no. 6, 1850, p. 220.

particular on family matters and the formal recognition of children of single mothers.

It is worth mentioning at this stage that there is a regular expression in the legal vocabulary close to the values that underpin social welfare in the broadest sense and associated with the practice of pro bono in law. The term means "for the public good". It reflects the approach of a lawyer voluntarily devoting part of their time, free of charge or for a small fee, to protecting the rights of disadvantaged people, assisting organisations representing the needs of marginalised members of the community, or being involved in improving the law and the administration of justice.

The problem of the de facto exclusion of poor citizens from the courts arose in the 1840s. It became central to a broader debate on balancing the rights and obligations of all participants in society[8]. Positions were formulated at the time emphasising the destructive impact of poverty as a threat to the realisation of formal legal capacity. It was argued that such a state of affairs requires public assistance, which becomes an ethical obligation, an imperative of contemporary governance. At the same time, the danger of abuse arising from too massive a capacity to bring cases dictated by bad faith, revenge or greed was signalled[9]. It was also pointed out that too easy access to courts, lack of proper control as to the validity of claims would contribute to the escalation of social conflicts. In turn, state control in this area would require the creation of new laws and institutions increasing the role and competences of the administrative apparatus, which was of particular concern to liberal circles. In this sense, the project to create a comprehensive legal aid programme highlighted the differences in views on the role of the State.

Finally, on 22 January 1851, a legal aid act was passed, which regulated the provision of assistance in civil, criminal and commercial cases. The act set out two necessary conditions for obtaining assistance: the poverty of the applicant

---

8 An important voice in the discussion was the work of a magistrate: J. C. M. G. du Beux, *Essai sur l'institution de l'avocat des pauvres et sur les moyens de défense des indigents dans les procès civils et criminels en France, en Sardaigne et dans les principaux pays de L'Europe,* Paris, 1847. Not long after the publication of this book, the Academy of Moral and Political Sciences began to conduct research based on Du Beux's analyses and recommendations, which provided a solid foundation on which the Chamber of Deputies relied to address the exclusion of poor citizens from access to the judiciary on the eve of the 1848 revolution.

9 S. Schafer, *L'assistance judiciaire et l'étranger civil (1840–1851),* 'Sociétés & Rperésentations', 2014/2, no. 38, p. 208.

and the credibility of their case. Potential beneficiaries were required to provide the relevant offices with their tax sheets or exemptions and written statements that poverty excluded them from access to justice[10]. The complainant's opponent could appear at the legal aid office to challenge the claim's validity or the claimed poverty[11]. An essential feature of the 1851 Act was the recommendation that offices handling applications for assistance should promote consensual dispute resolution, thus minimising the need to go to Court. The legal aid act of 1851 lasted 120 years, until the enactment of the Act of 3 January 1972 which provided for full or partial legal aid subject to income limits[12]. The new system was based on the payment of state compensation. In practice, however, it was criticised by lawyers who claimed that they bore most of the costs of their services. Potential aid recipients also signalled that too-low income thresholds prevented many citizens from benefiting from aid[13]. These comments contributed to changes in subsequent regulations, which already form the framework of the current legal aid system.

2.2. The current model of state-funded legal aid

The functioning of the current legal aid system in France is based on two normative acts: Act on Legal Aid of 10 July 1991 (A.1991)[14] as amended[15]; the Decree of 19 December 1991 concerning legal aid[16]. The last reform in this area took place in 2021[17]. Its aim was to simplify the procedure for applicants, guarantee greater

10 It is worth noting that the 1851 Act gave poverty a slightly different character than before. In the new legal framework, poverty no longer necessarily meant permanent deprivation, but lack of resources and estimated legal costs. S. Schafer, *L'assistance judiciaire…*, p. 221.

11 Loi du 22 janvier 1851 sur l'assistance judiciaire, articles 10, 11.

12 Loi no 72-11 du 3 janvier 1972 instituant l'aide juduciaire. The implementing act of this law was Décret No 72-809 du 1er septembre 1972 portant application de la loi No 72-11 du 3 janvier 1972 instituant l'aide judiciaire.

13 L. Cadiet, *Premières, et brèves, vues sur le nouveau droit de l'aide juridictionnelle*, 'Revue jurudique de l'Ouest', 1991, No. 3, p. 323.

14 Loi n° 97–647 du 10 juillet 1991 relative à l'aide juridique.

15 Loi n° 2006-911 du 24 juillet 2006 relative à l'integration; Loi n° 2007-210 du 19 février 2007 portant réforme de l'assurance de protection juridique.

16 Le décret no 91-1266 du 19 décembre 1991 portant application de la loi no 97–647 du 10 juillet 1991 relative à l'aide juridique.

17 Amendments made with: Décret No 2020-1717 du 28 décembre 2020 portant application de la loi No 91–647 du 10 juillet 1991 relative à l'aide juridique et relatif à l'aide juridictionnelle et à l'intervention de l'avocat dans les procédures non juridictionnelles.

fairness in the processing of applications, and gradually reduce the time taken to process applications. Generally, these regulations cover legal aid, advice and assistance in out-of-court proceedings. They provide for:

- appropriate legal aid: financial assistance in court proceedings and out-of-court settlements;
- assistance with costs related to activities ordered by the judge, e.g., expert opinion;
- assistance to cover lawyers' fees in criminal proceedings as an alternative to a court case (plea bargaining and mediation), for legal aid for persons detained by the police for questioning and disciplinary proceedings in prisons;
- access to the law, which includes the provision of general information on the rights and duties of persons, free legal advice and consultation, assistance in drafting and concluding legal acts (art. 53 A.1991)[18];
- Assistance in cross-border disputes[19] to cover the costs of translating the request for assistance and the documents needed to examine the case before referring it to the competent authority, as well as the costs of the translator when the proceedings take place in France (art. 40 A.1991).

Beneficiaries of legal aid may avail themselves free of charge of the services of a lawyer or other legal adviser (bailiff, avoué, notary, etc.) and of any official whose assistance is required for the proceedings in question. As a general rule, the right to choose a lawyer and officials lies with the beneficiary, who may also rely on the assistance of representatives of the jurisdiction concerned (art. 25 A.1991). Beneficiaries of legal aid may also apply for exemption from court costs. Legal aid is available to persons irrespective of their status in the justice system. Thus, assistance is available to defendants as well as plaintiffs, witnesses, suspects, defendants, convicted persons, etc. The assistance covers all categories of disputed or uncontested cases in courts of all instances. It therefore operates in civil, criminal and administrative proceedings. The costs of the assistance provided are borne by the State[20], which may finance it in full (100 %) or in part (55 % or

18 In 2016, the public authorities launched a dedicated website with the aim of facilitating access to justice for as many people as possible, streamlining procedures and providing information on legal aid. See. https://www.justice.fr/

19 A cross-border dispute in the context of legal aid concerns a situation where the habitual residence or domicile of the party applying for aid is in a Member State of the European Union other than the one in which the court having jurisdiction on the merits of the case is located or where the judgment has to be enforced.

20 Legal practitioners providing assistance to a beneficiary receive remuneration from the State, the amount of which is determined by a decree of the Council of State (art. 31

25 %) depending on the asset criterion. The assistance may also cover all or part of the proceedings. Its purpose may also be to facilitate a settlement before a court hearing or to enforce a court decision or other enforcement order (art. 10 and 11 of the 1991 Acts). Assistance may be requested both before and during proceedings (art. 18 of the 1991 Acts). In the event of an appeal, the beneficiary retains the right to defend himself (art. 8 of the 1991 Acts). If the beneficiary of legal aid loses the case, he should pay the costs of the case incurred by his opponent. However, the judge may decide, taking into account the principle of equity and the economic situation of the party, to leave part of the costs with the State (art. 42 A.1991).

Legal aid offices functioning in the courts of first and second instance as well as in the Court of Cassation, the Council of State, the National Asylum Law Court, the Supreme Court of Arbitration and the Refugee Appeals Commissions (art. 13 and 14 of the A.1991) deal with the settlement of applications. The decision to grant assistance is made once the requirements of material resources, nationality, place of permanent residence and legitimacy of the proceedings have been met. The conditions indicated can therefore be divided into procedural and substantive. In the first group, the requirements for applicants play a crucial role. Under French Law, legal aid is available to persons of French nationality, citizens of the European Union or foreign nationals with the right of permanent residence in France. The legislature also grants the right to legal aid in cases before French courts to persons not resident in France who are nationals of those countries that have concluded an international or bilateral agreement with France authorising legal aid. In principle, persons of foreign nationality may be eligible for legal aid provided that they permanently and regularly reside in France. It should be added, however, that this condition does not apply to litigants in cases that appear particularly noteworthy from the point of view of the subject matter or the anticipated costs (art. 3 A.1991). The residence requirement is also waived in the case of foreign nationals who are minors, subject to criminal proceedings or subject to the procedures laid down in the legislation on the entry and residence of foreign nationals and the right of asylum[21]. In exceptional

---

A.1991). The cost of legal aid may also be paid by a party who is not a beneficiary and loses the case. In that case, he or she is obliged to reimburse the State Treasury for the relevant amounts. However, the judge may fully or partially exempt a party from this reimbursement for reasons based on equity and the economic situation of that party (art. 43 A.1991).

21 In addition, the aforementioned law – Loi n° 2006-911 du 24 juillet 2006 relative à l'integration – modified the conditions for granting legal aid before the Refugee

circumstances, the president of the competent Court or the president of the legal aid office may decide to grant temporary legal aid if the proceedings threaten the applicant's living conditions, particularly in the case of an enforcement order or eviction (A.1991, art. 20). In criminal cases, the procedure allows for the provision of legal aid in urgent cases, e.g., police detention, preliminary hearing, immediate expedited hearing.

As a rule, the provision of free legal aid by the State concerns natural persons. Their applications account for the bulk of the applications and benefits granted, but the legislator has also provided for the possibility of providing assistance to legal persons (art. 2 A.1991). The condition is that they are not for profit, are established in France and do not have sufficient resources (e.g., associations). Consortia of co-owners of buildings covered by a protection plan and legal persons who are parties to cross-border disputes in civil or commercial matters may be the subject of assistance.

Legal aid is not available free of charge to persons covered by legal expenses insurance. An important condition for granting assistance is the asset criterion. According to it, legal aid may be granted to persons whose average total income in the previous calendar year did not exceed the threshold determined annually by a decree of the Council of State (art. 4 A.1991)[22]. At the same time, family allowances and certain social benefits are not included in income determination. Thus, persons who receive supplementary benefits from the National Solidarity Fund (*Fonds national de solodarité*) a salary supplement (*revenu minimum d'insertion*), a pension for veterans or war invalids are exempted from the requirement to submit a declaration of assets in order to obtain free legal aid. The presentation of material resources is also not required of minors interviewed in all types of cases, as well as victims of criminal and terrorist attacks and domestic violence (art. 9 A.1991). It should

---

Appeals Commission (La Commission des recours des réfugiés). The law abolished the condition of having entered France legally or having a residence permit for at least one year.

22 Data on the current asset criteria for legal aid can be found: http://www.cdad-moselle.justice.fr/informations-pratiques/aides-aux-victimes/aide-juridictionnelle/ From 1 January 2021, legal aid is granted on the condition that the applicant has a reference tax income of less than €11,262 per person. To benefit from partial legal aid or assistance with the intervention of a lawyer, this ceiling is set at €16,890. Décret n° 2020-1717 du 28 décembre 2020 portant application de la loi n° 91–647 du 10 juillet 1991 relative à l'aide juridique et relatif à l'aide juridictionnelle et à l'intervention de l'avocat dans les procédures non juridictionnelles.

be added that when looking at the property criterion, external elements that determine a certain standard of living are also taken into account. Possession of movable and immovable property, including property that does not generate income, is also assessed, with the exception of property that cannot be sold or mortgaged without causing significant harm to the life of the person concerned (e.g., loss of main residence or property needed for professional activities). The assessment of the applicant's assets also includes the resources of the spouse, as well as those of persons in a joint household, unless the action is brought against them.

An exception to the general rule of consideration of the asset criterion is the possibility for persons whose income exceeds the set limits to obtain legal aid provided that the case appears to be of particular interest from the point of view of its subject matter, the anticipated costs of litigation or cross-border disputes (art. 6 A.1991). In the latter case, proof must be provided that the applicants for assistance would not be able to meet the expenses due to differences in the cost of living between France and the Member State of their habitual residence.

The merits of the proceedings will be examined in the light of whether the actions of the potential beneficiary appear manifestly unjustified, unfounded or abusive, for example because of the number of applications made and their repetitive nature. Furthermore, in cassation cases, the applicant may not be granted legal aid if the cassation does not meet sufficient requirements (art. 7 A.1991). Legal aid is also not granted at the end of the court proceedings.

If legal aid is refused, the applicant may, either alone or with a lawyer, within 15 days of being notified of the decision, lodge an appeal stating the reasons for challenging the decision. The appeal can be addressed to the legal aid office that issued the decision, which in turn will forward it to the authority competent to hear the appeal. Depending on the jurisdiction, this will be: for courts of first instance, the President of the Court of Appeal; for the National Asylum Law Court, the President of the National Asylum Court; for the Administrative Court, the President of the Administrative Court of Appeal to which the Court is subordinate; for the Administrative Court of Appeal, the President of the Administrative Court of Appeal handling the case; for the Council of State, the President of the Litigation Section of the Council of State; for the Court of Cassation, the First President of the Court of Cassation; for the Court of Conflicts, the President of the Court of Conflicts. The second decision on the application is final, so it can no longer be appealed.

Since 1998, there have been special centres – *les maisons de la justice* (MJD) – near the big cities to provide access to justice, especially for victims of crime. To this end, they are assisted not only by lawyers, but also by police officers, local associations, social workers, etc.[23] In addition, there are departmental legal aid centres – *Les centres départementaux d'accès au droit* (CDAC) – which provide assistance in out-of-court proceedings with the possibility of requesting assistance through the courts, offer free legal consultations and assistance in drafting legislation. Also, some consumer associations provide free legal advice, generally defending the interests of consumers in the amicable or judicial settlement of a dispute. Citizens can also benefit from the assistance of local professional associations. Their affiliated bar members provide free, anonymous, confidential legal consultations to anyone, regardless of income. A National Council for Legal Aid (*Conseil national de l'aide juridique*) was set up to coordinate the operation of legal aid in France. Its task is to collect all quantitative and qualitative information on the functioning of and access to legal aid. The Council is to propose to the public authorities any measures to promote better access to legal aid (art. 65 A.1991).

3. Conclusions

Looking at legal aid in France from a historical perspective, it is fair to say that it is the heir to the practice of charity. The contemporary understanding of the importance of assistance in access to justice is more closely linked to the axiology of the revolutionary triad – liberty, equality and fraternity. These slogans guide us towards a kind of justice that does not unduly discriminate or favour anyone and justifies a duty of solidarity, especially towards the most vulnerable. Justice must therefore continue to be accessible to all, not just the wealthy, in addition to its value of neutrality. In this perspective, state institutions, insofar as they strive for justice, have a duty to help those who formally have legal capacity but whose power in practice is limited or thwarted by poverty.

Legal aid must therefore be seen as one element of public service. Here, the State must guarantee the functioning of the legal aid system, not only by financing it but also by creating its normative and institutional infrastructure, managing it and reforming it where necessary. This is also the case in France, which has created an assistance network operating through legal aid offices in civil, criminal and administrative jurisdiction at all levels of judicial proceedings. This assistance can also be used for non-judicial forms of dispute resolution, such as mediation.

23 See https://www.legalife.fr/guides-juridiques/conseil-juridique-gratuit-ou-trouver-une-assistance-gratuite/

The most controversial issue usually concerns the criteria for granting assistance. In France, in particular, representatives of the so-called middle-class signal that, on the one hand, they are too rich to count on state assistance in accessing justice and, on the other hand, too poor to act without concern for their ability to defend their rights within the broader justice system.

The recent changes to the state legal aid system introduced in 2020 focus on the goal of effective qualitative decision-making, favouring facilitating access to justice for the most vulnerable. One of the measures that will contribute to this task will be the increased use of modern technology, which will allow, for example, legal aid application documents to be downloaded online and the necessary explanations to understand its rules and mechanisms to be obtained. Secure digital platforms are therefore being created to exchange information and data between jurisdictions, lawyers and officials. Remote techniques such as videoconferencing are increasingly being used. This virtual infrastructure will speed up the flow of information and documents and promote the need for proximity between judicial authorities and citizens.

Literature

Blandin A., L'avocat des pauvres à Pau, *Annales de la Charité*, nr 6, 1850.

Cadiet L., Premières, et brèves, vues sur le nouveau droit de l'aide juridictionnelle, *Revue jurudique de l'Ouest*, nr 3, 1991.

Du Beux J.C.M.G, *Essai sur l'institution de l'avocat des pauvres et sur les moyens de défense des indigents dans les procès civils et criminels en France, en Sardaigne et dans les principaux pays de L'Europe*, Paris 1847.

Halpérin J.-L., *L'impossible Code civil*, Paris 1992, s. 293; K. Sójka-Zielińska, *Wielkie kodyfikacje cywilne. Historia i współczesność*, Warszawa 2009.

Lewaszkiewicz-Petrykowska B., Współczesne prawo cywilne a Code civil Napoleona jako dziedzictwo wielowiekowej kultury prawnej, *Czasopismo Prawno-Historyczne*, t. 57, 2005, z. 2.

Renaut M.H., L'accès à la justce dans la perspective de l'histoire du droit, *Revue historique de droit français et étranger*, Vol. 78, nr 3, 2000.

Schafer S., L'assistance judiciaire et l'étranger civil (1840–1851), *Sociétés & Rperésentations*, Vol. 2, nr 38, 2014.

Wawrzyniak J., O niektórych osobliwościach Konstytucji V Republiki Francuskiej, *Studia Iuridica Lublinensia*, nr 22, 2014.

Maria Kalinowska

Free Legal Aid in the United Kingdom

Abstract: This text provides an overview of the legal aid system in the United Kingdom, focusing on both criminal and civil matters. It highlights the historical development of legal aid in the UK, the governing legislation, and the role of the Legal Aid Agency (LAA) in administering legal aid services. The text discusses the provision of legal aid in criminal cases, including lower and higher crime categories, as well as the availability of civil legal aid in various areas such as child custody, asylum applications, housing issues, and domestic violence cases. It also outlines the Civil Legal Advice (CLA) service and other forms of legal aid, such as controlled legal representation, civil representation, family mediation, judicial review, and exceptional case funding. The text concludes by emphasizing ongoing efforts to improve the legal aid system and the significance of the UK's adversarial legal system and welfare state in shaping the development of state-funded legal aid.

Keywords: Legal aid, United Kingdom, Legal Aid Agency, Legal Aid, Sentencing and Punishment of Offenders Act, Civil Legal Advice

1. Introduction

Legal aid in the UK was first introduced in 1949 as a central pillar of the welfare state. Initially, the Law Society administered the legal aid system. Over the years, access to legal aid has steadily declined due to regulation, reaching only 29 % before the 2008 recession. Time after time, new regulations, i.e., in 2004, 2007 and 2010, introduced fixed fees for certain types of cases and led to the withdrawal of many legal aid providers for the more complex areas covered by legal aid, such as immigration or asylum[1].

At present, *the* governing legislation is the Legal Aid, Sentencing and Punishment of Offenders Act (LASPO) 2012. This Act of the UK Parliament creating reforms to the justice system is also revolutionary in terms of the provision of legal aid, as it introduced many innovative solutions, institutions, thus establishing a new system for the operation of legal aid. A factor indicating the scale of the issue in the public space of the UK citizens and at the legislative level is that no other country matches the UK in terms of the amount of expenditure

1 See https://www.chambersstudent.co.uk/where-to-start/newsletter/legal-aid-cuts-and-reforms (accessed 5.09.2021).

and the number of cases funded under legal aid[2]. However, it is worth noting that despite the government spending £1.76 billion on legal aid in 2019–2020, many experts have argued over the years that the proposed solutions will largely help an ever smaller proportion of the population in ever smaller cases[3].

When discussing the regulation of legal aid, it is important to note that the UK is a signatory to the ECHR as a Western European country[4], under which the ECtHR sets the framework for how states can provide legal aid to their citizens. This framework emphasises the role of legal aid in ensuring fundamental fairness (especially in criminal cases), stresses the importance of providing legal aid to suspects due to the "*particular vulnerability of the accused in the early stages of* proceedings"[5], as well as the principle of equality of defence, especially in criminal cases "*where the very nature of the proceedings involves fundamental inequality between the* parties"[6]. As regards legal aid in civil cases is concerned, the decision of the ECtHR in *Airey v. Ireland*[7] is decisive for many countries, stating that a defence counsel must be available in civil as in criminal cases, according to the premise of the "*interest of justice*"[8].

Key to this is the Legal Aid Agency (LAA), an executive agency of the UK Ministry of Justice, established under the above-mentioned Legal Aid, Sentencing and Punishment of Offenders Act to administer legal aid, which has been operating effectively since 1 April 2013. The legal aid services themselves in England and Wales are provided by law firms, *not-for-profit* organisations, mediators and barristers who the above-mentioned Legal Aid Agency pays to provide legal aid services. The schemes for providing these services require different types of contracts covering different kinds of work[9]. However, an online

---

2 See J.A. Flood, A. Whyte, *What's Wrong with Legal Aid? Lessons from Outside the UK*, December 2006, p. 83.

3 See House of Commons Justice Committee, *The Future* of *Legal Aid. Third Report of Session 2021–22*, 27 July 2021, p. 3.

4 Original text available: https://www.echr.coe.int/documents/convention_pol.pdf.

5 See *Salduz v. Turkey*, App. No. 36391/02, Judgment of 27 November 2008, ECHR 2008, para. 54.

6 See P. van Dijk, G.J.H. van Hoof, *Theory and Practice of the European Convention on Human Rights*, Hague 1998.

7 See *Airey v. Ireland*, App. No. 6289/73, Judgment of 9 October 1979, ECHR 3.

8 See United Nations Development Programme (UNDP), United Nations Office on Drugs and Crime (UNODC) *Global Study on Legal Aid – Global Report*, pp. 26–27.

9 See Ministry of Justice, Legal Aid Agency, *User Guide to Legal Aid Statistics, England and Wales*, 24 June 2021, p 9.

list of legal aid service providers[10] in the territory makes it easier for those in need to locate and identify them.

Given the subject of this article and the territorial extent and administrative division of the United Kingdom, it should be noted that the legal aid regime in England and Wales is discussed in some detail, with the proviso that the rules on legal aid in Scotland and Northern Ireland are different.

2. Legal aid in criminal matters

Legal aid in criminal matters mainly covers the range of activities carried out in police stations and criminal courts in relation to persons under investigation or charged with a criminal offence. In principle, it is possible to identify two categories of situations for the use of legal aid, namely: (1) crime lower and (2) crime higher. Lower crime cases include all matters relating to the stage taking place at the police station and the pre-charge stage, as well as the early court stage (including in the magistrates' courts) and assistance in prisons. This assistance is relatively characterised by operating on a larger scale and its lower labour costs of the criminal legal aid provided. Higher crime includes work in The Crown Courts) and the higher courts. The above assistance relates only to more serious criminal cases and includes a relatively smaller number of criminal legal aid situations, however, with higher costs. In most Crown Court cases, the work of both a solicitor and a barrister or higher solicitor advocate is required. A small proportion of the most complex cases in the Crown Court are classified by the Legal Aid Agency as Very High Cost (VHC) and are handled differently[11].

3. Civil legal aid

Civil legal aid covers areas and issues not *strictly* criminal in nature, but concerning citizens' rights and private relations that may also require legal aid. Thus, civil legal aid primarily covers child custody cases, assistance with asylum applications, housing issues (where there is a risk of demolition or homelessness), family mediation or assistance and counselling in domestic violence cases.

The Civil Legal Advice (CLA) service is critical in providing civil legal aid[12]. It can be provided either remotely (e.g., by telephone) or in person by a qualified

10 See https://find-legal-advice.justice.gov.uk (accessed 4.09.2021).

11 See Ministry of Justice, Legal Aid Agency, *User Guide to Legal Aid Statistics, England and Wales*, 24 June 2021, p 5.

12 See. https://www.gov.uk/civil-legal-advice (accessed: 4.09.2021).

lawyer. The above services are usually offered through a two-stage process. In the first stage, users of the service contact a central service office, the relevant persons diagnose the case of a particular person, which – if it potentially falls within the scope of the assistance provided and is financially eligible – is forwarded to a specialised advisor. The next step is for the specialist adviser to assess whether or not the case should be initiated (for example, because it was considered out of scope for financial or substantive reasons, or the notifier did not provide sufficient evidence). A large proportion of cases (including debt, discrimination, education, family and housing cases) are resolved by telephone consultation with a qualified adviser, but in a small number of cases, specialised experts may judge that the situation requires advice in a face-to-face meeting with a qualified lawyer. Another form of legal aid available is Controlled Legal Representation, which involves representation in tribunals. Still, unlike civil representation, the award of this legal aid is vetted against certain financial and legal conditions, and the work is usually funded alongside the initial advice and legal aid within the same case. The following solution is civil representation, which consists of legal aid for representation in courts or in the higher courts for issues such as family, housing or mental health matters, with complete investigations undertaken and cases prepared. Legal aid is then available as an application for civil representation in family law matters where there is a risk of domestic violence or child abuse. Applicants receive funding for legal aid in these cases if they can prove the presence or risk of domestic violence or child abuse by providing certain prescribed evidence. Legal aid solutions also include family mediation, where an independent, impartial and accredited mediator talks to the divorcing or separating couple and attempts to reach an agreement without taking the matter to Court. Other legal aid arrangements available include judicial review, which takes the form of civil legal representation whereby an application for judicial review legal aid is made by those needing assistance in challenging a previous government decision. The last legal aid institution discussed may be Exceptional Case Funding (ECF). This is because it is possible to obtain legal aid in civil cases in certain circumstances, even if their case does not fall within the scope of the other forms of legal aid available. Such cases are handled exceptionally by a separate organisational unit within the Legal Aid Agency[13].

13 See Ministry of Justice, Legal Aid Agency, *User Guide to Legal Aid Statistics, England and Wales*, 24 June 2021, pp 6–7.

4. Conclusions

Although the United Kingdom has a relatively extensive and well-developed system for access to legal aid, as the case analysis shows, the issue is subject to close scrutiny at several levels, both in the drafting of existing legislation and in its application. Namely, there is an ongoing effort to improve the functioning of this system. An illustration of this is the report on the future of legal aid[14], published on 27 July 2021 by the *House of Commons-appointed Justice Committee* (*The House of Commons*). Extensive analysis of the issue led to a number of conclusions and recommendations to improve the functioning of the legal aid system[15].

Furthermore, the analysis of this issue leads to the conclusion that, even though the legal aid system in England and Wales is in a constant process of change and improvement, which means constant attempts to reconcile the interests of so many parties, including those who need help, those who provide legal services and the State, it can be considered highly developed and rooted in many years of experience with a state-funded system. Moreover, the fact that the English legal system is based on adversarial principles and the common law tradition, combined with a commitment to the post-war welfare state, may partly explain why state-funded legal aid has developed more rapidly there than in many other European countries[16].

Literature

Flood J.A., Whyte A., *What's Wrong with Legal Aid? Lessons from Outside the UK*, December 2006.

Smith R., Legal Aid in England and Wales: Current Issues and Lessons, *Making Legal Aid a Reality Public Interest Law Institute. A Resource Book for Policy Makers and Civil Society.*

Van Dijk P., Van Hoof G.J.H., *Theory and Practice of the European Convention on Human Rights*, Hague 1998.

---

14 The original text of the report is available: https://committees.parliament.uk/publications/6979/documents/72829/default/

15 See House of Commons Justice Committee, *The Future* of *Legal Aid. Third Report of Session 2021–22*, 27 July 2021, p. 66.

16 See R. Smith, *Legal Aid in England and Wales: Current Issues and Lessons*, 'Making Legal Aid a Reality Public Interest Law Institute. A Resource Book for Policy Makers and Civil Society', p. 44.

Maria Kalinowska

Free Legal Aid in the United States of America

Abstract: This text provides an overview of free legal aid in the United States, focusing on both criminal and civil matters. It highlights the historical background of the right to counsel and the challenges of accessing justice for low-income individuals. The text discusses the provision of legal aid in criminal cases, including the right to counsel and the role of public defenders. In civil cases, it explains the absence of a general obligation to provide state-funded counsel and the concept of "civil right to counsel." It examines various legal aid programs and pro bono services that offer assistance to individuals experiencing poverty in civil matters. The text also explores the role of organizations such as the Legal Services Corporation (LSC) and the funding mechanisms, including Interest on Lawyers Trust Accounts (IOLTA). It concludes by acknowledging the ongoing efforts to address access to free legal aid while recognizing the challenges and limitations in providing equal access to justice.

Keywords: United States, free legal aid, access to justice, right to counsel, Legal Services Corporation, pro bono services, legal aid programs, IOLTA

1. Introduction

The United States of America (United States, USA) was one of the first countries to guarantee the right to counsel in its Constitution. However, it was not until 1963 in *Gideon v. Wainwright*[1]. the US Supreme Court ruled that the Constitution required individual states, i.e., state authorities through appropriate statutes, to provide defendants accused of serious crimes with the right to counsel. Subsequently, the Supreme Court extended the right to appointed counsel to misdemeanour and juvenile proceedings (see *Argersinger v. Hamlin*[2] and *In re Gault*)[3].

The phrase "*with liberty and justice for all*" used in the US Pledge of Allegiance[4] represents the idea that justice should be available to everyone, however, this

1 372 U.S. 335 (1963).

2 407 U.S. 25 (1972).

3 387 U.S. 1 (1967); See United Nations Development Programme (UNDP), United Nations Office on Drugs and Crime (UNODC), *Global Study on Legal Aid – Global Report*, p. 27.

4 The Pledge of Allegiance of the United States is an expression of allegiance to the flag of the United States and the republic of the United States of America.

idea is not always reflected in reality. Inequality of access to justice in the United States is the culmination of several factors that significantly limit access to justice for less affluent groups in society. The US legal system's complexity is a formidable barrier for low-income communities. The legal system is structured so that most, if not all, legal situations require a professional attorney. However, less affluent populations still cannot afford an attorney due to a lack of necessary income or assets[5].

Prepared in 2017 by the Legal Services Corporation, LSC in collaboration with the National Opinion Research Center (NORC) at the University of Chicago, the 2017 Justice Gap Report[6] indicates the scale of the issue. The report reveals that as many as 86 % of the civil legal problems reported by low-income Americans in 2016 received inadequate or no legal assistance. Additionally, in the same year, 2016, as many as 71 % of low-income households experienced at least one civil legal problem, including problems with health care, housing, disability access, veterans' benefits and domestic violence.

Due to the peculiarities of the US system, some of the issues related to free legal aid are regulated at the federal level and some are regulated at the state government level, so access to the legal aid provided varies by state jurisdiction. Currently, there are mixed state funding systems for private practitioners and public defenders funded by the federal, State or local government. At the outset, it should also be stressed that the legal aid provisions in the United States differ significantly in criminal and civil cases. In criminal cases, legal aid is guaranteed. In civil cases, however, there is no explicit obligation to provide legal aid (with strictly regulated exceptions). Free assistance in civil cases is still discretionary and depends on determining the merits of the claim of the party requesting such assistance[7]. As a result, many low-income US citizens are left without adequate legal assistance in disputes where they risk losing their jobs, livelihoods, homes or children, or seek a restraining order against their abuser[8].

---

5 L. H. Keith, *Poverty, the Great Unequalizer: Improving the Delivery System for Civil Legal Aid*, 66 Cath. U. L. Rev. 55 (2017), p. 65.

6 Original text available at: https://www.lsc.gov/our-impact/publications/other-publications-and-reports/justice-gap-report.

7 See United Nations Development Programme (UNDP), United Nations Office on Drugs and Crime (UNODC), *Global Study on Legal Aid – Global Report*, p. 27.

8 See https://www.lsc.gov/our-impact/publications/other-publications-and-reports/justice-gap-report.

2. Legal aid in criminal matters

The source of the guarantee of legal assistance in criminal cases is identified among the other rights of the accused in the criminal process in the Sixth Amendment to the United States Constitution, which states that: "The accused in criminal proceedings shall have the right … to have legal counsel for his or her defense"[9]. The indicated right to counsel is widely recognised as a component of the right to a fair trial. The Sixth Amendment regulation of the right to a fair trial cited above identifies five distinct rights: the right to counsel of one's own choosing, the right to appointed counsel, the right to counsel who is free (from conflicts of interest in this case), the right to effective assistance of counsel, and the right to self-representation[10]. The US Constitution thus explicitly guarantees free legal assistance to persons charged with a crime that could result in imprisonment and who, for financial reasons, are unable to use commercial legal services. In practice, however, it is necessary to complete the formalities in this regard when appearing in Court for the first time by requesting the appointment of a public defender. If the Court decides to declare a defendant "indigent" – a person who has few assets and cannot afford to pay a lawyer – the Court will usually either appoint a private lawyer, paid from the funds of the district in which the case is being heard, or appoint a public defender to represent the person. Some public defender programmes may charge clients a so-called "processing fee", although this is usually a small fee[11].

As mentioned above, due to the peculiarities of the US system, the system of regulation varies according to the applicable state regulations. The federal government and some states have offices of public defenders to assist indigent defendants, while other states have systems for outsourcing this work to private lawyers. Funding for criminal assistance comes from both US state authorities and the US federal government[12].

---

9 Original text available at: Parliament of the Republic of Poland, Constitution of the United States of America: http://libr.sejm.gov.pl/tek01/txt/konst/usa.html (accessed 31.08.2021).

10 See https://en.wikipedia.org/wiki/Right_to_counsel (accessed 31.08.2021).

11 See https://www.americanbar.org/groups/legal_services/flh-home/flh-faq/ (accessed 1.09.2021).

12 See George, P. James, *Acces to Justice, Costs, and Legal Aid, American Journal of Comparative Law*, vol.54, no Supplement Issue (Fall 2006), pp. 293–316.

3. Civil legal aid

The US Department of Justice defines civil legal aid as free legal assistance to low- and middle-income individuals with civil legal problems. This assistance covers civil legal issues, including assistance in accessing or securing basic needs such as health care, housing issues, government benefits, employment and educational services[13]. As mentioned, the United States has no general obligation to provide state-funded counsel in civil proceedings. There is no explicit right in the US Constitution to state-funded counsel in civil proceedings. However, the 14th Amendment prohibits the State from depriving "any person of life, liberty, or property, without due process of law" or denying "any person within its jurisdiction equal protection of the law"[14].

However, the aforementioned Supreme Court decision in *Gideon v. Wainwright*, which is seminal in this regard, has given rise to the idea of what is known as "civil right to counsel" and is also referred to as "civil Gideon," which refers to situations in which people who cannot afford an attorney in civil matters involving basic human needs such as shelter, livelihood, safety, health, and custody of children should have access to an attorney free of charge. The idea refers to the fact that the right to a lawyer in criminal cases is guaranteed, whereas in civil cases it currently exists only in very limited circumstances[15]. Although there is no constitutional right to counsel in civil proceedings, some state legislatures have enacted legislation and some state courts have ruled that certain parties should be entitled to state-funded counsel, usually in civil commitment or family law cases[16]. Significantly, in contrast to *Gideon v. Wainwright, in* which the US Supreme Court ruled that there must be counsel in criminal cases where the defendant faces imprisonment or loss of liberty, the Court declined to find a constitutional right to counsel in civil cases when it first encountered the issue in 1981. In *Lassiter v. Department of Social Services*[17], the US Supreme Court held that the due process clause of the federal Constitution does not provide for a guaranteed appointment of counsel for indigent parents facing termination of parental rights. Namely, "*the decision whether due process requires the*

13 See https://www.justice.gov/olp/civil-legal-aid-101 (accessed 31.08.2021).

14 See Alan W. Houseman, *Civil Legal Aid in the United States: An Update for 2017*, March 2018, p. 93.

15 See https://www.americanbar.org/groups/legal_aid_indigent_defense/civil_right_to_counsel1/ (accessed 31.08.2021).

16 See Houseman, *Civil Legal Aid in the United States: An Update for 2013*, p. 14.

17 452 U.S. 18 (1981).

appointment of counsel for indigent parents in proceedings to terminate parental rights is to be decided in the first instance by the court, subject, of course, to appellate *court review*"[18].

Even though there is no explicitly stated right to a free lawyer, there are a number of legal aid programmes and *pro bono* solutions that provide free legal aid to people experiencing poverty in civil cases. These programmes help people whose income is less than 125 % of the federal poverty level[19], although in some cases, it is also possible to help people whose income is slightly higher. Free legal aid is provided by all kinds of *non-profit* organisations, *pro bono* volunteers including lawyers, law students, paralegals, law schools, court-affiliated service centres such as legal aid centres, and online services such as websites for filing documents and obtaining legal information.

The above assistance can take many forms, including direct services such as legal representation in court proceedings and legal advice to identify legal problems and possible solutions, but also to identify and solve systemic issues, such as comprehensive information gathering and assistance in finding solutions to problems faced by large numbers of people, and community outreach and awareness-raising workshops, telephone helplines, medico-legal partnerships, information tools and online discussion, and downloadable court forms to help people understand their rights and responsibilities, when and where legal aid may be needed and where to seek it, and to get help for self-defence if needed[20]. Some of the most common issues that people seeking legal aid in the US are benefit denial, eviction, domestic violence, immigration cases, consumer protection and broad discrimination cases[21]. For those in need of solutions, it is also possible to find websites such as: www.lsc.gov or www.lawhelp.org, which offer assistance in identifying and locating available legal aid. In addition, American Bar Association, ABA) plays an essential role in providing free legal aid to those in need, by promoting the provision of pro bono services. The ABA website

18 *Ibid*, p. 32. See A.W. Houseman, *Civil Legal Aid in the United States: An Update for 2017* March 2018, p. 93.

19 An income indicator used to determine eligibility for certain programmes and benefits set annually by the Department of Health and *Human Services* (The *Department of Health and Human Services*).

20 See https://www.justice.gov/olp/civil-legal-aid-101 (accessed 31.08.2021).

21 See A. Cenzartowicz, *Legal aid – examples from the world*, https://nawokandzie.ms.gov.pl/numer-8/pomoc-i-edukacja-prawna/legal-aid-przyklady-ze-swiata.html (accessed 31.08.2021).

provides a package of information on how to obtain legal aid, as well as the entire spectrum of possibilities in this area.

The largest funder of legal aid for low-income Americans in the United States is the Legal Services Corporation (the LSC), created by Congress in 1974 to expand access to justice for low-income Americans. The organisation distributes more than 90% of its total Congressional appropriation to 134 independent non-profit legal aid programmes from more than 800 offices serving every county in the country. The LSC is governed by a bipartisan board of 11 members appointed by the President and confirmed by the Senate. LSC-funded organisations account for about 25 % of the country's total civil legal aid providers. In addition, there are hundreds of independently run non-profit legal aid programs that do not receive LSC funding and that focus on specific populations or special issues (such as children, the homeless, people with disabilities, and veterans) and provide more comprehensive services, such as legal aid, and coordinate all types of pro bono programmes. Many of these programmes and services are not limited to people earning up to 125 % of the federal poverty level mentioned earlier. Some programmes may have funding to serve all older Americans or victims of domestic violence, for example, regardless of income[22].

Interestingly, in addition to the above funding sources, there is a specific method of funding legal aid in the US legal culture (Interest on Lawyers Trust Accounts, IOLTA), which assumes that interest earned on lawyers' trust accounts is collected for civil legal aid to indigent individuals. When a lawyer in the United States receives funds belonging to a particular client, those funds must be deposited in a trust account that is separate from the lawyer's own funds. There are legal services in every US state that operate and are funded in this way[23]. IOLTA has played a leading role in financing several innovative programs that have positively impacted legal services for indigent persons[24].

4. Conclusions

As shown in the previous section of this chapter, the number of programmes and the associated access to free legal aid has increased over the years. This has mainly been driven by organizations providing legal services programmes to combat

22 See https://www.justice.gov/olp/civil-legal-aid-101 (accessed 31.08.2021).

23 See https://www.globaldisabilityrightsnow.org/tools/usa-vietnam/legal-aid-united-states [accessed 31.08.2021].

24 See https://www.americanbar.org/groups/interest_lawyers_trust_accounts/overview/ (accessed 31.08.2021).

poverty and the associated lack of access to justice. The question should be asked how effective the proposed solutions are. However, it is fair to acknowledge that this is still an ongoing process, as according to the Department of Justice, 63 million Americans[25] are eligible for free civil legal aid. In contrast, as many as 50 % of those seeking civil legal aid are turned away due to a lack of resources.

An analysis of the issue of access to free legal aid shows the full range of dependencies that exist and the problems facing US society. Social stratification, high wealth disparities and the inequalities in access to justice that are undeniably linked to them are among the conclusions that emerge. As the issue's history indicates, the provision of legal services to the poor has never been an uncontested issue. Depending on the political winds, support for legal services in the United States has risen and fallen. While equal access to justice is far from an ideal solution to ensure equality in this regard, solutions provided by federal agencies, state agencies, or legal professionals provide important legal assistance to Americans, especially to the low-income portion of the population[26].

Literature

Cenzartowicz A., *Legal Aid – Examples from the World*, https://pokojadwokacki.pl/pomoc-prawna-na-swiecie-agnieszka-cenzartowicz/ (accessed 20.05.2024).

George, James P. Acces to Justice, Costs, and Legal Aid, *American Journal of Comparative Law*, Vol. 54, no Supplement Issue, Fall 2006.

Houseman A., Perle L.E., *Securing Equal Justice for All. A Brief History of Civil Legal Assistance in the United States*, May 2018.

Houseman A.W., *Civil Legal Aid in the United States: An Update for 2017*, March 2018.

Houseman, *Civil Legal Aid in the United States: An Update for 2013.*

Keith L.H., Poverty, the Great Unequalizer: Improving the Delivery System for Civil Legal Aid, *66 Cath. U. L. Rev*, Vol. 55, 2017.

25 Status as of 20 November 2020. https://www.justice.gov/olp/civil-legal-aid-101 (accessed 1.09.2021).

26 See A. Houseman, L.E. Perle, *Securing Equal Justice for All. A Brief History of Civil Legal Assistance in the United States*, May 2018, p. 7.

Ivan Pankevych

Free Legal Aid in Ukraine

Abstract: The aim of the study is to present the issues of exercising the right to free legal aid in Ukraine. In the paper we used the dogmatic and the comparative methods. The Constitution of Ukraine provides that everyone has the right to legal aid. In the cases provided for by the Act, aid is provided free of charge. Despite the fact that the emergence of such legal aid was constitutionally provided for almost 25 years ago, it was not until June 2, 2011 that the Ukrainian parliament passed the law on free legal aid. On its basis, the Cabinet of Ministers of Ukraine established the Coordination Centre for Legal Aid Provision in January 2013. Currently in Ukraine there are 23 regional centers for presenting free legal aid, 84 local centers, 428 legal aid offices, 5 law societies "Prawokator". However, the system of free legal aid in Ukraine will need to be further refined. Its functioning was challenged by the substantial increase in the number of people entitled to receive free legal aid, in particular as a result of the ongoing Russian-Ukrainian hybrid war.

Keywords: free legal aid, legal protection, hybrid war

1. Introduction

After the proclamation of the Act of State Independence on August 24, 1991[1] Ukraine has started to implement international standards in the field of human and civil rights protection, among which the right to free legal aid is an important element. When considering the issue of free legal aid in Ukraine, it should first of all be mentioned that the provision of this type of legal aid was relatively precisely regulated less than 10 years ago. Indeed, art. 59 of the Constitution of Ukraine of 28 June 1996 states that "everyone has the right to legal aid. In the cases provided for by the Act, aid is provided free of charge. Everyone chooses their lawyer voluntarily. The bar works to ensure the right to defense in cases of accusation and when resolving cases in courts and other state authorities in Ukraine"[2]. The Ukrainian Parliament also ratified the ECHR on 17 July 1997[3]

1 Акт проголошення незалежності України (in:) Відомості Верховної Ради України. – 1991. – № 38. – Ст. 502.

2 Конституція України. Прийнята на п'ятій сесії Верховної Ради України 28 червня 1996 р. (in:) Відомості Верховної Ради України. – 1996. – № 30. – Ст. 141.

3 Закон України Про ратифікацію Конвенції про захист прав людини і основоположних свобод 1950 року, Першого протоколу та протоколів N 2, 4,

according to which it should have become not only the recognition of the jurisdiction of the Strasbourg Court, but also the reform of the entire system of legal protection bodies, as well as compliance with European standards in the field of human rights protection and their implementation into the national legal order. On the other hand, the settlement of the issue of detailed legal regulation of the provision of free legal aid was then postponed to a further perspective.

2. Provision of free legal aid – From the concept to the act

In the Concept of improving the operation of the judiciary in order to establish a fair trial in Ukraine in line with European standards, approved ten years later after the adoption of the Basic Law of Ukraine on the basis of the Regulation of the President of Ukraine No. 361/2006 of May 10, 2006, it was noted that the lack of an effective legal aid system access to justice, in particular free of charge for people on low incomes[4]. In the Concept of shaping the system of free legal aid in Ukraine, approved on the basis of the Regulation of the President of Ukraine No. 509 of 9 June 2006[5] regulates the general principles of its formation and operation, as well as the issues of full or partial financing of legal aid at the expense of the state budget. The concept concluded that at the current stage, the state of free legal aid in Ukraine is unsatisfactory and does not meet the main European requirements for ensuring access to justice[6]. After the amendment to the Constitution of Ukraine of 28 June 1996, by the Law of Ukraine of 7 February 2019[7] The preamble to the Basic Law was supplemented with a standard on the

---

7 та 11 до Конвенції (in:) Відомості Верховної Ради України (ВВР), 1997, N 40, ст.263.

4 Концепція вдосконалення судівництва для утвердження справедливого суду в Україні відповідно до європейських стандартів, затверджена Указом Президента України від 10 травня 2006 року № 361/2006. (in:) Офіційний вісник України. – 2006. – № 19 (24.05.2006). – Ст. 1376.

5 Концепція формування системи безоплатної правової допомоги в Україні, затверджена Указом Президента України від 6 червня 2006 року № 509/2006 (in:) Офіційний вісник України. – 2006. № 24 (29.06.2006). – Ст. 1764.

6 Концепція формування системи безоплатної правової допомоги в Україні, затверджена Указом Президента України від 6 червня 2006 року № 509/2006 (in:) Офіційний вісник України. – 2006. № 24 (29.06.2006). – Ст. 1764.

7 Про внесення змін до Конституції України (щодо стратегічного курсу держави на набуття повноправного членства України в Європейському Союзі та в Організації Північноатлантичного договору) (in:) Відомості Верховної Ради (ВВР), 2019, № 9, ст.50.

European identity of the Ukrainian people and the irreversibility of Ukraine's European and Euro-Atlantic course, the timeliness of the implementation of European standards has increased immeasurably.

At present, however, on many levels the situation in Ukraine is such that the proclamation of reforms and their implementation differ significantly in time. Unfortunately, this also applies to a situation that we would define as a global change in the concept of the state's attitude towards providing legal aid to its own citizens. The point is that in times of totalitarianism, a collectivist conception dominated the interests of the state over the interests of the individual. After independence and the proclamation of the development of a democratic state in Ukraine, an individualistic concept was implemented, according to which the state should act in the interests of the individual. As Professor O. Yanovska rightly points out, providing legal aid should not be seen as an act of charity towards people with low incomes, but as a duty of society as a whole. Each individual has the right to receive free legal aid from an attorney in court, as well as the right to voluntarily choose a qualified attorney. At the same time, the state is responsible for financing free legal aid[8]. Jeremy McBride, on the other hand, believes that the right to aid imposes an obligation on the state to provide a lawyer and pay for his services if the person does not have such an opportunity. This is especially true when the level of competence of the accused and/or the consequences of his conviction are such that it is in the interest of the administration of justice to provide legal aid in this way. However, the right to legal aid – whether granted by the state or not, does not mean that it is not subject to regulation, in particular in cases where there is a possibility of causing harm to court proceedings[9].

It is up to the state to ensure that the right to free legal aid can be exercised where this cannot be ensured by the private sector and civil society. Whether the state will undertake this obligation depends primarily on the political will and economic resources of individual states. Such a political will appeared in Ukraine only in 2011, when on 2 June 2011, the Verkhovna Rada of Ukraine

---

8 Яновська О. Г. Європейські стандарти надання безоплатної правової допомоги в кримінальному судочинстві: проблеми реалізації в Україні / О. Г. Яновська (in:) Науковий вісник Міжнародного гуманітарного університету. Юриспруденція. – 2013. – Вип. 6-1(2). – С. 202.

9 Макбрайд Джеремі. Європейська конвенція з прав людини та кримінальний процес [Текст]: [посібник] / Джеремі Макбрайд; [пер. Д. Шкрьоба]; Рада Європи, Ген. директорат з прав людини і прав. питань. – Київ, 2010. – С. 19–20.

passed the Law on free legal aid[10]. The main task of the act has become the creation of an effective system of free legal aid. The act defined the content of the right to receive legal aid, the grounds and procedure for presenting legal aid, and above all the competences of the competent organs of state authority and local self-government bodies in this field. art. 1 of the Act defines the concept of legal aid, which is the provision of legal services aimed at ensuring the implementation of human and civil rights and freedoms, protection of these rights and freedoms, and their restoration in the event of violation[11]. The aforementioned article of the Act also defines the concept of legal services as the provision of legal information, consultations and clarifications on legal issues; preparation of applications, complaints, procedural documents and other legal documents; representing the interests of the individual in court, other state authorities, local self-government, and in front of other persons; ensuring the protection of the unit against prosecution; helping to ensure her access to secondary legal aid and mediation[12]. The analyzed act establishes two types of free legal aid, distinguished by the criterion of access to justice: free primary legal aid and free secondary legal aid. Primary free legal aid is a type of state guarantee consisting in informing a person about their rights and freedoms, the procedure for their implementation, recovery in the event of a breach, and about the procedure of appealing against decisions, actions or inactivity of state authorities, local self-government and their employees. Pursuant to art. 7 of the Act, services under free primary legal aid include the provision of legal information, advice and clarifications on legal issues, aid in the preparation of applications, complaints and other legal documents (except procedural documents), aid in ensuring access to secondary legal aid and mediation[13]. Based on the analysis of the above-mentioned legal regulations, we can conclude that the basic free legal aid belongs to the group of services that are not related to court proceedings. The subjects of providing free legal aid in Ukraine are executive authorities, local self-government bodies, natural persons, legal entities of private law engaged by local self-governments, as well as specialized institutions established by local self-governments.

---

10 Закон України № 3460-VI від 2 червня 2011 року «Про безоплатну правову допомогу» (in:) Відомості Верховної Ради України (ВВР), 2011, № 51, ст.577.

11 Закон України № 3460-VI від 2 червня 2011 року «Про безоплатну правову допомогу» (in:) Відомості Верховної Ради України (ВВР), 2011, № 51, ст.577.

12 Закон України № 3460-VI від 2 червня 2011 року «Про безоплатну правову допомогу» (in:) Відомості Верховної Ради України (ВВР), 2011, № 51, ст.577.

13 Закон України № 3460-VI від 2 червня 2011 року «Про безоплатну правову допомогу» (in:) Відомості Верховної Ради України (ВВР), 2011, № 51, ст.577.

The second important type of free legal aid guaranteed by the aforementioned Act is secondary legal aid. Free secondary legal aid is a type of state guarantee consisting in equalizing the chances of access to justice and consisting of the following types of legal services: protection, representation of people's interests before courts, other state authorities, local self-government, other persons, preparation of procedural documents. As far as secondary legal aid is concerned, in this case the legislator, unlike primary legal aid, on the one hand limits the group of persons entitled to receive free legal aid. On the other hand, the above-mentioned group is, in our opinion, quite wide-ranging, namely art. 14 of the Law on Free Legal Aid of 2 June 2011 stipulates that the following categories of people have the right to receive it: (1) persons subject to the jurisdiction of Ukraine, if their average monthly income does not exceed two minimum levels of subsistence, calculated and approved in accordance with the Law of Ukraine On the minimum level of subsistence[14] for persons belonging to basic socio-demographic groups, as well as disabled persons receiving a pension or pension replacement benefits not exceeding two minimum subsistence levels for persons with disabilities[15]; (2) children, including orphans, children deprived of parental care, children in a difficult life situation, children injured as a result of military operations or armed conflict; (2^1) internally displaced persons; (2^2) citizens who have submitted an application for registration as internally displaced persons; (2^3) Ukrainian citizens – owners of plots of land, living in rural areas; (3) persons against whom administrative detention was imposed; (4) persons against whom administrative arrest was applied; (5) persons who, in accordance with the provisions of the law on criminal proceedings, consider themselves detained; (6) persons against whom a coercive measure in the form of detention was applied; (7) persons in criminal proceedings against whom, in accordance with the provisions of the Code of Criminal Procedure of Ukraine, the defender engages the investigator, prosecutor, investigating judge or court to defend themselves or appoint separate proceedings, as well as persons sentenced to imprisonment, detention in a disciplinary battalion of soldiers or restriction of liberty; (8) persons covered by the Act of Ukraine on Refugees and Persons

14 Закон України № 966-XIV від 15 липня 1999 року «Про прожитковий мінімум» (in:) Відомості Верховної Ради України (ВВР), 1999, № 38, ст.348.

15 So from 1 January to 30 June 2021, the average monthly income should not exceed UAH 4,540 for non-disabled people and UAH 3,538 for disabled people.

in Need of Additional or Temporary Protection[16]; (8[1]) persons who have applied for recognition as stateless; (9) veterans and persons covered by the Law of Ukraine On the Status of War Veterans, guarantees of their social protection[17], persons of particular merit towards the Homeland, persons who were victims of Nazi persecution; (9[1]) persons under the jurisdiction of Ukraine who applied for the status of a person covered by the Law of Ukraine On the Status of War Veterans, guarantees of their social protection[18]; (10) persons against whom the court examines a case on limiting the capacity to perform civil acts of a natural person, for recognizing a natural person as incapacitated and for restoring legal capacity to a natural person; (11) persons against whom the court is considering a case concerning compulsory psychiatric care; (12) rehabilitated persons in accordance with the legislation of Ukraine; (13) persons who have experienced domestic violence or gender-based violence; (14) persons who have reported corruption or a crime related to corruption[19].

As we can tell, the list of people eligible for free secondary legal aid is very extensive. The Russian-Ukrainian hybrid war, which has been going on for more than seven years, contributed to the increase in the catalog. According to information from the Ministry of Social Policy of Ukraine, as of 22 February 2021, 1,460,806 internally displaced persons from the temporarily occupied territories of Donetsk and Luhansk oblasts and the Autonomous Republic of Crimea were registered in the unified database of internally displaced persons[20]. Simply put, in order to ensure the legally guaranteed right to free secondary legal aid, the state budget is to provide for a pool of resources and the development of an appropriate mechanism for the provision of free legal aid. The lack of budgetary resources or the "intricate" mechanism of providing free legal aid, combined with the

16 Закон України № 3671-VI від 8 липня 2011 року «Про біженців та осіб, які потребують додаткового або тимчасового захисту» (in:) Відомості Верховної Ради України (ВВР), 2012, № 16, ст.146.

17 Закон України № 3551-XII від 22 жовтня 1993 року «Про статус ветеранів війни, гарантії їх соціального захисту» (in:) Відомості Верховної Ради України (ВВР), 1993, № 45, ст.425.

18 Закон України № 3551-XII від 22 жовтня 1993 року «Про статус ветеранів війни, гарантії їх соціального захисту» (in:) Відомості Верховної Ради України (ВВР), 1993, № 45, ст.425.

19 Закон України № 3460-VI від 2 червня 2011 року «Про безоплатну правову допомогу» (w:) Відомості Верховної Ради України (ВВР), 2011, № 51, ст.577.

20 Обліковано 1 460 806 внутрішньо переміщених осіб (in:) https://www.msp.gov.ua/news/19676.html

Ukrainian whip of corruption for many years, may lead to the deterioration of the legislator's good intentions, resulting in additional social tensions. Art. 4 of the Law of Ukraine On Free Legal Aid expressly states that when exercising the right to free legal aid, it is forbidden to apply privileges or restrictions to persons on the basis of race, color, political, religious and other beliefs, sex, ethnic and social origin, place of residence. residence, language or other characteristics[21]. The next article of the aforementioned Act, which defines the policy of the state in the field of free legal aid, postulates that it is based on the principles of the rule of law; legality; the availability of free legal aid, as well as ensuring its quality and guaranteeing state funding[22]. However, in our opinion, due to various Ukrainian "traditions", in order to make the system of free legal aid more effective and to increase the degree of trust in it on the part of civil society, an independent system for monitoring its functioning is needed.

3. System of free legal aid in Ukraine

After the Ukrainian legislator passed the law on free legal aid, which we briefly analyzed, the proper institutional system began to be shaped. By order No. 504 of 6 June 2012[23] the Cabinet of Ministers of Ukraine established the Legal Aid Coordination Center – the first institution of the free legal aid system. On 1 January 2013, regional centers of free secondary legal aid began operating, which ensure the presentation of legal aid to suspects and accused persons in criminal proceedings, detained, arrested and sentenced[24]. In December 2013, a memorandum of cooperation was signed between the Plenipotentiary of the Supreme Council of Ukraine for Human Rights (Ombudsman) and the Legal Aid Coordination Center. Both parties to the above-mentioned memorandum have agreed to consolidate actions aimed at eliminating violations of human rights and freedoms, including the right to use free secondary legal aid and

---

21 Закон України № 3460-VI від 2 червня 2011 року «Про безоплатну правову допомогу» (in:) Відомості Верховної Ради України (ВВР), 2011, № 51, ст.577.

22 Закон України № 3460-VI від 2 червня 2011 року «Про безоплатну правову допомогу» (in:) Відомості Верховної Ради України (ВВР), 2011, № 51, ст.577.

23 Постанова Кабінету Міністрів України № 504 від 6 червня 2012 року «Про утворення Координаційного центру з надання правової допомоги та ліквідацію Центру правової реформи і законопроектних робіт при Міністерстві юстиції» // Офіційний вісник України від 15.06.2012. – 2012 р., № 43, стор. 29, стаття 1668, код акта 61973/2012

24 Огляд системи безоплатної правової допомоги в Україні. Проект доступна та якісна правова допомога в Україні. – Київ, 2014, с. 18.

support in the implementation of the citizens' right to equal and free access to state-guaranteed legal aid in criminal proceedings[25].

In 2014, the Open Public Platform for the Development of the Ukrainian Free Legal Aid System was established. It gathered a wide group of non-governmental organizations, representatives of the Ministry of Justice of Ukraine, independent lawyers, as well as representatives of international projects in the field of human rights protection. Among them, we can mention the Center for Political and Legal Reforms, the Ukrainian Foundation for Legal Aid, the United Nations project "Without Borders", etc. Such "accumulation" of governmental and non-governmental institutions resulted in the expansion of activities in the field of providing free legal aid. Already on July 1, 2015, 100 local centers of free additional legal aid started operating in all regions of Ukraine (except for the temporarily occupied territories). Completed the institutional development of free legal aid systems by establishing, as of 1 September 2016, more than 400 legal aid offices in district (poviat) centers and small towns. Currently in Ukraine there are 23 regional centers for presenting free legal aid, 84 local centers, 428 legal aid offices, 5 law clubs "Prawokator", about 7,000 lawyers involved in the provision of free legal aid; approximately 1,500 lawyers of the free legal aid system. In 2019, UAH 390.5 million was transferred from the state budget in 2019 to ensure the establishment and operation of the free legal aid system, and another UAH 337.7 million was allocated to the payment of services and reimbursement of funds for the provision of free legal aid. In fact, the Ukrainian free legal aid system is currently the largest in Europe. It can also be concluded that it is one of the most successful projects of the Ministry of Justice of Ukraine, the Cabinet of Ministers of Ukraine and international partners.

4. Supervisory Board of the Legal Aid Coordination Center

Pursuant to the Regulation of the Ministry of Justice of Ukraine № 2551/5 of August 14, 2019, in order to ensure the independence of the management of the free legal aid system, transparency of its activities and the effective implementation of the state policy in the field of free legal aid, the Regulations of the Supervisory Board of the Coordination Center for Legal Aid were approved[26].

---

25 Огляд системи безоплатної правової допомоги в Україні (in:) Проект доступна та якісна правова допомога в Україні. – Київ, 2014, с. 74.

26 Наказ Міністерства юстиції України № 2551/5 від 14 серпня 2019 року «Про затвердження Положення про Наглядову раду Координаційного центру з надання правової допомоги» (in:) Офіційний вісник України від 20.08.2019. – 2019 р., № 63, стор. 298, стаття 2208, код акта 95677/2019.

Nine members of the Supervisory Board on a voluntary basis for a five-year term of office are composed of various professional specializations and selected on the basis of a competition by committees composed of representatives of key partners and stakeholders of the free legal aid system. At the same time, it should be mentioned that one-third of the composition of the Supervisory Board is renewable once every two years on the basis of the criteria set out in the regulations, and its members may not include employees of state authorities, the Coordination Center for Legal Aid and its territorial branches[27]. In December 2019, a competition was announced for the selection of members of the Supervisory Board of the Coordination Center for Legal Aid, after which, based on the order of the Ministry of Justice of Ukraine No. 662/7 of 17 March 2020, its composition was approved[28]. The aforementioned Supervisory Board has a fairly broad range of competences, including supervision over the operation of the free legal aid system, preparation of proposals for the appointment and dismissal of the head of the Coordination Center, listening to the annual report on the operation of the free legal aid system, including financial aid. In addition, her important competences include identifying and assessing political, financial or other risks, as well as presenting opinions on their prevention and resolution.

5. Conclusions

To conclude our considerations, we would like to state that at the moment the situation around the issue of free legal aid in Ukraine can be described as positive. An important and valuable feature of access to free legal aid is not only the existence of the possibility to provide the above-mentioned type of legal aid to a wide range of eligible persons. Free legal aid – an important component in the development of civil society in Ukraine. The further progress of reforms in the country depends on whether the constitutional guarantees in the field of free legal aid will become reality. The more so as guaranteeing the implementation of the right to legal aid is not only a constitutional obligation of the state, but also the observance of international, primarily European, standards in the field of human and civil rights protection.

---

27 Наказ Міністерства юстиції України № 2551/5 від 14 серпня 2019 року «Про затвердження Положення про Наглядову раду Координаційного центру з надання правової допомоги» (in:) Офіційний вісник України від 20.08.2019. – 2019 р., № 63, стор. 298, стаття 2208, код акта 95677/2019.

28 У Координаційному центрі з надання правової допомоги затверджено склад наглядової ради (in:) Юридична газета. 19.03.2020.

Literature

Акт проголошення незалежності України (w:) Відомості Верховної Ради України, № 38. – Ст. 502, 1991.

Конституція України. Прийнята на п'ятій сесії Верховної Ради України 28 червня 1996 р. (w:) *Відомості Верховної Ради України*, № 30, Ст. 141, 1996.

Концепція вдосконалення судівництва для утвердження справедливого суду в Україні відповідно до європейських стандартів, затверджена Указом Президента України від 10 травня 2006 року № 361/2006. (w:) *Офіційний вісник України*, № 19 (24.05.2006). Ст. 1376, 2006.

Концепція формування системи безоплатної правової допомоги в Україні, затверджена Указом Президента України від 6 червня 2006 року № 509/2006 (w:) *Офіційний вісник України*, № 24 (29.06.2006), Ст. 1764, 2006.

Закон України Про ратифікацію Конвенції про захист прав людини і основоположних свобод 1950 року, Першого протоколу та протоколів N 2, 4, 7 та 11 до Конвенції (w:) *Відомості Верховної Ради України (ВВР)*, N 40, ст.263, 1997.

Про внесення змін до Конституції України (щодо стратегічного курсу держави на набуття повноправного членства України в Європейському Союзі та в Організації Північноатлантичного договору) (w:) *Відомості Верховної Ради (ВВР)*, № 9, ст.50, 2019.

Яновська О.Г. Європейські стандарти надання безоплатної правової допомоги в кримінальному судочинстві: проблеми реалізації в Україні, О.Г. Яновська (w:) *Науковий вісник Міжнародного гуманітарного університету. Юриспруденція*, Вип. 6-1(2). – С. 202, 2013.

Макбрайд Джеремі. Європейська конвенція з прав людини та кримінальний процес [Текст]: [посібник]/Джеремі Макбрайд; [пер. Д. Шкрьоба]; Рада Європи, Ген. директорат з прав людини і прав. питань, Київ, С. 19–20, 2010.

Закон України № 3460-VI від 2 червня 2011 року «Про безоплатну правову допомогу» (w:) *Відомості Верховної Ради України (ВВР)*, № 51, ст.577, 2011.

Закон України № 966-XIV від 15 липня 1999 року «Про прожитковий мінімум» (w:) *Відомості Верховної Ради України (ВВР)*, № 38, ст.348, 1999.

Закон України № 3671-VI від 8 липня 2011 року «Про біженців та осіб, які потребують додаткового або тимчасового захисту» (w:) *Відомості Верховної Ради України (ВВР)*, № 16, ст.146, 2012.

Закон України № 3551-XII від 22 жовтня 1993 року «Про статус ветеранів війни, гарантії їх соціального захисту» (w:) *Відомості Верховної Ради України (ВВР)*, 1993, № 45, ст.425.

Обліковано 1 460 806 внутрішньо переміщених осіб (w:) https://www.msp.gov.ua/news/19676.html

Постанова Кабінету Міністрів України № 504 від 6 червня 2012 року «Про утворення Координаційного центру з надання правової допомоги та ліквідацію Центру правової реформи і законопроектних робіт при Міністерстві юстиції» (w:) *Офіційний вісник України від* 15.06.2012, 2012 р., № 43, стор. 29, стаття 1668, код акта 61973/2012.

Огляд системи безоплатної правової допомоги в Україні (w:) *Проект доступна та якісна правова допомога в Україні*, Київ, 2014.

Наказ Міністерства юстиції України № 2551/5 від 14 серпня 2019 року «Про затвердження Положення про Наглядову раду Координаційного центру з надання правової допомоги» (w:) *Офіційний вісник України від*, 20.08.2019. 2019 р., № 63, стор. 298, стаття 2208, код акта 95677/2019.

У Координаційному центрі з надання правової допомоги затверджено склад наглядової ради (w:) *Юридична газета*. 19.03.2020.

Ilnytskyi Oleh

University Legal Clinic in Ukraine

Abstract: The aim of the study is to highlight the issue of university clinics in Ukraine. In the study we used the dogmatic and the comparative methods. The university movement of legal clinics has been actively developing in Ukraine since the beginning of the 1990s. University legal clinics are an obligatory part of the faculty of law in Ukraine, on which the practical training of law students is based. Their activities are conducted both on the basis of self-organization, through the trade union of the counseling center, and based on centralized legal regulation of the Ministry of Education and Science of Ukraine. Thus, university legal clinics form a part of the professional training system for lawyers in Ukraine.

The statistics of the clinics' activity also demonstrate that university legal clinics are an organizational form of providing and receiving free legal aid. In some cases, students and professors of legal specialties provide citizens with free legal aid in courts.

Unfortunately, this aspect of the activity of university legal clinics is not yet adequately examined in theory and devoid of any attention in practice. That said, the potential of development of this system permits the provision of effective and affordable free legal aid, which will contribute to the development of the system of protection and defense of the rights, freedoms and interests of individuals.

Keywords: faculty of law, lawyer, free legal aid

1. Introduction

Legal clinical movement constitutes an important element of the legal system of Ukraine, which gave birth, as one of the important ontological sources, to the system of pro bono legal aid in this country. Supported by non-governmental funding, for quite a period of time it used to be the catalyst of changes in the "legal landscape", directed at the democratization of the legal system that was in the making, the driving engine of the reform in the fundamental human rights areas via problem statement and development of law enforcement practice aiming to deviate from the state-oriented Soviet system of law and implement the law proclaiming the rule-of-law principle.

Besides this national and mental aspect, the legal clinical movement throughout the world is an important practical component of the system of education of students-lawyers. Therefore, "penetration" of legal clinics into the educational process and lawyer training curriculum in Ukraine has obviously been just the matter of time. And currently legal clinics have become the bases for practical training and testing of the acquired knowledge, abilities and skills of the students of higher legal educational institution almost in all schools of law in Ukraine. However, to tell the truth, the degree of their efficiency and integration into the educational process is different.

Under such circumstances of importance is determination of further prospects of the university student clinic development in Ukraine, through the study of the dualistic nature of their operation: as the centres of practical educational training and as the elements having some synergic relation with the pro bono legal aid system.

2. University legal clinics in the process of education of students-lawyers in Ukraine

The legal clinic movement in higher educational institutions has a long general history caused by the realization of the acute need for ensuring access for it in the course of training to "live" cases with "legal pathologies" (according to professor George Frommhold who was the first to introduce the term into official use[1]), through improvement of the quality of training of student-lawyer as a specialist in an applied specialty. The long history of development of this educational and applied tool[2] has led to the appearance and shaping of one of the modern educational training methodologies – "legal clinic education" (comes from the English "legal clinic education"), the aim of which is student's acquisition of practical skills of acting in the professional field via provision of pro bono aid to residents. Legal clinic education is a way for students to obtain practical lawyer's skills via pro bono legal aid provision to residents within their academic internship and

---

1 *Cit. according to:* Гончаренко В.О. Юридична клініка: історія і визначення. *Практика діяльності «юридичних клінік» України*. 2004. № 1. С. 3. [Honcharenko V. O. Legal Clinic: History and Definition. *Praktyka Diyalnosti 'Yurydychnykh Klinik' Ukrayiny*. 2004. No. 1. P. 3]

2 *See detailed information:* Лоджук М.Т. Юридичні клініки в Україні: освіта та правова допомога. Одеса, 2015. С. 6–37; Фігель Ю.О. Роль юридичних клінік у формуванні вмінь реалізації права студентами юридичних спеціальностей: дис. … канд. юрид. наук: 12.00.01 «Теорія та історія держави і права; історія політичних і правових учень». Львів, 2011. 198 с. [Lodzhuk M. T. Legal Clinics in Ukraine: Education and Legal Aid. Odesa, 2015. pp. 6–37; Fihel Yu. O. The Role of Legal Clinics in the Development of Law Implementation Abilities by Students of Legal Specialties: thesis… candidate of legal sciences: 12.00.01 'Theory and History of State and Law; History of Political and Legal Teachings'. Lviv, 2011, 198 pp.]

other types of internship on the basis of a legal clinic within a higher educational institution[3].

At the same time, it should be noted that currently university legal clinics in Ukraine have a much wider institutional recognition and regulation than educational and methodological ones.

Long-term work at the development of the university legal clinic movement ended up in the approval of the Typical Regulation on the Legal Clinic of a Higher Educational Institution of Ukraine[4] (referred to as Regulation 592), which made it binding for rectors of higher educational institutions of the IIIrd–IVth accreditation levels, training specialists in the direction "Law", regardless of forms of ownership and subordination, to secure establishment of legal clinics and their operation under the Regulation. And paragraph 2, part 7, art. 33 of the Law of Ukraine *On Higher Education* as of 1 July 2014 defined legal clinics already at the legislative level as possible structural units of higher educational institutions.

At the same time, p. 2.3 of Regulation No. 592, according to the goal and tasks of a legal clinic of a higher educational institution, for the sake of ensuring its complete and efficient functioning, makes it binding for the management of the legal clinic and the higher educational institution to organize and ensure teaching of a special course "Fundamentals of Practice in Legal Clinics", which embraces the principles and functions of the legal clinic operation as well as focuses on the key aspects of legal practice.

However, the study of the core documents on the academic process organization in higher educational institutions in Ukraine, performed on the basis of open sources, shows that such special course is taught in just a few schools of law. And where such special course is taught, it is included to the list of optional subjects, thus not guaranteeing gaining of the respective knowledge, abilities and competences by all students getting their education under the respective educational and professional curriculum.

One more problem in the legal clinic functioning within the structure of professional training of specialists in law is availability of a branched system of specialists in Ukraine, with similar academic and professional rights both for the graduates of specialty 081 "Law" – graduates in specialty 293 "International

3 Лоджук М.Т. Юридичні клініки в Україні: освіта та правова допомога. Одеса, 2015. С. 173. [Lodzhuk M. T. Legal Clinics in Ukraine: Education and Legal Aid. Odesa, 2015. P. 173]

4 Order of the Ministry of Education and Science of Ukraine as of August 03, 2006 No. 592 (registered by the Ministry of Justice of Ukraine as of August 08, 2006 at No. 956/ 12830)

Law" – and in specialty 262 "Law Enforcement" (as a rule, in the departmental higher educational institutions of the police system or resident civil protection services).

Regulation No. 592 is not valid for them either in form, or in meaning, though the unity of the professional status of the graduates of the above specialties in the system of specialties in the labour market requires a unified approach to ensuring the content of professional training in legal aid provision to people. Availability of a legal clinic at the respective faculty which claims that it trains students in the professional qualification "lawyer", regardless of the specific specialty of the educational and professional curriculum, is an unwritten "decency".

Still, available regulatory documents determining the content of educational training focus on the integrity of the practical training component, ensuring its role in the overall structure of the educational and professional program. The above goal is reached through regular (annual) academic internship and externship of students in the bodies and institutions of the respective professional direction.

However, such internship and externship, particularly, for freshmen and for second-year students, in most cases does not correspond to its original designation. It could hardly be the case that a freshman who, in the best case, possesses some general theoretical knowledge of the system of law, can independently perform the externship base supervisor's substantive task in the respective law enforcement institution. At the same time, externship supervisors from the respective institutions rather often do not possess sufficient knowledge, pedagogical skills or do not have enough time to teach the student, and they consider externship supervision to be an additional load for them, overburdening leveraging of the function related to educational training of specialists on them by higher educational institutions. Due to this, they are reluctant to accept students for externship. In such conditions, the student does not get enough practical skills and abilities, besides the aspect of familiarization with the operation of such externship base, and the practical component is almost ignored in student training.

Still, the advantage of practical training at the university legal clinic is ensuring the consistency of academic education (the possibility of allocating clinic clients' cases, with due account of the achieved level of educational and professional training of students, between the respective years of study); permanent involvement of professional pedagogical staff in student training, who, both independently and involving experts, exercise control over the quality of task performance by students; acquisition and development of professional skills and abilities generated through direct communication during consultations (communicative skills, development of the sense of responsibility for the exercising of professional rights, analytical, law enforcement, etc.).

However, in spite of this fact, many of the leading Ukrainian schools of law, the clinics of which are included into the Association of Legal Clinics of Ukraine, even deny participation in the clinic's operations as a way of undergoing student internship and externship.

Due to this, I think that legal clinic education should become one of the obligatory training methods and must be reflected as a standard element of lawyer training in the theoretical and practical components of the respective curricula and syllabi. The institutional preconditions for bringing of this proposal into life in Ukraine have already been established in the format of a branched network of university legal clinics.

Such proposals correspond to the draft Legal Education Development Concept published by the Committee for Education, Science, and Innovations of the Verkhovna Rada of Ukraine[5], as far as achievement of one of the strategic goals – "Schools of law ensure acquisition of a high level of applied practical skills and abilities by the recipients of higher legal education" – is concerned. The following is mentioned among the ways of its achievement: increase in the scope of practical lawyer training to 30 ECTS credits and guaranteeing of its quality as well as promotion of the legal clinic development in the form of separate structural units of higher educational institutions and implementation of educational courses in legal clinic practice in the educational process, active implementation of cases into the educational process as innovative forms and methods of teaching, promotion of the participation of the recipients of higher legal education in educational probations in the state authorities, courts, notarial bodies, the prosecutor's office, the bar and other legal entities of public and private law.

Legal clinic education constitutes an important element of educational and professional training as to as acquisition of the necessary professional competences by the recipients of higher education in the professional qualification "lawyer", the capacity of which is insufficiently unleashed in the Ukrainian system of education. Introduction of the respective educational course as well as its introduction as an obligatory component of the system of the general scope of practical training of lawyers can really improve its efficiency.

---

5 Draft Legal Education Development Concept (06.11.2020) [Electronic resource]. URL: http://kno.rada.gov.ua/news/main_news/75465.html (date of access: 11.12.2020)

3. Relationship between university legal clinics and pro bono legal aid system in Ukraine

The functioning of university legal clinics by its essence clearly meets the regulatory definition of legal aid – as provision of the legal services aiming to ensure exercising of the rights and freedoms of humans and citizens, protection of those rights and freedoms, their redress in case they are infringed. Such legal services, according to the Ukrainian legislator, include: provision of legal information, consultations and clarifications in legal matters; drawing up of applications, complaints, procedural and other documents of legal nature; representation of the person's interests in courts, other state authorities, local self-government bodies, to other persons; ensuring the person's protection against accusations; provision of assistance to a person in accessing secondary legal aid and mediation (paragraphs 3 and 4, part 1, art. 1 of the Law of Ukraine *On Pro Bono Legal Aid* as of 2 June 2011[6]).

The statistics published by the non-governmental self-governing public organization "The Association of Legal Clinics of Ukraine", which now unites 57 university legal clinics of the leading higher educational institutions training lawyers for the year 2019 proves that over this period the Association members have provided 8,648 legal certificates in the form of informing clients, 8,960 legal consultations, prepared 1,946 legal non-judicial documents as well as conducted 2,285 legal awareness events. But the activities of the clinics lie not just in the forms of primary legal aid (non-judicial), but in the provision of secondary legal aid in the form of drawing up documents of procedural nature (2,672) and representation of the interests of people entitled to pro bono secondary legal aid in courts, other state authorities, local self-government bodies, to other persons (326 cases)[7].

The unity of the principles of operation of the legal clinics established in higher educational institutions with the regulatory pro bono legal aid principles and a special focus on the pro bono nature of legal services provision by legal clinics makes their activities, in fact, an element of the pro bono legal aid system.

And still such actual unity is not confirmed by the regulatory framework. The legislative list of subjects of the pro bono legal aid system in Ukraine does not contain any mention of university legal clinics.

---

6 The Bulletin of the Verkhovna Radda of Ukraine, 2011, No. 51, page 2136, art. 577.

7 Official site of the Association of Legal Clinics of Ukraine. URL: https://legalclinics.in.ua/ (date of address: 11.12.2020)

Absence of the official status creates, in our opinion, further challenges in the integration of university legal clinics into the educational process as far as official recognition of the practical skills obtained, limitation of possible forms of activity and types of legal services that can be provided by them (particularly, in the conditions when the requirements on representation in courts in most cases by professional lawyers are valid in Ukraine), the procedure of regulation and organization of their activities from the point of view of ensuring quality standards and responsibility for legal services provision to clients are concerned.

While some of these problems can be solved by own clinics' effort through self-organization (for example, the Association of Legal Clinics of Ukraine has got clear and categorical Legal Clinic Operation Standards approved by the All-Ukrainian Congress of the Association held on 19 June 2014 and the mechanism of regular and systemic monitoring of their compliance in the activities of legal clinics) or through academic autonomy of the higher educational institution where they operate (inclusion and recognition of the legal clinics as the bases for practical student training and introduction of the respective educational courses into the curricula and syllabi), but without systemic legislative changes participation of clinics in pro bono legal aid provision (particularly that of secondary level) still lies in the "grey" regulatory area.

4. Conclusion

Currently, there are almost no occupations in the qualification "lawyer" that could be held on the basis of obtained first (bachelor) level of higher education. And that proves that even completion of the bachelor program does not yet grant professional rights to carry out legal practice in the format of legal services provision in Ukraine. Therefore, formal activity of students, trained under the respective educational programs, within legal services provision to clients by clinics requires additional legal determination and regulation both from the point of view of interaction with clients, and from the point of view of taking this legal aid beyond classrooms and classes – for representation purposes.

Several legislative initiatives have been directed at this, in particular, one of the most fundamental ones – draft Law on amending some legislative acts of Ukraine (concerning determination of the status of legal clinics as subjects of the pro bono legal aid provision) No. 9502 as of 25 November 2011[8], which

8 Official site of the Verkhovna Rada of Ukraine: Legislation of Ukraine: Law-Making. URL: http://w1.c1.rada.gov.ua/pls/zweb2/webproc4_2?pf3516=9502&skl=7 (date of address: 13.12.2020)

presupposed provision of the legal clinics in higher educational institutions of Ukraine of the legal profile with the status of subjects of the pro bono primary and secondary legal aid provision, as well as simplification of the procedure and reduction of financial costs for vulnerable strata of our society during their exercising of the right to a representative in a court hearing in civil and administrative cases as well as in cases on administrative offences.

However, the conclusion of the Main Scientific and Expert Administration of the Verkhovna Rada of Ukraine concerning the content of that draft Law was negative. It mentioned in general that inclusion of university legal clinics into the range of subjects of the pro bono legal aid provision will not solve the problem of the quality of legal services provided by such clinics and will not provide any additional preferences (including financial ones) in terms of fulfillment by the higher educational institutions having such clinics, in this case, already – of the obligations – on legal aid provision and will lay down the regulatory basis for shifting the responsibility of the state for fulfillment of this function onto educational institutions[9].

In our opinion, this conclusion is not well-grounded in terms of ensuring adequacy in the functioning of the legal system institutes, and its arguments replace objective reality related to the involvement of the clinics in the pro bono legal aid provision in Ukraine through justification with the deficit of funding for the development of state legal institutions in Ukraine, traditional for Ukraine. However, inclusion of university legal clinics will not only add some duties for higher educational institutions as far as ensuring the organization of their operation in accordance with the pro bono legal aid standards is concerned (by the way, familiarization with the Legal Clinic Operation Standards, implemented within the self-governed Association or the respective requirements of Regulation No. 592 has shown that already now they meet state requirements and standards set for legal aid), but also opens up opportunities for the implementation of legal educational space in Ukraine within the practical field of future activities of graduates in the form of their probation and acquisition of the requires skills, abilities and experience in the basics of professional activity during the period of studies under the supervision of experienced supervisors-mentors, acquisition of additional budget funding and non-state financial support for the arrangement and ensuring of the activity of such clinics within the programs dealing with the institutionalization of the pro bono legal aid network in Ukraine.

9 Ibid.

However, currently the above draft Law is not under consideration, and since 2012 no serious regulatory developments aimed to solve the above issues have been made.

Therefore, university legal clinics in Ukraine remain among the informal pro bono legal aid provision centres, focusing mainly on consultations and legal awareness-raising. However, their institutional, staff and functional resource could be used more efficiently in the system, both for the sake of better ensuring implementation of the human rights advocacy function and development of the pro bono legal aid system, via the use of the academic and scientific, student and educational capacity, and for the sake of improving the efficiency and quality of student training, via provision of an opportunity to gain empirical experience of working with the legal system cases.

Literature

Fihel Yu. O, The Role of Legal Clinics in the Development of Law Implementation Abilities by Students of Legal Specialties: Thesis… Candidate of Legal Sciences: 12.00.01, *Theory and History of State and Law; History of Political and Legal Teachings*, Lviv 2011.

Honcharenko V.O., Legal Clinic: History and Definition, *Praktyka Diyalnosti 'Yurydychnykh Klinik' Ukrayiny*, No. 1, 2004.

Lodzhuk M.T., *Legal Clinics in Ukraine: Education and Legal Aid*, Odesa 2015.

Agnieszka Gloria Kamińska

Navigating Equitable Horizons: The Evolution and Prospects of Legal Aid in the Republic of Malta

Abstract: The free legal aid system in the Republic of Malta stands as a testament to the country's commitment to accessible justice. In the pursuit of an equitable legal framework, this article meticulously examines the foundations, evolution, and operational intricacies of Malta's legal aid system. This study delves into the historical trajectory of legal aid in Malta, tracing its development from nascent provisions to its contemporary form. Through a rigorous analysis of legislative structures, the article unravels the intricate web of statutes and regulations that underpin the system. Additionally, the operational dimensions are scrutinized, encompassing eligibility criteria, the role of legal practitioners, and the synergy between state intervention and private sector participation. With a sober and scholarly approach, this exploration sheds light on the core tenets that define Malta's free legal aid landscape, inviting contemplation on the broader themes of justice, equality, and the pivotal role of legal aid in society.

Keywords: Free legal aid, Republic of Malta, accessible justice, legal framework, evolution, legislative structures, operational intricacies, eligibility criteria, legal practitioners, state intervention, private sector participation, justice, equality, societal welfare.

1. Introduction

In the realm of legal systems, each nation weaves its distinct narrative of justice, presenting a mosaic of adaptations and innovations. One such mosaic comes into focus as we turn our scholarly gaze toward the free legal aid system in the Republic of Malta. As we embark on this academic exploration, our journey will traverse the labyrinthine passages of Malta's legal aid framework[1]. Against the backdrop of Malta's historical and cultural tapestry, the free legal aid system emerges as a mechanism striving to uphold the ideals of justice, especially for those facing financial constraints. The objective of this discourse is to delve into the contours of this legal aid system, capturing its evolution through time,

1 Law Relating to Legal Aid: Presented to the Honourable Professor Guido de Marco, Deputy Prime Minister and Minister of Foreign Affairs and Justice. (1991). Malta: Malta University Services Limited for the Permanent Law Reform Commission pp. 1–5.

examining the legislative foundations, and deciphering the practical dynamics that render it operational[2].

The historical trajectory of legal aid in Malta beckons us to trace its origins and developmental arc. From modest beginnings to its contemporary form, the system's transformation embodies a responsive approach to the evolving needs of its citizens. As we navigate the legislative landscape, the statutes and regulations that underpin Malta's legal aid structure become prominent landmarks. Our analysis will illuminate the interplay between legal principles, policy considerations, and the pragmatic machinery that breathes life into the provision of legal aid. Yet, beyond the legislative framework lies the realm of implementation – an arena where eligibility criteria, the role of legal practitioners, and the equilibrium between state-sponsored initiatives and private sector participation coalesce. These facets form the gears that set the legal aid machinery in motion. The sections that follow will navigate this intricate tapestry of Malta's free legal aid system, characterized by its sobriety and steadfast commitment to justice[3]. With a measured approach, we shall unravel the layers that constitute this vital pillar of Malta's legal infrastructure. In doing so, we hope to cast light not only on the legal aid system itself but also on the broader themes of access to justice and the symbiotic relationship between law and societal welfare. As we commence this academic odyssey, our intention is to enrich our understanding, stimulate discourse, and lay the groundwork for a profound exploration of the free legal aid landscape in the Republic of Malta[4].

2. History of the institution of legal aid in Malta

The historical underpinnings of legal aid in the Republic of Malta weave a narrative of responsive evolution within the fabric of its legal system. Dating back to its earliest legislative provisions, the institution of legal aid has traversed a dynamic trajectory, shaped by societal needs, legal developments, and a persistent commitment to ensuring access to justice for all. The origins of legal aid in Malta can be traced to the beginnings of XX century, when the first rudimentary measures were introduced to cater to the legal needs of individuals who lacked the means

2 Newman, D. (2013). Legal Aid Lawyers and the Quest for Justice. Regno Unito: Hart Publishing pp. 21–34.

3 Histories of Legal Aid: A Comparative and International Perspective. (2022). Svizzera: Springer International Publishing pp. 55–74.

4 Wilding, J. (2023). The Legal Aid Market: Challenges for Publicly Funded Immigration and Asylum Legal Representation. Regno Unito: Policy Press pp. 75–84.

to engage in the intricacies of the legal process. These early provisions, though modest, laid the groundwork for a more comprehensive legal aid system that would emerge over the ensuing years. A significant milestone in the evolution of legal aid was marked by the enactment of Legal Aid Agency(Establishment) Order, in 2014[5]. This seminal legislation crystallized the principles of legal aid within the Maltese legal framework, acknowledging the necessity of safeguarding the rights of individuals who faced economic constraints in accessing legal representation[6]. This foundational legal act established the groundwork for subsequent developments, including the delineation of eligibility criteria and the establishment of mechanisms for the provision of legal aid services.

The historical journey of legal aid in Malta also reflects a parallel progression in response to evolving legal challenges. In the legal aid sector, the sending and receiving authority is the Advocate for legal aid (the lawyer responsible for the legal aid institute), who carries out his activity at the registry of the civil court, located in the Palace of Justice of the Republic Street, in Valletta (Malta)[7]. Notably, the 2014 reform introduced provisions to address the growing complexities of legal disputes, ensuring that individuals facing intricate legal matters were not impeded by financial limitations. This marked a pivotal moment in the institution's history, aligning it more closely with the intricate demands of modern legal proceedings. The legislative landscape continued to evolve, with subsequent years witnessing refinements to the legal aid framework. The 2014 brought forth amendments that sought to streamline the process of accessing legal aid, enhancing the efficiency and accessibility of the system. These amendments were a testament to the responsiveness of the legal system to the evolving needs of citizens, as well as a recognition of the crucial role legal aid plays in upholding the principles of justice and fairness.

The historical trajectory of legal aid in Malta is a testament to the country's commitment to nurturing a system that aligns with the principles of accessible justice. As the legal landscape adapted to societal changes and emerging legal complexities, so too did the legal aid system undergo transformations[8]. This evolution stands as a testament to Malta's unwavering dedication to ensuring

5 Legal Notice: 414 of 2014 – Legal Aid Agency (Establishment) Order, 2014. Government Gazette of Malta No. 19,349 - 28.11.2014

6 Wilding, J. (2023). The Legal Aid Market: Challenges for Publicly Funded Immigration and Asylum Legal Representation. Regno Unito: Policy Press pp. 84–111.

7 https://e-justice.europa.eu/431/IT/about_the_network?MALTA&member=1

8 Wilding, J. (2023). The Legal Aid Market: Challenges for Publicly Funded Immigration and Asylum Legal Representation. Regno Unito: Policy Press pp. 155–172.

that justice remains within reach for all its citizens, regardless of their financial circumstances. In the subsequent sections of this article, we delve deeper into the legislative architecture that supports the legal aid framework, as well as the operational dynamics that bring this system to life. Continuing on this historical journey, it becomes evident that the evolution of legal aid in Malta has been characterized by a blend of legislative refinements and pragmatic adaptations. The Legal Aid Agency Order, in 2014 laid a cornerstone, firmly establishing legal aid as an integral component of Malta's legal infrastructure. However, the journey was far from static, and subsequent years witnessed a series of legislative reforms designed to enhance the efficacy and inclusivity of the legal aid system[9].

The turn of the 2010–2020 brought forth a period of heightened legal consciousness, coinciding with societal shifts and a growing recognition of the significance of legal rights. In response to this changing landscape, Malta witnessed a series of legal reforms aimed at bolstering legal aid provisions. Notably, 2014 marked a milestone with the enactment of Legal Aid Agency Order, which introduced pivotal changes to the eligibility criteria, expanding the scope of individuals who could access legal aid. This expansion was a direct response to the evolving socio-economic dynamics and a determination to address the needs of marginalized and vulnerable segments of society. The dynamic nature of legal aid's historical trajectory is also reflected in the increasing diversification of legal services offered. As the legal landscape broadened, so did the complexity of legal disputes. 2014 saw the introduction of specialized legal aid provisions for certain categories of cases, such as family law matters or cases with public interest implications. This nuanced approach exemplified Malta's dedication to not only broadening access to justice but also tailoring legal aid to suit the intricacies of specific legal contexts. Moreover, a pivotal moment of adaptation occurred in the decade now ending 2014–2024 with the advent of technological advancements. The integration of digital platforms into legal aid applications streamlined processes, minimizing procedural obstacles and enhancing the accessibility of legal aid services. This shift toward digital engagement echoed the broader global trend of harnessing technology to foster efficiency and inclusivity within legal systems.

The historical narrative of legal aid in Malta underscores a proactive stance toward inclusivity and justice[10]. The system's evolution, propelled by a

9 Access to Justice and Legal Aid: Comparative Perspectives on Unmet Legal Need. (2017). Regno Unito: Bloomsbury Publishing pp. 84–100.

10 Perspectives on Legal Aid: An International Survey. (1979). Regno Unito: Frances Pinter pp. 55–86.

commitment to equitable access, is testament to Malta's responsiveness to changing societal needs and legal complexities. As the historical exploration continues, we now shift our focus to the legislative underpinnings that substantiate the framework of legal aid in the Republic of Malta. Delving into the statutes and regulations that define and govern this system will shed light on the legal foundations that sustain the pursuit of accessible justice for all.

3. Administrative oversight of legal aid provision

The intricate orchestration of legal aid provision within the Republic of Malta extends beyond its legal framework to encompass administrative bodies entrusted with its oversight. These pivotal entities, often referred to as "Administrative Oversight Authorities," assume a central role in shaping and facilitating the functioning of the legal aid system. This section of the article delves into the composition, responsibilities, and operational significance of these authorities, shedding light on their pivotal role in ensuring the equitable and effective delivery of legal aid services. These Administrative Oversight Authorities, which may be organized at both national and local levels, represent the strategic arm of the legal aid system. Their composition typically includes representatives from the legal community, judiciary, and relevant governmental bodies. This inclusive approach brings together diverse perspectives, fostering a collaborative and comprehensive approach to overseeing legal aid provision.

The responsibilities shouldering upon these authorities are multifaceted. They range from establishing eligibility criteria that align with evolving legal dynamics and societal realities to the management of financial resources allocated to the legal aid system[11]. Striking a balance between prudent resource allocation and the imperatives of justice remains a critical undertaking for these bodies. Additionally, the establishment of transparent procedures, performance evaluation mechanisms, and continuous feedback loops further exemplify their proactive engagement. Operational significance underscores the essence of these Administrative Oversight Authorities. Their decisions, deliberations, and policy recommendations influence the accessibility, efficiency, and quality of legal aid provision. Moreover, they bridge the gap between the legislative intentions and on-the-ground implementation, ensuring that the lofty goals of equitable access to justice are translated into practical realities. As we navigate the labyrinthine corridors of administrative oversight within Malta's legal aid ecosystem, it

11 Aquilina, K. (2018). Constitutional Law in Malta. Paesi Bassi: Wolters Kluwer pp. 24–35.

becomes evident that these authorities constitute a linchpin for the system's functionality. In the subsequent sections, we will expound upon the eligibility criteria they formulate, the financial mechanisms they navigate, and the collaborative efforts they orchestrate. The intricate interplay between the legislative framework, administrative oversight, and the operational machinery truly underscores the comprehensive nature of Malta's legal aid architecture. Within the intricate framework of legal aid provision in the Republic of Malta, the administrative oversight entities play a pivotal role that transcends mere governance. As guardians of the equitable access to justice, these entities function as the guardians of the system's integrity, efficacy, and inclusivity. At the heart of their responsibilities lies the calibration of eligibility criteria. With an astute awareness of evolving legal dynamics and societal sensitivities, these oversight bodies refine and adapt the criteria that govern who can avail themselves of legal aid. This sensitive task reflects a nuanced balance between accommodating changing needs and safeguarding the system's sustainability[12]. Financial stewardship forms another cornerstone of their mandate. The allocation and utilization of financial resources within the legal aid domain are meticulously overseen to ensure that the available resources are channeled judiciously to cater to the diverse needs of individuals seeking assistance. This financial guardianship bridges the gap between financial prudence and the core imperative of upholding justice.

Moreover, these oversight entities foster transparency and procedural clarity. The establishment of clear, transparent mechanisms for application, assessment, and disbursement cultivates an environment of trust and confidence. This resonates not only with applicants seeking assistance but also with the broader legal community and society at large.

Collaboration emerges as a hallmark of these oversight entities' modus operandi. Their role in facilitating cooperation between legal professionals, civil society organizations, and other stakeholders serves as a testament to their commitment to fostering a holistic legal aid ecosystem[13]. By acting as bridges of dialogue, they not only streamline processes but also enrich the quality of legal aid provision. As we delve deeper into the operational dimensions of these oversight entities, we are reminded of their indispensable contribution to Malta's legal aid

12 Gerard, A. (2014). The Securitization of Migration and Refugee Women. Regno Unito: Taylor & Francis pp. 55–84.

13 Law Relating to Legal Aid: Presented to the Honourable Professor Guido de Marco, Deputy Prime Minister and Minister of Foreign Affairs and Justice. (1991). Malta: Malta University Services Limited for the Permanent Law Reform Commission pp 34–55.

architecture. Their responsibilities extend far beyond administrative tasks; they are the custodians of justice's accessibility and fairness.

4. Legal aid beyond the state: Exploring legal support mechanisms

In the realm of ensuring accessible justice, the Republic of Malta presents a diverse array of legal support mechanisms that extend beyond the conventional purview of state-sponsored initiatives[14]. Among these mechanisms, "Legal Aid Beyond the State" emerges as a distinctive facet that merits meticulous exploration. This segment of the article delves into the realm of legal support mechanisms beyond direct state intervention, shedding light on the role of private entities, legal insurance, and collaborative models in enhancing access to justice. The landscape of legal aid in Malta is not confined solely to the traditional paradigms governed by state provisions. Instead, it embraces innovative approaches that harness the power of private sector engagement. One such avenue is legal insurance – a mechanism that empowers individuals to secure legal support through private arrangements. By subscribing to legal insurance policies, individuals safeguard themselves against unforeseen legal challenges, thereby augmenting their access to legal expertise when the need arises.

The dynamics of legal insurance hinge on a proactive approach[15]. Individuals, cognizant of the potential legal exigencies they might face, invest in policies that mitigate the financial barriers typically associated with legal representation. This proactive approach echoes the broader ethos of Malta's legal framework, which emphasizes foresight and preparation in the pursuit of justice. Furthermore, the legal insurance model fosters a symbiotic relationship between the legal and insurance sectors. Legal practitioners collaborating with insurance providers establish a bridge that aligns legal expertise with the needs of policyholders. This collaborative alliance, though fundamentally rooted in the private domain, contributes to the broader objectives of equitable legal support. Collaboration manifests not only between legal practitioners and insurance providers but also among various stakeholders. Collaborative legal aid models, emerging as a promising trend, involve partnerships between legal professionals, civil society organizations, and institutions of higher learning. These alliances embody a shared

14 Histories of Legal Aid: A Comparative and International Perspective. (2022). Svizzera: Springer International Publishing pp 88–98.

15 Aquilina, K. (2018). Constitutional Law in Malta. Paesi Bassi: Wolters Kluwer pp. 45–96.

commitment to expanding the horizons of accessible justice, transcending the conventional boundaries of legal aid. As we traverse the terrain of legal support mechanisms beyond the state, we embark on a journey that captures the fusion of private enterprise, legal expertise, and societal collaboration. The subsequent sections will delve into the mechanics of legal insurance, the nuances of collaborative models, and the intricate tapestry that interweaves these elements within Malta's legal aid landscape. Through this exploration, we endeavor to uncover the layers that enrich the pursuit of justice, ensuring that access to legal support resonates as a holistic endeavor that transcends traditional boundaries.

In delving further into the realm of legal support mechanisms that extend beyond state-sponsored initiatives, it becomes evident that the landscape of accessible justice in the Republic of Malta is multifaceted and dynamic. The exploration of legal insurance and collaborative models underscores the nuanced approach that Malta adopts to ensure justice is within reach of all its citizens.

Legal insurance, as a distinctive avenue within this landscape, exemplifies a proactive stride towards accessible legal assistance. The notion of individuals preemptively securing legal support through private arrangements is a testament to both the evolving legal climate and the proactive stance of citizens. By subscribing to legal insurance, individuals navigate the intricate web of legal complexities with a safety net in place, fortified against potential legal challenges. A notable aspect of legal insurance lies in its seamless convergence of legal expertise and private sector enterprise[16]. Legal practitioners collaborating with insurance providers create a bridge that connects the expertise of legal professionals with the financial underpinnings of insurance mechanisms. This synergy benefits individuals seeking legal recourse by alleviating the financial burden often associated with legal representation. Collaborative legal aid models, another dimension of Malta's approach, epitomize a communal commitment to accessible justice. These partnerships between legal practitioners, civil society entities, and educational institutions forge a collective front against barriers to justice. By pooling resources, knowledge, and expertise, these models broaden the spectrum of legal support and enrich the quality of legal aid services. It is within the interplay of these mechanisms that the mosaic of Malta's legal aid landscape is unveiled[17]. The intersection of state-sponsored initiatives, private sector involvement, and

16 Aquilina, K. (2018). Constitutional Law in Malta. Paesi Bassi: Wolters Kluwer pp. 194–214.

17 Access to Justice and Legal Aid: Comparative Perspectives on Unmet Legal Need. (2017). Regno Unito: Bloomsbury Publishing pp. 25–41.

collaborative frameworks weaves a tapestry that resonates with the principles of inclusivity and equity. The subsequent sections of this article will continue to dissect the operational dynamics of these mechanisms, unveiling the intricacies that shape their functionality and exploring the convergence of these diverse avenues toward a unified pursuit of accessible justice. As we proceed, we delve deeper into the tangible manifestations of these mechanisms within the Maltese legal framework, uncovering their impact on the fabric of justice and underscoring their role in advancing the societal mandate of equal access to legal support.

Within this intricate interplay of mechanisms, the intricate mosaic that forms Malta's legal aid landscape is unveiled. The convergence of state-sponsored endeavors, private sector participation, and collaborative frameworks intertwines to create a tapestry resonant with the fundamental principles of inclusivity and equity. As the subsequent sections of this article unfold, the exploration will persist in its endeavor to meticulously dissect the operational dynamics underpinning these mechanisms. By unveiling the intricate mechanisms that shape their functionality, this analysis aims to uncover the convergence of these diverse avenues, all harmonizing in a concerted endeavor for the pursuit of accessible justice.

As our exploration progresses, the narrative delves further into the tangible manifestations of these mechanisms within the contours of the Maltese legal framework. Through this lens, we endeavor to reveal their profound impact on the very fabric of justice. This exploration underscores their pivotal role in advancing the societal imperative of providing equal access to essential legal support. As the discourse unfolds, the intricate threads of Malta's legal aid tapestry converge into a comprehensive and holistic perspective, reflecting the multidimensional pursuit of justice for all[18].

As we peer into the temporal horizon of 2023 and 2024, the trajectory of Malta's legal aid landscape appears poised for both evolution and refinement. The dynamic interplay of state-sponsored initiatives, private sector engagement, and collaborative endeavors is set to steer this landscape toward new horizons of accessibility and effectiveness. In 2023, the ripple effects of technological advancements are anticipated to manifest more profoundly. The integration of digital platforms and online interfaces could redefine the accessibility paradigm, bridging geographical distances and simplifying the application process. This digital evolution may also catalyze the establishment of comprehensive databases, streamlining the management of legal aid applications and facilitating

18 The New International Directory of Legal Aid. (2021). Paesi Bassi: Brill, pp. 154–182.

real-time data analysis for better resource allocation. Simultaneously, 2023 envisages a more pronounced synergy between legal practitioners and insurance providers[19]. The legal insurance model, fortified by the expertise of legal professionals, might become a cornerstone for many seeking preemptive legal support. This collaborative liaison, rooted in private sector dynamism, could see legal insurance policies tailored to address emerging legal complexities and societal nuances. The collaborative models, which found their footing in earlier years, are projected to flourish in 2024. These models, fueled by the shared objectives of legal professionals, civil society actors, and educational institutions, could evolve into comprehensive networks that comprehensively address diverse legal needs. This collaborative spirit could lead to the establishment of legal aid clinics, workshops, and public outreach programs, creating a symbiotic ecosystem that nurtures legal awareness and empowerment.

However, this journey is not without its challenges. The evolution of legal aid mechanisms demands stringent quality control measures to ensure consistency and reliability. Resource allocation becomes an intricate puzzle to solve, with careful consideration required to balance the demands of immediate cases against the broader sustainability of the system. The potential for information disparities among different mechanisms necessitates proactive efforts to ensure that individuals are well-informed about the full spectrum of legal aid options.

In the horizon of 2023 and 2024, Malta's legal aid landscape stands on the cusp of transformative change. The intertwining of private and public efforts, guided by a shared commitment to justice, holds the promise of a more accessible, equitable, and responsive legal aid system. As these years unfold, they will undoubtedly inscribe a chapter of innovation and progress within the annals of Malta's legal framework, further solidifying its reputation as a beacon of accessible justice[20].

5. Conclusions

The journey through the intricate landscape of the free legal aid system in the Republic of Malta has illuminated a landscape characterized by responsiveness, adaptability, and an unwavering commitment to justice. As the threads of

19 Perspectives on Legal Aid: An International Survey. (1979). Regno Unito: Frances Pinter pp. 84–96.

20 Aquilina, K. (2018). Constitutional Law in Malta. Paesi Bassi: Wolters Kluwer, pp. 78–45.

historical evolution, administrative oversight, and innovative mechanisms intertwine, a rich tapestry emerges – a tapestry that echoes the core tenets of accessible justice.

In our exploration, we have witnessed how Malta's legal aid system has evolved from modest beginnings to a dynamic and comprehensive framework. The administrative oversight entities, serving as vigilant custodians, have navigated the delicate balance between efficiency and equity, safeguarding the integrity of the system. The embrace of legal insurance and collaborative models has expanded the horizon of accessible justice, inviting a diverse array of stakeholders to join hands in the pursuit of this noble endeavor. As we stand on the threshold of the next decade, the prospects for Malta's free legal aid system appear both promising and complex. The system's evolution may witness refinements that align with the ever-evolving legal landscape. These advancements may seek to leverage technology for even more seamless access to legal aid, transcending geographical barriers and optimizing the application process. Advantages lie in the potential to achieve a more inclusive legal ecosystem. The collaboration between state-sponsored initiatives, private sector engagement, and community-driven approaches can foster a holistic support structure that caters to a spectrum of legal needs. The diverse avenues of legal aid can, collectively, mitigate the challenges arising from financial constraints, leveling the playing field and ensuring that justice remains accessible to all. However, these opportunities are not devoid of challenges. Striking a balance between sustainability and the expansion of legal aid initiatives may prove intricate. The allocation of finite resources requires judicious management to address both immediate and long-term legal needs. Moreover, ensuring uniformity in the quality of legal aid services across different mechanisms necessitates vigilant monitoring and quality assurance. The way forward demands innovative solutions. A concerted effort to enhance public awareness of legal aid options could ensure that individuals are informed of the resources at their disposal. Continuous dialogue among legal practitioners, administrative authorities, and stakeholders can foster a symbiotic environment that nurtures the evolution of the legal aid landscape.

In envisioning the trajectory of legal aid in Malta for the next decade, the compass points towards an expansive landscape of possibilities. As the legal system advances, so too does the responsibility to ensure that its benefits are equitably distributed. Malta's journey towards accessible justice stands as a beacon for other legal systems, exemplifying the potential for harmonizing public and private efforts to sculpt a legal landscape where the scales of justice are truly balanced for all.

Envisioning the trajectory of legal aid in Malta over the next decade evokes a sense of boundless potential. The compass of progress points toward an expansive landscape of possibilities, shaped by the evolving legal landscape and the societal imperatives of justice. As Malta's legal system advances, the parallel responsibility of ensuring the equitable distribution of its benefits becomes increasingly crucial. In the immediate term, the year 2023 promises to be a crucible of transformative change. The seeds sown in preceding years are set to bear fruit, manifesting in streamlined digital interfaces, collaborative legal aid models, and the amplification of legal insurance's role. The symbiotic relationship between state-sponsored efforts and private sector dynamism is poised to fortify accessibility and responsiveness. Zooming out to the next two decades, the compass aligns with a vision of sustainability and expansion. By 2043, Malta's legal aid landscape could have evolved into a comprehensive ecosystem where seamless digital interfaces, sophisticated eligibility criteria, and a dynamic collaborative network intertwine. The integration of artificial intelligence might bring forth tools for legal aid assessment, enhancing efficiency while ensuring equitable support. However, this journey is accompanied by the challenges of maintaining equilibrium. Resource management, quality control, and continuous public awareness efforts remain vital. Over the next two decades, addressing these challenges could lead to a legal aid landscape characterized by finely tuned mechanisms, informed by both the past and the potential of emerging technologies.

Malta's trajectory towards accessible justice stands as a beacon, illuminating the path for other legal systems. It serves as a living testament to the harmonization of public and private endeavors, a model where the scales of justice are balanced for all. This beacon extends its light not only over the next 10 years but also over the ensuing two decades. As the legal aid landscape matures, it has the potential to radiate justice, fairness, and inclusivity – a legacy that stands as a testament to the enduring power of legal innovation.

Literature

Access to Justice and Legal Aid: Comparative Perspectives on Unmet Legal Need, Regno Unito: Bloomsbury Publishing 2017.

Aquilina, K., *Constitutional Law in Malta*. Paesi Bassi: Wolters Kluwer 2018.

Gerard, A., *The Securitization of Migration and Refugee Women*. Regno Unito: Taylor & Francis 2014.

Histories of Legal Aid: A Comparative and International Perspective, Svizzera: Springer International Publishing 2022.

Ibp, I., *Malta Company Laws and Regulations Handbook Volume 1 Strategic Information and Basic Laws*. Stati Uniti: IBP USA 2017.

Law Relating to Legal Aid: Presented to the Honourable Professor Guido de Marco, Deputy Prime Minister and Minister of Foreign Affairs and Justice, Malta: Malta University Services Limited for the Permanent Law Reform Commission 1991.

Newman, D., *Legal Aid Lawyers and the Quest for Justice*. Regno Unito: Hart Publishing 2013.

Perspectives on Legal Aid: An International Survey, Regno Unito: Frances Pinter 1979.

The Implementation and Enforcement of European Union Law in Small Member States: A Case Study of Malta, Germania: Springer International Publishing 2021.

The New International Directory of Legal Aid, Paesi Bassi: Brill 2021.

Wilding, J., *The Legal Aid Market: Challenges for Publicly Funded Immigration and Asylum Legal Representation*. Regno Unito: Policy Press 2023.

Agnieszka Piskorz-Ryń

Access to Information on the Law from the Perspective of the Access to Public Information Act

Abstract: This article presents access to information about the law in Poland from the perspective of the Access to Public Information Act of 6 September 2001. To this end, three levels have been distinguished. The first relates to lawmaking (transparency of the legislative process), the second to access to legislation and the third to access to interpretation of the law in individual cases. Information about the law is regulated in the Access to Public Information Act to a limited extent The Act on Access to Public Information refers most broadly to the course of the legislative process. Public information is information on draft normative acts. Citizens may also participate in the meetings of public authorities coming from universal elections. The rules of access to the content of legal acts are regulated in special laws and the Access to Information Act does not apply to them. The Act does not apply when it comes to the interpretation of the law in individual cases.

Keywords: legislative process, access to public information, transparency of public life, public information

1. Introduction

In a democratic state, information about the law is part of the transparency of public life[1]. Transparency consists of a pattern and a state of the facts. The latter is influenced by norms, values and facts. The pattern is descriptive in nature. It is subject to transformation with changes in public life. According to the pattern, one of the elements of transparency in public life is access to information about the law. The extent of information that should be available in a democratic state can only be considered. There should be access to information on the legislative process, access to meetings of collegiate bodies of public authority from

1 In the introduction, I refer to the concept I have formulated of a multifaceted scheme of transparency A. Piskorz-Ryń, *Jawność i ograniczenia jawności publicznych zasobów informacyjnych,* in: A. Piskorz-Ryń (ed.) *Dostęp i wykorzystywanie,* Warszawa 2015, p. 11.

universal suffrage, the content of normative acts and information on procedures for dealing with specific matters should be ensured. Transparency should also be considered as a de facto state of affairs. In this view, it is assessed at a specific place and time from the perspective of the said pattern. Thus, the state of implementation of the pattern can be examined, also in terms of information about the law.

This article will present access to information about the law in Poland from the perspective of the Access to Public Information Act of 6 September 2001[2]. Three levels can be distinguished for this purpose. The first relates to the creation of law (transparency of the legislative process), the second to access to legal acts, and the third to access to interpretation of the law in an individual case. Accordingly, I will shortly describe them in this article. In addition, I will undertake an attempt to answer the question to what extent in the Polish legal order information about the law can be obtained on the basis of the Access to Public Information Act.

2. Transparency of the legislative process

The right to public information in Poland is regulated by the Constitution[3]. A citizen shall have the right to obtain information on the activities of organs of public authority as well as persons discharging public functions. Such right shall also include receipt of information on the activities of self-governing economic or professional organs and other persons or organizational units relating to the field in which they perform the duties of public authorities and manage communal assets or property of the State Treasury (Article 61 § 1). The right to obtain information shall ensure access to documents and entry to sittings of collective organs of public authority formed by universal elections, with the opportunity to make sound and visual recordings (Article 61 (2)). The procedure for the provision of Information, referred to in paras. 1 and 2 above shall be specified by statute, and regarding the Sejm and the Senate by their rules of procedure (Article 61

2 Access to Public Information Act of September 6, 2001. As published in *Dziennik Ustaw* of 2022 item 902. *Dziennik Ustaw* further cited as *Dz.U.* Text of the Act in English https://archiwum.informacjapubliczna.org.pl/wwwdane/files/foia before amendment in2011 ygyp.pdf This text does not take into account the amendments to the Act. The provisions quoted in this article have not been amended.

3 The Constitution of the Republic of Poland of 2nd April 1997. As published in *Dz.U.* No. 78, item 483, https://www.sejm.gov.pl/prawo/konst/angielski/kon1.htm (Access: 1.02.2024).

(4)). At a statutory level, the issue of access to information in Poland is regulated by the Act on Access to Public Information. It regulates the principles and procedure of access to public information. According to Article 1(1) of the Act, public information is any information about public matters. This definition is criticized because defining what is a public matter and what is not is debatable. M. Jaskowska understands by the term public information any kind of documents relating to, associated with or in any way concerning public authorities[4].

At the same time, Article 6(1) of the Act contains an enumeration of information that is public information. This enumeration is indicative.

Turning to the issue of openness of the legislative process, public information is information on draft normative acts that have been officially published by a public body. Until officially published, they constitute an internal document[5]. Internal documents are not qualified as public information by administrative courts[6]. The purpose of internal document construction is to protect the decision-making process[7]. In Poland, the jurisprudence of administrative courts is of great importance for the application of the Act. It influences the practice of

---

4 M. Jaśkowska, *Dostęp do informacji publicznych w świetle orzecznictwa Naczelnego Sądu Administracyjnego*, Toruń 2002, p. 28–29.

5 For the internal document, see more on A. Piskorz-Ryń, Komentarz do art.1 in: *Ustawa o dostępie do informacji publicznej. Komentarz*, ed. A. Piskorz-Ryń, M. Sakowska-Baryła Warszawa 2023, p.42–48.

6 *Trybunał Konstytucyjny* (The Constitutional Tribunal of the Republic of Poland) considers internal documents to be information of a working nature (notes, memos) that have been recorded in traditional or electronic form and represent a certain thought process, a process of deliberation, a stage in the development of a final concept, the adoption of a final position by an individual employee or team. Internal documents are distinguished from official documents within the meaning of Article 6(2) of the Act by the fact that they serve to carry out some public tasks, but do not prejudge the directions of the authority. Internal documents are intended to exchange information, collect necessary materials, agree on views and positions. However, they are not an expression of the position of the authority and therefore do not constitute public information Judgment of *Trybunał Konstytucyjny* of 13.11.2013, P 25/12 OTK-A 2013/ 8, item 122 (https://ipo.trybunal.gov.pVipo/Sprawa?&pokaz=dokumenty&sygnataa= P%2025/12 Access: 1.02.2024).

7 Article 3(1k) of the Council of Europe Convention on Access to Official Documents (CETS No. 205). In accordance with Explanatory Report to the Council of Europe Convention on Access to Official Documents section 34 It should be noted that, even if the aim of the Convention is to encourage public participation in decision-making, the purpose of this limitation is to preserve the quality of the decision-making process by allowing a certain free "space to think".

law application. The construction of the internal document is not supported by the law and is based solely on case law.

Public information according to the jurisprudence of administrative courts are opinions on a specific draft legal act on which the legislative process is ongoing. This also applies to opinions prepared for the President of the Republic of Poland as part of his participation in the legislative process[8]. Remaining legal opinions are internal documents.

Public information published in the Public Information Bulletin is also information on draft normative acts (Article 6(1)(b)). Details concerning the subject matter or text of the project, persons responsible for work on the project and, if possible, the content of the findings or assumptions of the project should be published in this way[9]. The Bulletin also publishes information on the intentions of the legislature and the executive (Article 6 (1)(1a)). For this reason, public information will be information on ongoing legislative proceedings. The entity will then be obliged to provide public information based on its knowledge at the date of the reply. This knowledge must be derived from existing sources, for example developed and adopted assumptions, enacted programs or projects, official speeches, and positions[10].

Everyone has the right of access to meetings of collegiate bodies of public authority derived from universal suffrage[11]. They are open and available (Article 18 (1)). These bodies are obliged to provide the premises or technical means for the exercise of the right. Where necessary, audiovisual or digital transmission of the meetings of these bodies shall be provided (Article 18(3)). Restricting access to meetings of the bodies on the grounds of premises or technical facilities must not lead to unjustified provision of access only to selected persons (Article 18(4)). The Act, due to the limited premises or technical reasons, allows for the selection of interested parties. This should be done according to the clear criteria. Representatives of the media and persons whose interest may be affected by the

8 Judgment of the *NSA* of 27.01.2012, I OSK 2130/11, *CBOSA*. https://orzeczenia.nsa.gov.pl/doc/9B0E75BB3F (Access: 1.02.2024). *Naczelny Sąd Administracyjny* further cited as *NSA*.

9 Judgment of the *NSA* of 10.01.2014, I OSK 2213/13, *Centralna Baza Orzecznictwa Sądów Administracyjnych* further cited as *CBOSA* https://orzeczenia.nsa.gov.pl/doc/2A4509A725 (Access: 1.02.2024).

10 Judgment of the *NSA* of 27.05.2014, I OSK 2374/13, *CBOSA* https://orzeczenia.nsa.gov.pl/doc/A275D42F97; Judgment of the *NSA* of 27.05.2014, I OSK 2350/13, *CBOSA*, https://orzeczenia.nsa.gov.pl/doc/7CBAB403E8 (Access: 1.02.2024).

11 Article 3(1)(3) of Access to Public Information Act.

case should be admitted first. In the event that such selection is inadequate, the drawing of lots for places should not be ruled out[12].

Transparency is widely regarded as an element of due process. The openness of proceedings of collegially elected public authorities is not exclusively meant for the purpose of obtaining information on the activities of the elected members of those bodies. It is not exclusively meant to obtain information that can be used as a basis for the voters' decision in the next election. It also affects the fairness of the decision-making process[13]. Local laws are enacted in the Polish legal system at meetings of the municipal council, the district council, and the voivodship assembly. The openness of meetings allows proceedings to be monitored. This means that all actions taken by these bodies must take place in public, with the participation of those concerned.

According to Article 11b (1) of the Act on Communal Self- Government of 8 March 1990 [14], the activities of municipal council are public. Restrictions to openness may only result from laws. The openness of the activity of the municipal council includes the right of citizens to obtain Information, access to sessions of the municipal council and meetings of its committees, as well as access to documents, including protocols of meetings of the municipal council and committees of the municipal council. Similar regulations apply to the county council and the voivodship assembly[15]. Those participating in deliberations have the right to know how a councillor votes. The laws governing local government in Poland stipulate that open voting is the norm. Secret votes apply to personal matters. They are carried out only if the law permits it[16]. At the same time, according to Article 20 (1b) of the Act on Communal Self- Government the deliberations of the municipal council are transmitted and recorded by means of audio and video recording equipment. Recordings of the proceedings are made available in the Public Information Bulletin and on the website of the municipality as well

---

12 M. Bernaczyk, *Prawo do informacji publicznej w Polsce i na świecie*, Warszawa 2014, p. 439.

13 Judgment of the *NSA* in Gdansk of 20.03.2003, II SA/Gd 1529/02, *CBOSA* https://orzeczenia.nsa.gov.pl/doc/C8FC2A604B (Access: 1.02.2024).

14 *Dz.U.* 2023, item 40, as amended.

15 Article 8a (1), of the Act of 5 June 1998 on county self-government *Dz.U.*2024, item 107; Art. 8a (1), of the Act of 5 June 1998 on voivodship self-government *Dz.U.*2022, item 2094, as amended.

16 See more M. I. Ulasiewicz, *Jawność obrad organów kolegialnych jednostek samorządu terytorialnego*, in: *Zasady w prawie administracyjnym. Teoria, praktyka, orzecznictwo*, ed. *Z. Duniewska, A. Krakała, M.* Stahl, Warszawa 2018, p. 228–241.

as in other customary ways. It is therefore possible to be present at a session of the municipal council, to observe it in real time or to watch broadcasts at a later date. Similar regulations apply to the county council and the provincial assembly[17]. The indicated laws supplement the provisions of the Access to Public Information Act.

Meanwhile, the rules of access to the sittings of the Sejm and the Senate are regulated by their regulations[18]. This follows from Article 61(4) of the Constitution of the Republic of Poland. This is a manifestation of what is known as parliamentary procedural autonomy. Rules of procedure are autonomous acts issued based on the Constitution and are acts implementing it[19]. This solution is justified by the principle of organizational autonomy of both chambers of parliament and presupposes independence in determining the manner of procedure[20]. The transparency of Sejm sessions shall be ensured in particular by: informing the public about the Sejm sessions, allowing the press, radio and television to report on Sejm sessions, allowing the public to observe the Sejm sessions from the gallery overlooking the Sejm floor, on the terms specified by the Speaker of the Sejm in the rules of order. The Sejm, at the request of the Presidium of the Sejm or at least 30 MPs, may decide to make its proceedings secret if the well-being of the State so requires (Article 172(2) of the Rules of Procedure of the Sejm). The Sejm decides on the secrecy of debates without the participation of the public and representatives of the press, radio, or television, after hearing the reasons for the motion without debate. A resolution on secrecy of deliberations shall be adopted by an absolute majority of votes in the presence of at least half of the total number of Members (Article 172(3)). The Rules of Procedure of the Sejm enumerative list in Article 170(1)-(3) the bodies that may attend meetings.

---

17 Art. 15 (1a), of the Act on county self-government; Art. 21 (1a) of the Act on voivodship self-government.

18 Resolution of the Sejm of the Republic of Poland of 30 July 1992 Rules of Procedure of the Sejm of the Republic of Poland (*Monitor Polski* 2022, item 990, as amended).

19 M. Zubik, *W sprawie dostępu do informacji w Kancelarii Sejmu, Opinie,* Przegląd Sejmowy 2003 No 154, p. 59.

20 M. Florczak-Wątor, Komentarz do art. 61, w: *Konstytucja RP., Komentarz,* ed. P. Tuleja, Warszawa 2019, Lex, Art. 61 point 4.

3. Access to information on legal acts and access to interpretation of the law in an individual case

Access to information on legal acts being in force is regulated by the Act on 20 July 2000 on the promulgation of normative acts and certain other legal acts[21]. From the perspective of the Access to Public Information Act, this is *lex specialis*. It regulates the principles and procedure of announcing normative acts and the principles and procedure of publishing official journals. These are, within the meaning of the Act: the Journal of Laws of the Republic of Poland *'Dziennik Ustaw'*, the Official Journal of the Republic of Poland *'Monitor Polski'*, official journals of ministers heading divisions of government administration, official journals of central offices, the Official Journal of the Financial Supervision Commission and provincial official journals[22]. This law 'monopolises' the official promulgation of normative acts and makes the texts promulgated in the manner described therein the exclusive proof of the content established by the legislator. They are treated as original texts[23]. The rules and procedure for the promulgation of normative acts of the European Union are set out in European Union regulations.

The Access to Public Information Act is not for obtaining an interpretation of the law in an individual case. A request for public information is not a request for interpretation of the law[24]. A polemic against a decision made[25] and applications

21 Dz. U. 2019 item 1461.

22 Article 8 of the Act on promulgation of normative acts and certain other legal acts.

23 G. Wierzyński, *Komentarz do ustawy o ogłaszaniu aktów normatywnych i niektórych innych aktów prawnych* in: *Redagowanie i ogłaszanie aktów normatywnych. Komentarz*, Warszawa 2016, Komentarz do art. 1, LEX.

24 Judgment of the *NSA* of 31.03.2022, III OSK 1717/21, CBOSA https://orzeczenia.nsa.gov.pl/doc/D2CAC8C57B (Access:1.02.2024); Judgment of the *NSA* of 27.08.2018, I OSK 2149/16, CBOSA https://orzeczenia.nsa.gov.pl/doc/DB48CCA8D0(Access: 1.02.2024); Judgment of the WSA in Gdańsk of 28.09.2023, III SAB/Gd 147/23, CBOSA https://orzeczenia.nsa.gov.pl/doc/1E32598766 (Access: 1.02.2024); Judgment of the *WSA* in Warszawa of 16.03.2022, II SAB/Wa 789/21, https://orzeczenia.nsa.gov.pl/doc/03CAD857BB (Access: 1.02.2024); Judgment of the *WSA* in Rzeszów of 1.02.2011, II SAB/Rz 50/10, https://orzeczenia.nsa.gov.pl/doc/662E66E0E1 (Access: 1.02.2024). *Wojewódzki Sąd Administracyjny* further cited as *WSA*.

25 Judgment of the *NSA* of 24.01.2006 r., I OSK 928/05, CBOSA https://orzeczenia.nsa.gov.pl/doc/9CC1C79A14 (Access: 1.02.2024); Judgment of the *WSA* in Rzeszowie of 5.10.2021, II SAB/Rz 100/21, CBOSA https://orzeczenia.nsa.gov.pl/doc/0D1D1D3898 (Access: 1.02.2024); Judgment of the *NSA* in Warszawie of 11.12.2002, II SAB 105/02, LEX No 137863. Judgment of the *NSA* of 19.01.2011, I OSK 8/11, CBOSA https://orzeczenia.nsa.gov.pl/doc/0F7908771B (Access: 1.02.2024).

in an individual case containing a request for clarification of the content of acts do not constitute public information.

4. Conclusions

Information about the law is regulated in the Access to Public Information Act to a limited extent. The rules of access to the content of legal acts are regulated in special laws and the Access to Information Act does not apply to them. The Act does not apply when it comes to the interpretation of the law in individual cases. The Act only requires the publication of information on how cases are resolved by the public administration. The right to information is a political right in Poland. It serves to protect the interests of the community, not to protect individual interests. The Act on Access to Public Information refers most broadly to the course of the legislative process. Public information is information on draft normative acts. Citizens may also participate in the meetings of public authorities coming from general elections. These in turn have the competence to legislate laws in Poland. In this respect, one is entitled to speak of extended transparency. Not only are meetings of these bodies open to the public, available via streaming, but they offer the possibility of participation. They should be regarded as an instrument to counteract the abuse of power by public authorities. In this way, the legislator has guaranteed the possibility of controlling the legislation process. Both at the parliamentary level and at the local government level. In the case of the latter, entitlements are widest.

Literature

Bernaczyk M., *Prawo do informacji publicznej w Polsce i na świecie*, Warszawa 2014. Jaśkowska M., *Dostęp do informacji publicznych w świetle orzecznictwa Naczelnego Sądu Administracyjnego*, Toruń 2002.

Piskorz-Ryń A. (ed.), *Dostęp i wykorzystywanie*, Warszawa 2015.

Konstytucja RP. Komentarz, ed. P. Tuleja, Warszawa 2019.

Ustawa o dostępie do informacji publicznej. Komentarz, ed. A. Piskorz-Ryń, M. Sakowska- Baryła Warszawa 2023.

Wierzyński G., *Komentarz do ustawy o ogłaszaniu aktów normatywnych i niektórych innych aktów prawnych w: Redagowanie i ogłaszanie aktów normatywnych. Komentarz*, Warszawa 2016.

Zasady w prawie administracyjnym. Teoria, praktyka, orzecznictwo, ed. Z. Duniewska, A. Krakała, M. Stahl, Warszawa 2018.

Zubik M., *W sprawie dostępu do informacji w Kancelarii Sejmu, Opinie*, „Przegląd Sejmowy" 2003 No 154.

Authors

Małgorzata Augustyniak
University of Warmia and Mazury in Olsztyn; ORCID: 0000-0002-5958-1992

Agnieszka Franczak
Jagiellonian University in Kraków; ORCID: 0000-0001-9393-634X.

Michał Bożek
University of Silesia in Katowice; ORCID: 0000-0002-2057-8921

Marian Grzybowski
Jan Dlugosz University in Czestochowa; ORCID: 0000-0001-7915-2653

Marcin Grzybowski
Krakow University of Economics; ORCID: 0000-0003-1905-8942

Oleh Ilnytskyi
Franko National University of Lviv (Ukraine); ORCID: 0000-0001-7343-8810

Jerzy Jaskiernia
Jan Kochanowski University in Kielce; ORCID: 0000-0001-9401-5999

Ksenia Kakareko
University of Warsaw; ORCID: 0000-0003-3707-4479

Maria Kalinowska, ORCID: 000-0003-3251-8528

Agnieszka Gloria Kamińska
Jagiellonian University in Kraków; ORCID: 0000-0002-0762-6829

Dorota Kottmann
University of Zurich; ORCID: 0009-0005-8017-5445

Grzegorz Krawiec
University of the National Education Commission, Krakow; ORCID: 0000-0003-2949-5361

Beata Nuzzo
Krakow University of Economics; ORCID: 000-0001-9320-5627

Marta Osuchowska
Cardinal Stefan Wyszyński University in Warsaw; ORCID: 0000-0001-9950-7458

Ivan Pankevych
University of Zielona Góra; ORCID: 0000-0003-2826-9610

Agnieszka Piskorz-Ryń
Cardinal Stefan Wyszyński University in Warsaw; ORCID: 0000-0001-9788-0988

Bogusław Przywora
Jan Dlugosz University in Czestochowa; ORCID: 0000-0002-8809-3971

Aleksandra Syryt
Cardinal Stefan Wyszyński University in Warsaw; ORCID: 0000-0002-7501-0786

Grażyna Szpor
Cardinal Stefan Wyszyński University in Warsaw; ORCID: 0000-0002-3264-9360

Dávid Tóth
University of Pécs; ORCID: 0000-0002-2179-7587

Aleksander Wróbel
Jan Dlugosz University in Czestochowa; ORCID: 0000-0001-5314-5906

Ius, Lex et Res Publica
Studies in Law, Philosophy and Political Cultures

Edited by
Barbara Janusz-Pohl
Anna Jaron

Vol. 1 Anna Jaron: Socio-Economic Constitutional Rights in Democratisation Processes. An Account of the Constitutional Dialogue Theory. 2012.

Vol. 2 Stanisław Filipowicz: Democracy – The Power of Illusion. 2013.

Vol. 3 Teresa Dukiet-Nagórska (ed.): The Postulates of Restorative Justice and the Continental Model of Criminal Law. As Illustrated by Polish Criminal Law 2014.

Vol. 4 Agnieszka Kupzok: Enforcement of Patents on Geographically Divisible Inventions. An Inquiry into the Standard of Substantive Patent Law Infringement in Cross-Border Constellations. 2015.

Vol. 5 Alicja Jagielska-Burduk / Wojciech Szafrański: Legal Issues in Cultural Heritage Management. A Polish Perspective. 2016.

Vol. 6 Maciej Mataczyński (ed.): The Takeover of Public Companies as a Mode of Exercising EU Treaty Freedoms. 2017.

Vol. 7 Maciej Barczewski (ed.): Value of Information. Intellectual Property, Privacy and Big Data. 2018.

Vol. 8 Pawel Smoleń, Marcin Burzec: Introduction to Polish Tax Law. 2018.

Vol. 9 Łukasz Pohl, Konrad Burdziak: Judicial Interpretation of the 1997 Criminal Code Provisions on Self-Defence. 2019.

Vol. 10 Adam Szot: Judicial Review of Administrative Discretion. The Influence of Court Decisions on Administrative Actions. 2019.

Vol. 11 Michał Peno / Konrad Burdziak (eds.): The Concept of Modern Law. Polish and Central European Tradition. 2019.

Vol. 12 Leszek Leszczyński / Bartosz Liżewski / Adam Szot (eds.): Potential of Precedent in the Statutory Legal Order. 2019.

Vol. 13 Łukasz Bolesta: In Search of a Model for the Legal Protection of a Whistleblower in the Workplace in Poland. A legal and comparative study. 2020.

Vol. 14 Paweł Chmielnicki / Adam Sulikowski (eds.): New Perspectives on Legislation. A Comparative Approach. 2020.

Vol. 15 Marcin Burzec / Beata Kucia-Guściora / Paweł Smoleń: Agricultural Activity in Poland: A Fiscal and Legal Study. 2020.

Vol. 16 Magdalena Półtorak / Ilona Topa (eds.): Women, Children and (Other) Vulnerable Groups. Standards of Protection and Challenges for International Law. 2021.

Vol. 17 Josef Albert Fox: Die polnische Verfassung vom 3. Mai 1791. Hintergründe der Entstehung und der Außerkraftsetzung. Stellung Polens im Zeitalter der Aufklärung. 2021.

Vol. 18 Barbara Janusz-Pohl (ed.): Juvenile Justice Systems: Poland-Brazil-Portugal. 2021.

Vol. 19 Leszek Leszczyński: General Reference Clauses in the Judicial Process. Context of Legislative Intentions Interpretative Discretion. 2021.

Vol. 20 Francisco J. Campos Zamora: Das Problem der Begründung richterlicher Entschei- dungen. Eine Analyse auf der Grundlage der Theorie der juristischen Argumentation. 2021.

Vol. 21 Aneta Skorupa-Wulczyńska: Language Rights of the Citizen of the European Union. 2022.

Vol. 22 Mateusz Osiecki: International Legal Aspects of Aerial Terrorism. Methods of Law Enforcement in Avia-tion. 2022.

Vol. 23 Vladimír Sharp / Gabriela Blahoudková / Jakub Handrlica (eds.): Law, Pandemics and Ownership Restrictions. 2022.

Vol. 24 Piotr Kasprzyk / Anna Konert: Drones – Future of Aviation Law? Interference of Public Law in Private Law. 2023.

Vol. 25 Szymon Pawelec (ed.): Consensual Procedures in Criminal Law – Comparative Perspective. 2023.

Vol. 26 Dorota Pudzianowska: The Statelessness in Public Law. 2023.

Vol. 27 Bogusław Przywora / Aleksander Wróbel: Formalised Access to Pre-jurisdictional Free Legal Aid. Analysis based on Example of Ukraine, Poland, Great Britain and Sweden. 2023.

Vol. 28 Ewa Dawidziuk / Patricia Panero / Anna Tarwacka (eds.): Family, Law, and Society: from Roman Law to the Present Day. 2023.

Vol. 29 Marian Grzybowski / Bogusław Przywora / Aleksandra Syryt (eds.): Free Legal Aid, Theory, Legal Basis and Practice. European Standards. 2023.

Vol. 30 Karolina Gmerek: Trial as a Social Communication Occurrence. Interactions Between Professional and Non-professional Participants of a Trial. 2023.

Vol. 31 Paweł Wiliński (ed.): Effective Legal Remedies in Criminal Justice System. European Perspective. 2024.

Vol. 32 Olga Sitarz / Anna Jaworska-Wieloch / Jakub Hanc : On the (Non)existence of the Right to Religious Freedom of Persons Deprived of Liberty. A Reconstruction of the Normative Standard Based on Polish and German Regulations in Comparison With Empirical Studies. 2024.

Vol. 33 Marian Grzybowski / Bogusław Przywora / Aleksandra Syryt (eds.) : Free Legal Aid – A Comparative Approach. Volume 2. 2024.

www.ingramcontent.com/pod-product-compliance
Ingram Content Group UK Ltd.
Pitfield, Milton Keynes, MK11 3LW, UK
UKHW021832100926
8556IPUK00004B/300

9 783631 905333